Finance for IT Decision Makers

A Practical Handbook for Buyers, Sellers and Managers

The British Computer Society

The BCS is the leading professional body for the IT industry. With members in over 100 countries, the BCS is the professional and learned Society in the field of computers and information systems.

The BCS is responsible for setting standards for the IT profession. It is also leading the change in public perception and appreciation of the economic and social importance of professionally managed IT projects and programmes. In this capacity, the Society advises, informs and persuades industry and government on successful IT implementation.

IT is affecting every part of our lives and that is why the BCS is determined to promote IT as the profession of the 21st century.

Joining the BCS

BCS qualifications, products and services are designed with your career plans in mind. We not only provide essential recognition through professional qualifications but also offer many other useful benefits to our members at every level.

BCS membership demonstrates your commitment to professional development. It helps to set you apart from other IT practitioners and provides industry recognition of your skills and experience. Employers and customers increasingly require proof of professional qualifications and competence. Professional membership confirms your competence and integrity and sets an independent standard that people can trust. Professional Membership (MBCS) is the pathway to Chartered IT Professional (CITP) status.

www.bcs.org/membership

Further Information

Further information about the BCS can be obtained from: The British Computer Society, First Floor, Block D, North Star House, North Star Avenue, Swindon SN2 1FA, UK.

Telephone: 0845 300 4417 (UK only) or +44 01793 417 424 (overseas)
Email: customerservice@hq.bcs.org.uk
Web: www.bcs.org

Finance for IT Decision Makers

A Practical Handbook for Buyers, Sellers and Managers

Michael Blackstaff

Second Edition

 BCS

Second edition
First edition published by Springer Verlag 1999

Michael Blackstaff has asserted his right under the Copyright, Designs and Patents Act 1988, to be identified as author of this Work.

The British Computer Society
Publishing and Information Products
First Floor, Block D
North Star House
North Star Avenue
Swindon SN2 1FA
UK
www.bcs.org

ISBN 10 1-902505-73-5
ISBN 13 978-1-902505-73-2

British Cataloguing in Publication Data.
A CIP catalogue record for this book is available at the British Library.

Typeset by Tradespools, Chippenham, Wiltshire.
Printed at Antony Rowe Ltd., Chippenham, Wiltshire.

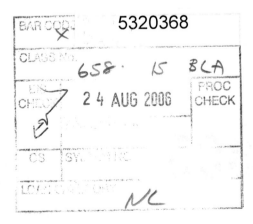

Contents

Part One: Finance for IT Decision Makers

List of Figures and Tables

Authors

Michael Blackstaff FCA MBCS CITP
Michael Blackstaff has over thirty years' finance, marketing and training experience of the information technology (IT) industry and its customers. For nine years he was a financial marketing specialist with IBM United Kingdom Ltd, developing business cases for complex projects, selling leasing, teaching salespeople the finance of selling and advising customers on financing and accounting for IT. His published work includes two technical booklets (with S Nasser) published by the Faculty of Information Technology of the Institute of Chartered Accountants in England and Wales, *The Leasing of IT Acquisitions* (1995) and *The Depreciation of IT Equipment* (1993). Self-employed since 1993, he teaches courses on finance and accounting for non-financial managers and salespeople in IT and other industries. His courses have been successfully adapted and taught in other countries.

Website: www.financial-trainer.com

Hugh Pike BSc MBA (Co-author of Chapter 9)
Hugh Pike is a consultant and trainer in commercial negotiations, specializing in outsourcing engagements. He was a senior commercial negotiator in IBM's Global Services division for more than ten years, prior to becoming freelance in 2005. During his time in IBM, Hugh developed a wealth of experience in outsourcing during deal negotiations with customers in a wide variety of businesses. For the last two years prior to leaving IBM, he had responsibility for outsourcing engagements across Europe, in particular those involving outsourcing consultants. In addition he organized and delivered courses in various aspects of outsourcing.

Hugh can be contacted at: hugh_pike@yahoo.co.uk.

Foreword

Michael Blackstaff has produced a practical, readable and enjoyable guide to the financial factors that IT decision makers should consider when making an investment and how these relate to business operations. For many years this has been a contentious area, particularly in the IT sector, where, on the one hand, technological considerations have sometimes been allowed to override business sense; while, on the other hand, insufficient knowledge of the black arts of financing have sometimes been known to lead to poor IT decisions.

Michael sets out a logical, ordered, way of approaching the subject, which, when used by IT and accounting professionals, will provide a common base of understanding. The book provides a sound basis for the achievement of better business decision making about investments in IT.

I worked with Michael in IBM United Kingdom Limited for over ten years. We were colleagues in IBM's Financial Marketing Department (of which I was Manager) where, in collaboration with clients seeking both to justify IT investments and manage their cash flow, we used many of the techniques described in this book. Later, as Manager of IBM's Business School, I collaborated with Michael in providing financial training for IBM's staff and clients. This book is the fruit of that practical experience.

Geoff Berridge
Director
Parataxis Ltd
London
March 2006
www.parataxis.co.uk

Acknowledgements

I should like to thank the following people for their contributions to this book:

- Mr Hugh Pike BSc MBA, the co-author of Chapter 9: *Outsourcing: Financial aspects*
- Mrs Barbara Penney ACA for her technical help regarding financing and leasing
- Mr Richard Barfield BSc FCA CMC, of the Valuation & Strategy group at PricewaterhouseCoopers LLP (www.pwc.com/uk) in London, for his technical help regarding those sections of the book that contain references to 'shareholder value added' (SVA). His suggestions of simple ways of describing this evolving subject for the non-specialist reader, and of how SVA can be related to more well-established ways of evaluating investments in Information Technology (IT), have, I believe, added significantly to the usefulness of the book. Richard's comments are made in a personal capacity and do not necessarily represent the views of PricewaterhouseCoopers LLP.

I should also like to thank the four organizations that have kindly granted permission for extracts from their published Accounts to be reproduced in the book and used for illustrative purposes. In alphabetical order they are the following:

- Aga Foodservice Group plc
- Hampshire County Council
- LogicaCMG plc
- Tesco plc.

Extracts from International Accounting Standard No. 17 (IAS 17) are reproduced by kind permission of the International Accounting Standards Board.

Extracts from 'Accounting Standards 2005/2006' are reproduced by kind permission of the Accounting Standards Board Limited. For further information please visit www.frc.org.uk/asb.

The diagram in Figure 10.1 is reproduced, slightly modified, from Lock, D. (2003) *Project Management*, 8th edition, Gower/Ashgate Publishing, Aldershot, by kind permission of the publishers.

I should like also to thank the following:

Matthew Flynn, Commissioning Editor of the Books Programme of the British Computer Society (BCS); Florence Leroy, Suzanna Marsh, Sue McNaughton also of the BCS; Geoff Berridge, Barbara Eastman, Javaid Punwar and Alex Sharpe.

Finally, 'thank you' to my wife Jenny for commenting on drafts and for her willingness to be a book widow during the writing.

Michael Blackstaff

Abbreviations

AEA	Annual equivalent annuity
ARR	Accounting rate of return
CA	Capital allowance
DCF	Discounted cash flow
EPS	Earnings per share
EVA®	Economic Value Added
FASB	Financial Accounting Standards Board (USA)
FRS	Financial reporting standard (UK)
FV	Future value
IAS	International accounting standard
IRR	Internal rate of return
IT	Information technology
NPV	Net present value
PC	Personal computer
P/E	Price/earnings
PI	Profitability index
PLC	Public limited company
PV	Present value
ROCE	Return on capital employed
ROE	Return on equity
ROI	Return on investment
RV	Residual value
SOYD	Sum of the years' digits
SSAP	Statement of standard accounting practice (UK)
SVA	Shareholder value added
TBV	Tax book value
TUPE	Transfer of Undertakings (Protection of Employment) Regulations 1981
VAT	Value added tax
WACC	Weighted average cost of capital

Preface

Some 'IT' people that I know, don't like 'finance' very much. At best it leaves them indifferent; at worst they just wish it would go away. This is because 'finance' is the thing that has incomprehensible jargon, charges their budget with costs that they never incurred and kills their pet projects by shrinking the benefits but never the costs.

Some finance people that I know, don't like IT very much. It has incomprehensible jargon, stretches the rules of accounting up to and sometimes beyond their natural limits and has an insatiable appetite for spending money on machines that never wear out but nevertheless always seem to need replacing after about eighteen months.

The purpose of this book, written by one who has had a foot in both camps for many years, is to promote mutual understanding by throwing some light on to the twilight zone where these two professions meet. Whichever camp you are in, I believe that you will find it useful.

Organization

There are many examples with detailed workings. If you can't stand numbers, then ignore them and just follow the logic in the narrative. The book consists of two parts and some appendices. Each part stands alone.

Part One is the main part of the book, and everything in it has relevance, direct or indirect, to making financial decisions about IT. It should be understandable to people with little prior knowledge of finance or accounting, while also perhaps being useful to non-specialist financial people for whom decisions about IT are not an everyday occurrence.

Part Two is called 'Finance fundamentals in a nutshell'. It is for people who have no prior knowledge of the subject, or who wish to brush up on knowledge that they once had. If needed, it should be read before Part One.

Preface to the second edition

The format and almost all the content of the first edition have been retained and updated. New topics include IT outsourcing, the financial characteristics of different kinds of business, examples of company and local authority published Accounts, the accounting treatment of long-term contracts (Appendix 5) and an introduction to budgeting, costing and pricing.

Michael Blackstaff

Part One
Finance for IT Decision Makers

1 Decisions, Decisions...

Objectives

When you have studied this chapter you should be able to:

- *define 'cash flow' and explain its importance in financial decision-making;*
- *build a simple financial case from a given set of data;*
- *explain the importance of determining which cash flows are relevant to the investment being evaluated;*
- *describe the concept known as 'discounted cash flow' and apply it to a simple financial case;*
- *explain what is meant by 'cost of money' and 'opportunity cost';*
- *describe the relationship between interest rates and inflation, and explain its relevance to financial decision-making.*

WHAT IS CASH FLOW?

From time to time we do what we call back-of-envelope calculations to test whether a particular idea is worth pursuing or not. For example, should we stay in this house that is cheap to run but involves expensive commuting costs, or move nearer to work, but to a more expensive area? Should we keep the old car that is getting expensive to maintain or replace it with a newer one that will involve an initial cost but will be cheaper to run? Most such decisions, whether personal or business, have the following characteristics:

- There is a choice of two actions – stay as we are or make a change.
- We are strongly, though not exclusively, influenced by the effect on our cash flow.

Cash flow means the movement of money (cash) to or from an individual or into or out of a business.

A FINANCIAL CASE

We shall use as an example the decision whether to keep the old car or to change it. Our approach would probably be to choose a reasonable evaluation period, perhaps three years, and then jot down estimates of the costs of each alternative. The estimates might look like those in Table 1.1. Please look at it. We would usually try, by taking into account expected

3

price increases, to estimate the amounts of actual cash that will have to be spent on these costs.

TABLE 1.1 *New car versus old – the data*

	Old car (£)	New car (£)
Cost of old car three years ago	7000	
Trade-in value of old car today	2000	
Cost of new car today		10 000
Trade-in values three years from today	600	4000
Running costs in first year (then increasing at 5% per annum):		
fuel	3300	2000
maintenance	1000	600
road tax	200	200
insurance	400	500

If you have an envelope handy, please now use the back of it to work out which of the alternatives you think is the best deal. Should you keep the old car or trade it in for the new one? Table 1.2 shows you an answer. Note that for clarity in Table 1.2 and throughout the book I have adopted the convention of showing cash outflows and (later) expenses as negative numbers.

TABLE 1.2 *New car versus old – the 'whole project' approach*

	Yr 0 (£)	Yr 1 (£)	Yr 2 (£)	Yr 3 (£)	Total (£)
Keep old car					
Fuel		− 3300	− 3465	− 3638	− 10 403
Maintenance		− 1000	− 1050	− 1103	− 3153
Road tax		− 200	− 210	− 221	− 631
Insurance		− 400	− 420	− 441	− 1261
Sell after three years				600	600
Net cash flows		− 4900	− 5145	− 4803	− 14 848
Trade in for new					
Cost now	− 10 000				− 10 000
Sell old now	2000				2000
Fuel		− 2000	− 2100	− 2205	− 6305
Maintenance		− 600	− 630	− 662	− 1892
Road tax		− 200	− 210	− 221	− 631
Insurance		− 500	− 525	− 551	− 1576
Sell after three years				4000	4000
Net cash flows	− 8000	− 3300	− 3465	361	− 14 404

The 'whole project' approach

However you did the calculations, they probably look something like those in Table 1.2. If we wanted a commonly used term that describes Table 1.2, we could call it a 'financial case'. What does it tell us? If we keep the old car our net cash expenditure over the chosen period will be £14,848. If we trade it in, it will be only £14,404. By trading in, we should therefore be better off in cash terms by £444. Note the phrase 'in cash terms'. Whether this means that the trade-in is actually the best deal financially remains to be seen. Meanwhile, a few comments about Table 1.2 itself will be helpful: how it is set out, what it contains and what it excludes.

First, Table 1.2 probably looks much like the back of your envelope, except possibly for one thing. In the case of the 'new' project I have separated (into 'Year 0') those cash flows – the initial expenditure and receipt – that could be said to represent the start of the 'project', from the others, such as running costs, that represent the consequences of a decision to proceed with it. This is both a conventional and convenient way of setting out project cash flows, for reasons that will become clear later.

Second, just as you probably did, I have excluded the original cost of the old car. Why? One reason is that it would be the same in both cases. However, another reason is that we can only make decisions about the future, not the past. We may possibly regret having spent £7,000 on the old car three years ago, but nothing can bring that money back. Past expenditure, whether of £7,000 or £7 billion, that cannot be recovered is called a 'sunk cost'. For those who had to make decisions about whether to continue with it, once started, the tunnel under the English Channel would have provided a constant reminder of the meanings, both real and metaphorical, of 'sunk cost'.

Sunk costs are irrelevant to decision-making and should therefore be excluded from cash flow estimates designed to assist it. They are, of course, relevant for other purposes. For example, we may wish to know the total costs incurred on the old car from when we bought it until today. Although these are all sunk costs, they are relevant for that particular purpose. However, they are not relevant for the purpose of deciding on a future course of action. We shall come across other examples of things that should be excluded from financial cases that are to be used as aids to decision-making.

The third thing to notice about Table 1.2 is that it shows two cash flow estimates, one for each course of action. This is not the shortest way of setting out project cash flows, neither is it necessarily the most convenient, especially when, as in this case, there are only two alternatives. However, it may be the only practicable approach for complex financial cases or where there are more than two alternatives to consider. Aptly, it is sometimes called the 'whole project' approach.

The 'combined' approach

There is, however, a shorter and sometimes more convenient way of producing cash flow estimates. With the car 'project', as with many business examples, we are comparing only two alternatives – 'continue as we are' or 'do something different'. Where this is so, we could combine everything into one case. Where this can conveniently be done it may be easier to use and be more informative than the whole project approach. An example of the combined approach is shown in Table 1.3. It lies between the whole project approach and the fully 'incremental' approach that we shall consider shortly. With one exception, Table 1.3 contains the same level of detail, and of course gives the same result, as did the 'whole project' approach. However, similar items are now paired, thus making it easier to compare them.

TABLE 1.3 *New car versus old – the 'combined' approach*

	Yr 0 (£)	Yr 1 (£)	Yr 2 (£)	Yr 3 (£)	Total (£)
Cash flows arising from trading in old car for new					
Cost of new now	−10 000				−10 000
Trade-in of old now	2000				2000
Fuel					
old costs avoided		3300	3465	3638	10 403
new costs incurred		−2000	−2100	−2205	−6305
Maintenance					
old costs avoided		1000	1050	1103	3153
new costs incurred		−600	−630	−662	−1892
Insurance					
old costs avoided		400	420	441	1261
new costs incurred		−500	−525	−551	−1576
Proceeds of sale after 3 years:					
old – benefit forgone				−600	−600
new – benefit gained				4000	4000
Net incremental cash flows	−8000	1600	1680	5164	444

The exception referred to in the previous paragraph is that road tax has been excluded. It could have been included, but to do so would be a waste of space, because it is the same in each option. Whichever option is chosen, it would be unchanged by the decision. We have thus identified something else that should be excluded from financial cases to be used as aids to decision-making – things that, although cash flows and although in the future, will be unaffected by the decision.

The 'incremental' approach

Given a choice of more numbers to look at or fewer, most people would choose fewer. The fully incremental approach, illustrated in Table 1.4, allows us to present the cash flow estimates with a minimum of detail. It shows only the incremental changes to cash flows that would occur if the 'new' project were to be decided upon. A glance at Table 1.4 will, I think, prove the point that it is easier to read and digest than the other formats, while giving the same result.

TABLE 1.4 *New car versus old – the fully incremental approach*

	Yr 0 (£)	Yr 1 (£)	Yr 2 (£)	Yr 3 (£)	Total (£)
Incremental cash flows arising from trading in old car for new					
Cost of new, less trade-in	−8000				−8000
Fuel		1300	1365	1433	4098
Maintenance		400	420	441	1261
Insurance		−100	−105	−110	−315
Proceeds of sale after 3 years				3400	3400
Net incremental cash flows	−8000	1600	1680	5164	444

Both the 'combined' and the 'incremental' forms (Tables 1.3 and 1.4) have the added advantage over the 'whole project' form that their bottom lines show the net changes to cash flow year by year. They show in which years we shall need more cash, and how much. From this we can determine how much we shall have to borrow, or by how much our own cash resources will be depleted, and when. We can also see when we can expect net cash inflows that will allow borrowings to be repaid or cash mountains to be replenished.

Checkpoint

So far in this chapter we have covered the first three of its objectives. In particular:

● we have defined 'cash flow';

● we have examined three possible approaches to setting out financial cases;

● we have identified the two main characteristics of cash flows that are relevant to decision-making – they will occur in the future, and they will differ among the alternatives.

WHAT IS DISCOUNTED CASH FLOW?

Whichever of the three approaches we choose, if our estimates prove to be exactly right (which would of course be extremely unlikely), then by trading in, we should be better off in cash terms by £444 compared with keeping the old car. I raised earlier the question of whether this means that the trade-in is actually the best deal from a financial point of view. It would be a pity to have done all this work, or the much greater amount of work involved in evaluating a real IT investment, only to use it inappropriately in making the decision.

What does 'better off' mean?

You might ask how there could possibly be any ambiguity. The numbers show clearly that by trading in we should be £444 better off in cash terms. Indeed they do. However, we have first to seek the answers to two questions: what do we mean by 'better off' and what do we mean by 'pounds'? In the answer to the second question lies the answer to the first, so what *do* we mean by pounds?

Please look closely at Table 1.5. It shows three amounts of money, 100 units each, receivable today. But units of what? The answer is 100 each of pounds, dollars and Swiss francs. It may be nice to know that we are to receive these sums, but we should also like to know what it all amounts to in pounds today. So we apply conversion factors (exchange rates) to convert units of foreign money to pounds. Please now look at Table 1.6. Supposing there are currently $2 to a pound, and SFr2.5 to a pound, we can now see the answer to what we wanted to know. Expressed in the units that tell us how much better off we shall be today, namely pounds, the answer is £190.

TABLE 1.5 *Similar amounts receivable (or payable), but in different currencies*

	£	$	SFr
Amounts receivable (or payable)	100	100	100

TABLE 1.6 *Using exchange rates to convert cash flows occurring in different currencies*

	Ref	£	$	SFr	Total (£)
Amounts receivable (or payable)	a	100	100	100	
Conversion factors (exchange rates)	b	1	2	2.5	
Amounts receivable (or payable) in pounds (a/b)		100	50	40	190

By looking at the headings in Table 1.5 we knew immediately that we were dealing with amounts that were being expressed in unlike units. We knew, therefore, that to make sense of what they might mean to us in real terms, we would have to convert them all to a single unit of our choosing, using appropriate conversion factors. The obvious single unit to choose was pounds.

When is a pound not a pound?

What, you may wonder, was the point of that rather trivial little exercise? To answer that question, now please look at Table 1.7. It too represents three amounts of money, 100 units of each. However, unlike Table 1.5, in which the amounts were all receivable today but in different currencies, now the amounts are all receivable in pounds but at different times – today, one year from today and two years from today.

TABLE 1.7 *Similar amounts receivable (or payable), but at different times*

	Yr 0 (£)	Yr 1 (£)	Yr 2 (£)
Amounts receivable (or payable)	100	100	100

The question is: do we have a similar problem to the one that we faced in Table 1.5? Indeed we do, but the nature of the problem is less obvious. In Table 1.5, we knew that we were dealing with unlike amounts because they had different signs. In Table 1.7, the same units (£s) are being used to represent values that are in fact as different in real terms as they would be if they were in different currencies. Why are the values different? The reason is that money received (or paid) in the future is not worth as much as money received today. If it were, and I were offering to give you £100, you would be indifferent whether you received it today, a year from today, or ten years from today.

THE COST OF MONEY

The fact is, however, that you would not be indifferent to when you received my £100; you would like it now, thank you very much. But why? The reason is as follows. Suppose that you have an overdraft of £100 from a bank that is charging you 10 per cent per annum interest. We could say that your current 'cost of money' is 10 per cent per annum. However, let us also suppose that you would like to pay off the overdraft. If you received my £100 today you could do so; if you did not receive it until a year from today you could not. The reason is that a year from today the overdraft will have grown, with interest, to £110, while my gift will not.

PRESENT VALUE

So, £100 today will enable you to extinguish exactly a debt that would require £110 to extinguish one year from today. We could say, therefore, that £100 today is worth exactly the same to you as £110 would be worth one year from today, if your cost of money is 10 per cent per annum during the intervening period.

Putting it the other way round, we could say that if your cost of money is 10 per cent per annum then £110 received one year from today is actually worth only ten elevenths (100 / 110) of what it would have been worth had it been received today. The same holds true, of course, if the £110 were payable one year from today rather than receivable. Finally, we could generalize and say that if the cost of money is 10 per cent per annum, then any sum receivable or payable one year from today is actually worth only ten elevenths (0.9091) of what it would have been worth had it been received or paid today.

Not all jargon is bad. If it were, then we IT people would be high on the list of culprits. Financial people use a few shorthand phrases that shorten considerably the last sentence in the previous paragraph. They would use 'future value' to mean the amount of cash receivable or payable in the future; they would use 'present value' instead of the rather long-winded 'what it would have been worth had it been received or paid today'; and they would use the term 'discount' to describe the process of taking a larger number and turning it into a smaller one.

So, with respect to our specific example, financial people would say that the present value of £110 receivable one year from today, discounted at 10 per cent is £100. To describe the generalization, they would say that the present value (PV) of a cash flow one year from today, discounted at 10 per cent, is equal to 0.9091 (ten elevenths) of its future value (FV). Notice that the phrase 'discounted at 10 per cent' is not strictly accurate, but it is widely used, and generally understood, to mean 'reduced to ten elevenths', or 100 / (100 + 10). If the discount rate used had been eight per cent, then 'discounted at eight per cent' would mean 'reduced to 100 / (100 + 8)', and so on.

Nothing but simple arithmetic

Tedious it may have been, but in the above example and its explanation we needed nothing but simple arithmetic, and that is the most difficult mathematics that you will encounter in the whole book. Finance is not a difficult subject, and I intend to keep proving the point. It is true that the numbers were easy. The arithmetic would certainly have been more tedious if the cash flow had been £537, the cost of money 14.25 per cent and the period seventeen years.

To cater for the majority of situations, where the numbers are indeed not so easy, tables of discount factors were developed. You will find such a table on page 277 in Appendix 1, which also gives the formula from which the table was derived. Table 1.8 shows a part of the table of present values.

TABLE 1.8 *Table of discount factors for* n *periods at discount rate* i

n	1	2	3	4	5	6	7	8	9	10	11
i											
5	0.9524	0.9070	0.8638	0.8227	0.7835	0.7462	0.7107	0.6768	0.6446	0.6139	0.5847
6	0.9434	0.8900	0.8396	0.7921	0.7473	0.7050	0.6651	0.6274	0.5919	0.5584	0.5268
7	0.9346	0.8734	0.8163	0.7629	0.7130	0.6663	0.6227	0.5820	0.5439	0.5083	0.4751
8	0.9259	0.8573	0.7938	0.7350	0.6806	0.6302	0.5835	0.5403	0.5002	0.4632	0.4289
9	0.9174	0.8417	0.7722	0.7084	0.6499	0.5963	0.5470	0.5019	0.4604	0.4224	0.3875
10	0.9091	0.8264	0.7513	0.6830	0.6209	0.5645	0.5132	0.4665	0.4241	0.3855	0.3505
11	0.9009	0.8116	0.7312	0.6587	0.5935	0.5346	0.4817	0.4339	0.3909	0.3522	0.3173
12	0.8929	0.7972	0.7118	0.6355	0.5674	0.5066	0.4523	0.4039	0.3606	0.3220	0.2875
13	0.8850	0.7831	0.6931	0.6133	0.5428	0.4803	0.4251	0.3762	0.3329	0.2946	0.2607
14	0.8772	0.7695	0.6750	0.5921	0.5194	0.4556	0.3996	0.3506	0.3075	0.2697	0.2366
15	0.8696	0.7561	0.6575	0.5718	0.4972	0.4323	0.3759	0.3269	0.2843	0.2472	0.2149

If we did not already know the answer, and we wanted to use the discount table to solve the problem discussed above, the question, to remind you, would be this: what is the present value of £110 receivable or payable one year in the future if we are discounting at 10 per cent? The way to use the table is to look down the left-hand side until you come to the 10 per cent row, then to look along until you come to the 'one year' column. The number that you find is 0.9091. What answer do you get if you then multiply 110 by 0.9091? The answer, of course, is 100.

Now please glance back to Table 1.7. It showed three amounts of £100 receivable (or payable) respectively today, a year from today and two years from today. While in cash terms, the value of the amounts in total is of course £300, we now know that, in real terms, it is rather less. How much less depends on the 'cost of money' of the receiver or payer. Supposing this to be 10 per cent, you may like to work out the answer for yourself. Table 1.9 shows the answer. It is £273.55.

TABLE 1.9 *Using discount factors to convert cash flows occurring at different times*

	Discount rate	Ref	Yr 0 (£)	Yr 1 (£)	Yr 2 (£)	Total (£)
Amounts receivable (or payable)		*a*	100	100	100	
Conversion factors (discount factors)	10%	*b*	1	0.9091	0.8264	
Amounts in 'today pounds' or 'present values' (*a* × *b*)			100	90.91	82.64	273.55

A common currency

The use of discount factors in the above example was analogous to the use of exchange rates in the previous one. Exchange rates were the means whereby we were able to represent cash flows expressed in unlike currencies (and therefore having different values) in a single common unit – pounds. Discount factors are the means whereby we can represent cash flows occurring at different times (and therefore having different values) in a single common unit – 'today pounds' or present values. Understanding this concept is vital if you are to understand what follows. It is even more important if you are to make sound judgements, or understand the judgements of others, about IT or other investment decisions in which you are involved.

Checkpoint

Since the previous checkpoint we have covered the fourth objective and part of the fifth objective of this chapter. In particular:
- we have discussed the main principles of discounted cash flow, and have seen how they are applied to a financial case;
- we have discussed what is meant by 'cost of money' and its importance in discounted cash flow calculations.

We can now return to our little problem of whether to keep the old car or trade it in for a newer one. Please turn back to Table 1.4. You will recall that in cash terms the numbers tell us that trading in old for new is the best option.

The real cost of trading in

Now assume that you expect your overdraft or credit card to cost 13 per cent per annum for the next three years. Let us now ask again: which is the best option financially – to keep the old car or to trade it in? A comparison of the cash numbers told us that the trade-in option would be cheaper by £444 than would keeping the old car. Taking into account what we now know about what is often called the 'time value of money', is £444 the number upon which we should base our decision? I think not. What number should our decision be based on? Table 1.10 shows the solution, but try to avoid looking at it before you have attempted the answer for yourself. Assume for this exercise, and in practice for most present value calculations, that the cash flows in each year occur on the last day of that year.

Now please look at Table 1.10. First, notice that in order to work out the answer, we only need to use the bottom line of numbers from Table 1.4 – the totals of the incremental cash flows. For the purpose of present value calculations, the detail from which those totals were derived has become irrelevant. If you enjoy this kind of thing, you could work out the present value of each individual cash flow and then add up all the answers.

However, your final answer would be the same, so such an approach would need to be strictly for pleasure.

TABLE 1.10 *New car versus old – applying discounted cash flow (incremental approach)*

	Yr 0 (£)	Yr 1 (£)	Yr 2 (£)	Yr 3 (£)	Total (£)
Incremental cash flows arising from trading in old car for new					
Net incremental cash flows	− 8000	1600	1680	5164	444
Discount factors @ 13%	1	0.8850	0.7831	0.6931	
Present values (PV)	− 8000	1416	1316	3579	− 1689

Note – the total of − £1,689 is called the 'net present value' (NPV), because it is the sum of a series of both positive and negative present values.

What we did was to look up the 13 per cent discount factors for one, two and three years and multiply the net cash flows in each year by the respective discount factors. The result was the present values of the cash flows in each year. We then added together those present values to arrive at a total. This total is called the 'net present value' (NPV), because it is the sum of a series of individual present values, of which some are positive and some are negative. The NPV of these cash flows, discounted at our cost of money of 13 per cent, is − £1,689.

Before we ask what that number actually means, let us perform one check on its correctness by doing present value calculations on the total cash flows of the two separate projects that we compiled earlier using the 'whole project' approach. Refer back to Table 1.2 and do the calculations yourself if you would like more practice at them. The result is shown in Table 1.11. Not surprisingly, the result is − £1,689, the same as the one obtained by using the incremental method.

TABLE 1.11 *New car versus old – applying discounted cash flow ('whole project' approach)*

	Ref	Yr 0 (£)	Yr 1 (£)	Yr 2 (£)	Yr 3 (£)	Total (£)
Keep old car						
Net cash flows			− 4900	− 5145	− 4803	
Discount factors @ 13%		1	0.8850	0.7831	0.6931	
Present values (PV)	*a*	0	− 4337	− 4029	− 3329	− 11 695
Buy new						
Net cash flows		− 8000	− 3300	− 3465	361	
Discount factors @ 13%		1	0.8850	0.7831	0.6931	
Present values (PV)	*b*	− 8000	− 2921	− 2713	250	− 13 384
Difference between PVs (*b* − *a*)		− 8000	1416	1316	3579	− 1689

INTERPRETING PRESENT VALUES

The question is what does that number −£1,689 actually mean? Remember that we are looking at two alternative projects: continue as we are (keep the old car) or do something different (trade it in). Remember also that we used the 'incremental approach'. This was in order to determine the incremental effect on cash flows of trading in rather than choosing the alternative. Remember, finally, that by discounting the cash flows at our 'cost of money' we have taken into account that cost. By doing so, we have reflected the fact that later cash flows are worth less than earlier ones. In cash terms we worked out that we should be better off by £444 trading in old for new. The net present value (NPV) of −£1,689 tells us that by contrast, in real terms, we should actually be −£1,689 worse off by trading in, and that therefore we should keep the old car. 'In real terms' means after taking into account what the money being used is costing us.

Why is there such a big difference, in this case as in many real ones, between the net incremental cash flow of 'plus' £444, and the net present value of 'minus' £1,689? Turning back to Table 1.10, the following factors in this particular example have contributed to it. First, 13 per cent is quite a high cost of money; overdrafts, and especially credit cards, do not come cheaply. Second, the biggest number in the financial case is the net cash outflow of £8,000 in Year 0 – today. Because it occurs today it is not discounted. By contrast, the biggest cash inflow, of £5,164, does not occur until Year 3, and it is therefore discounted quite heavily. This is an example of an unfortunate fact: that the universe was not constructed in a way that favours long-term projects. Why are the dice loaded against projects? It is because usually, although not necessarily, most of the big costs of projects occur at or near their beginning, and so are discounted hardly at all. By contrast, most of the benefits occur later in time, and they are therefore discounted more heavily.

Why we assumed an overdraft

In the examples considered so far we have assumed that the individual evaluating the project has an overdraft. This is because our ultimate purpose will be to apply these principles to real business, specifically real IT, project evaluations. As we shall discuss shortly, all the money that any business has at its disposal is 'on loan' in one way or another. Businesses, and organizations in general, may certainly own the assets that they use, in the sense of having legal title. However, they do not 'own' the money – the financial resources – used to acquire them. They are custodians of money invested or lent by others.

However, since we as individuals can and do own money, it is reasonable to ask how we should evaluate the car project were we 'cash rich', as the jargon has it – if we were using our own, rather than borrowed, money? If we were using our own money, could it be said to have a 'cost' for the purpose of doing present value calculations? The answer is that all money has a cost. This is most obvious if it is borrowed, but it is equally true if it is owned.

OPPORTUNITY COST

If money is owned, it is capable of earning interest by being invested (whether it is actually invested or not). The cost of using owned money to invest in something else, such as a new car, is therefore the lost opportunity of earning income from the best alternative investment. The cost of this lost opportunity is usually called the 'opportunity cost'.

Suppose that the best currently available investment of acceptable risk for your money is a high interest savings account paying seven per cent per annum, and that you would use this money to finance the new car. At what rate, then, should the project cash flows be discounted? The answer would appear to be seven per cent; that is, until we recall that tax is payable on interest received. What matters to us ultimately is not the quoted rate of interest, but what is left after tax, and that will be nearer five per cent. You may like to do the calculation, using a five per cent discount rate, and see if it makes any difference to the 'advice' offered by the financial model. Table 1.12 shows the answer of −£491. As you will have discovered, the NPV is still negative, but it is a much smaller negative number. It is a fact, although hardly a surprising one, that the lower the discount rate, the smaller will be the discount. The smaller the discount, then the smaller the difference between the cash numbers and their present values. The subject of tax, in the context of IT investment, is dealt with in Chapter 6.

TABLE 1.12 *New car versus old – effect of a lower discount rate*

	Yr 0 (£)	Yr 1 (£)	Yr 2 (£)	Yr 3 (£)	Total (£)
Incremental cash flows arising from trading in old car for new					
Net incremental cash flows	−8000	1600	1680	5164	444
Discount factors @ 5%	1	0.9524	0.9070	0.8638	
Present values (PV)	−8000	1524	1524	4461	−491

'FINANCIAL CASH FLOWS'

Assuming that you did not do so earlier, it would be reasonable to ask why we have not included in the car project the 'cash inflow' from the bank of £8,000, representing the increased overdraft if we were to buy the new car, and the 'cash outflows' represented by the interest payable and the eventual repayment of the loan. It could be argued that these are indeed cash flows attributable to the project. The answer is that they could be included, but that it would be pointless to do so because, as Table 1.13 illustrates, they would be cancelled out by the discounting process. Please look at the table and make sure that you agree.

TABLE 1.13 *Illustration of 'financial cash flows'*

	Yr 0 (£)	Yr 1 (£)	Yr 2 (£)	Yr 3 (£)	Total (£)
Financial cash flows arising from the car project					
Loan received from the bank	4000				4000
Interest paid @13% (simple interest		−520	−520	−520	−1560
because assumed paid each year)					
Loan repaid to the bank				−4000	−4000
Net cash flows	4000	−520	−520	−4520	−1560
Discount factors @ 13%	1	0.8850	0.7831	0.6931	
Present values (PVs)	4000	−460.2	−407.2	−3132.6	0

INFLATION

So far we have not considered inflation. What is inflation? A working definition is that inflation is the erosion over time of the purchasing power of money. Suppose that you lend £1 for a year at an interest rate of eight per cent, how much money will you have at the end of the year when the loan is repaid? The answer is, of course, £1.08. If, during the year of the loan, inflation was five per cent per annum, then how much have you gained in terms of the purchasing power of your money? It is tempting to say three pence (eight pence less five pence) and that is very nearly right. In fact, the answer is about 2.85 pence, because the calculation is not 1.08 minus 1.05, but 1.08 divided by 1.05. The reason is that percentage rates of things such as interest and inflation are always applied multiplicatively, not additively.

Consider the following example. Suppose that you are thinking of taking out an IT maintenance contract for three years. The first year costs £4,000, payable today. It is not a fixed price contract, but you believe that payments will increase in line with inflation, which you assume will average five per cent over the period. You could produce your cash flow estimate in either of two ways, as follows:

- You could, using your estimate of five per cent inflation, work out what the actual future cash outflows would be, and it is this that you would then put into your financial case. If your cost of money is, say, 12 per cent, then you would use 12 per cent as the discount factor in discounting the cash flows. That is exactly what we did in the car example, and it is usually the simplest method to adopt, as we shall see in Chapter 9 when we consider financial aspects of outsourcing. Or,

- You could ignore inflation and use current, uninflated, numbers in your cash flow estimate. In this case, since the cash flows exclude inflation, then the discount rate should also exclude inflation, otherwise you would not be comparing like with like. If your cost of money is 12 per cent and inflation is five per cent, then what is your 'real' cost of money? 1.12 divided by 1.05 comes to 1.0667, so the answer is that your real cost of money is 6.67 per cent. This is not a nice number to work with, but it is nevertheless the one that you should use in this case to discount the uninflated cash flows.

Table 1.14 demonstrates both of these approaches and shows, as you would expect, that both give the same present value (PV) for the cash flows. This means that you could use either method, and provided you use each correctly you will get the same answer.

TABLE 1.14 *Inflation and discounted cash flows*

	Yr 0 (£)	Yr 1 (£)	Yr 2 (£)	Total (£)
Maintenance contract – cash flows include inflation, discount rate includes inflation				
Cash flows inflated at 5%	−4000	−4200	−4410	−12 610
Discount factors @ 12%	1	0.8929	0.7972	
Present values (PV)	−4000	−3750	−3516	−11 266
Maintenance contract – cash flows exclude inflation, discount rate excludes inflation				
Cash flows uninflated	−4000	−4000	−4000	−12 000
Discount factors @ 6.67% (1.12 / 1.05)	1	0.9375	0.8789	
Present values (PV)	−4000	−3750	−3516	−11 266

The importance of consistency

The important thing is consistency. You can use quoted or 'nominal' cost of money rates to discount 'actual money' cash flows, as we did in evaluating the car project; or you can use 'real' cost of money rates to discount uninflated cash flows, that is cash flows at today's prices. Whichever method is used there will, of course, be inconsistencies, because in any real situation not all prices will increase at the general inflation rate, even if we could estimate accurately what that would be. Bearing in mind that every figure in a financial case is itself an estimate, such inconsistencies are unlikely to destroy its validity.

As an illustration of the relationship between quoted or 'nominal' interest rates, inflation rates and the resulting 'real' interest rates, Figure 1.1 shows what they were in the UK between 1988 and 1996. Those particular years have been chosen because, during that period, UK interest and inflation rates rose and fell quite sharply. Since 1996 both interest and inflation rates have remained quite low, in the UK and in many other countries, and their use for illustration would have made for a rather boring chart.

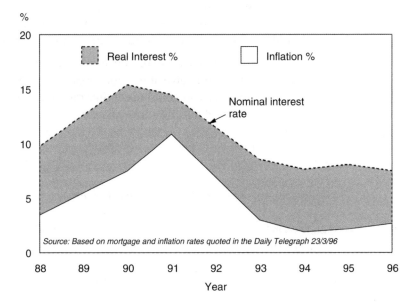

FIGURE 1.1 *Interest rates & inflation rates*

Summary

The main points covered in this chapter, linked to its objectives, have been the following:

- *'Cash flow' means the movement of cash to or from an individual, or into or out of a business.*
- *There are three possible approaches to setting out estimates of investment cash flows. They are:*
  - *the whole project approach, suitable in complex situations or where more than two alternatives are to be considered;*
  - *the combined approach;*
  - *the incremental approach.*

Of these, the incremental approach is usually the shortest, and the most informative, but it may be unsuitable for complex situations.

- *The two main characteristics of cash flows that are relevant to the decision process are that they will occur in the future and that they differ among the alternatives being considered.*
- *The 'real' value of a cash flow depends on when it occurs. The further into the future, the less the cash flow's real value in today's terms. The way to determine this real value is to discount the cash flows, using a discount rate based on the individual's or firm's cost of money.*
- *All money has a cost. This is true of both borrowed and 'owned' money. The cost of using owned money is the 'opportunity cost' – the benefit forgone by not investing it in the best available alternative.*
- *Either discount 'actual money' cash flows using a quoted or 'nominal' discount rate, or discount uninflated cash flows using the equivalent 'real' discount rate. Compare like with like.*

2 Financial Cases and Business Cases

Objectives

When you have studied this chapter you should be able to:
- *explain why businesses should attempt to quantify both the benefits and costs of a proposed investment;*
- *explain the difference between a financial case and a business case;*
- *describe some ways in which it may be possible to quantify 'intangible benefits';*
- *list four kinds of financial benefit;*
- *describe the difference between cash flow and profit, and explain why cash flow is usually regarded as the fundamental basis for investment decision-making.*

The achievement of these objectives is a necessary prerequisite for understanding how to build a financial case to justify a proposed IT investment.

COST CASES

The financial case that we considered in the previous chapter is what would usually be called a 'cost case', because with the exception of amounts receivable for selling the respective cars we have only considered expenditures. We have made no attempt to quantify the benefits of owning cars in general or these cars in particular. This is because we as individuals have generally come to regard a car as either a necessity or at least as highly desirable.

Many people no longer bother to work out how much the alternatives – public transport, taxis or occasional hiring – would cost, and consequently whether owning a car is the most cost-effective option. Neither do we generally even try to quantify the 'intangible' benefits of what we might perceive as our better image or enhanced status from having a superior car rather than an inferior one.

It is true that not every business decision is an 'investment decision'. For example, we shall see in Chapter 9 that a decision whether or not to outsource IT (or any other function) is essentially a 'cost reduction decision'.

However, in this and the next three chapters we shall be considering aspects of financial cases in the context of 'investment decisions'.

Whose money is it anyway?

The reason why we can afford the luxury of not quantifying the benefits of (for example) car ownership is that we are spending our own money. The reason why a business cannot afford the same luxury was introduced in the previous chapter. It is that a business is always spending someone else's money: the money invested by the proprietor(s) and lenders. This is most obviously true in the case of limited companies, whose proprietors are the shareholders. However, it is also helpful to think of it as being true of any other business, including a one-person business, and indeed of other kinds of organization, such as charities, the public sector and other non-profit-making bodies.

The more such organizations adopt good business practices, the more sound financially are they likely to be. Governments recognize this truth. For example, in the UK both national and local government now use what are known as 'generally accepted accounting principles', particularly in their accounting for assets. In what follows in this book, I shall mostly refer to companies, by which I mean limited companies. However, the principles and practices described can be applied in any kind of organization, including the public sector.

In the case of a limited company the shareholders – the investors – appoint directors to act as custodians of their money and to run the business on their behalf. The directors in turn delegate some of this authority to managers. Investors have a free choice in deciding where to invest their money. Rational investors invest it where they believe they will obtain the highest 'return' commensurate with an acceptable level of risk. If the company in which they have, for the time being, invested ceases to produce what they regard as the highest return available, then they will take out their money and put it elsewhere.

FINANCIAL CASES

The 'return' on the shareholders' money will be the sum total of the returns on all the individual investments that the company makes. Examples of investments made by companies might be any of the following: building a new manufacturing plant, developing a new product, entering a new market, taking over a competitor, buying shares in a supplier, or undertaking an IT investment. Each discretionary investment by a company, in IT systems for example, should only be made if it can reasonably be shown that, of all the possible uses of the limited funds available, it is likely to produce the highest return. The investment may deliver a return directly, or as an enabling project, not itself profitable but facilitating other investments that will be.

In business therefore, no longer should the question be 'which course of action costs least?' but 'which course of action returns the most?' To answer that question it is necessary to compare the costs associated with an investment with the benefits that will be generated. So, in business we are usually concerned with building, not just a cost case, but a cost–benefit case, and it is this that is usually being referred to when business people talk of a 'financial case'. However, a financial case is an aid to decision-making, it is not a decision maker. While most businesses produce a financial case for any significant investment, there are wide variations in the extent to which it is actually relied upon in making the decision whether to proceed or not. A financial case is usually part of something bigger, called a business case.

BUSINESS CASES

A business case sets out all the arguments for and against a proposed course of action, including the financial arguments. Whereas the financial case only includes those matters that it has been possible to express in numeric terms of benefit and cost, the business case, on the other hand, includes such matters as:

- Do we have to do this for legal or regulatory reasons?
- Is this proposal in accordance with the business strategy? This will itself have been formulated with a view to maximizing the long-term return on shareholders' money.
- Is this an enabling project, not profitable in itself, but an essential foundation for others that will be?
- Can we afford not to do this? Can we afford not to enter a new market that a competitor has entered (for example, a supermarket going into financial services), or not to adopt a new technology that a competitor has adopted (for example, a retailer installing electronic point of sale systems)?

Intangible or soft benefits

A business case will also usually include what are called intangible or soft benefits. Examples of words often used to describe these are:

- improved company image;
- increased brand awareness;
- improved employee morale or loyalty;
- better service to customers.

Note that it is benefits that are usually soft; costs have a habit of being depressingly hard, and to get bigger as the full implications of the investment become apparent.

Some investment decisions may be taken wholly on consideration of the financial case. Others may be taken with little or no consideration of it. Which approach is favoured will depend partly on a particular company's way of doing things. Some companies are heavily driven by numbers, others are not. Within a particular company, the approach taken will depend partly on the nature of the proposed investment or project and partly on the personalities of the decision makers. For example, a decision whether to replace old IT technology with new, with no strategic overtones, will often be heavily influenced by numbers. By contrast, a decision whether to develop a new product or enter a new market is more likely to be driven by gut-feel and entrepreneurial flair.

Hardening soft benefits

Since many investment decisions are in fact influenced, at least to some extent, by the numbers, it makes sense to ensure that whatever benefits can be quantified are quantified by the proposer of the idea. Two particular and related techniques are useful here. The first is the repeated use of those two most useful words – 'So what?' The second is to get the potential 'buyer' of the idea (internal or external) to do your selling for you. Smart sellers know that their objective should be the same as the buyer's – and the business buyer's objective should be to maximize the return on shareholders' money. Taking as an example the soft benefit 'better service to customers', a useful conversation to have, with yourself if nobody else wants to play, might go as follows:

'A benefit of this system will be better service to customers.'
'So what?'
'Customers will be happier with us as a supplier.'
'So what?'
'Where they have a choice, customers will be more inclined to buy from us than from our competitors.'
'So what?'
'So our sales will increase.'

Having established that if the cited benefit means anything it means that sales will increase, the question then becomes 'by how much?' This is where you get the 'buyer' to do your selling for you by pleading from ignorance – an idea described as 'the power of one' by Mack Hanan (2004). Choose the sort of percentage increase in sales that you believe the other person thinks is achievable, and then suggest a much smaller number. Suppose you believe that your 'buyer' actually anticipates a sales increase of five per cent as a result of your proposal, then suggest one per cent. If this smaller number will itself make your case, so much the better. In any event, if your original estimate of what is in the other person's mind was about right, then they may start to talk you up. Continuing with the above example, the conversation might proceed as follows:

'Suppose as a result of the proposed investment we can increase sales by one per cent?'
'Oh, I'm sure the increase would be more than that.'

To this the reply is, of course:

'Really, how much more?'

– and you are well on the way to having quantified the previously unquantifiable.

WHAT IS A BENEFIT?

From a financial point of view, a benefit is not a benefit unless it has a positive number attached to it, and it is financial matters with which we are concerned in this book. There are only four ways in which a financial benefit can arise in the case of a typical business investment, such as IT. These are:

- an increase in income;
- a decrease in, or avoidance of, outgoings;
- bringing forward income;
- postponing outgoings.

For the sake of completeness it should be added that another kind of financial benefit is represented by the appreciation in value that may occur with some kinds of asset. Land, buildings and shares are examples. Land and buildings may feature in IT investments but since the likelihood of their appreciation is unpredictable it would be unwise to count on it in the process of trying to justify an investment.

For the time being we shall concentrate on the first two items in the above list: increasing income and reducing or avoiding outgoings. The last two items in the list represent one reason why discounted cash flow is such an important factor in investment justification, and why it was one of the first principles that we covered in this book. The last of the four, postponing outgoings, is one reason, but often not the most important reason, why leasing can be such a useful way of financing IT. See Chapter 8: IT financing and leasing.

> ### Checkpoint
>
> So far in this chapter, we have covered the first four of its objectives. In particular:
>
> - we have discussed why businesses have to be more rigorous in justifying investments than do we as individuals;
> - we have considered financial cases in the context of business cases;
> - we have looked at ways that may help to put a financial value on so-called intangible benefits;
> - we have listed the four kinds of financial benefit likely to be relevant to an IT investment.

CASH FLOW AND PROFIT

In the above, I have mentioned 'income' and 'outgoings'. What, in business terms, do these words mean? In business, there are two ways of looking at income and outgoings. They are:

- cash flow, which means receipts and payments of cash;
- profit, which means revenues earned less expenses incurred, whether they have been received or paid for in cash or not.

Ultimately, the most important of these two meanings in business is the same one that is important to us as individuals, namely cash flow. We have already established that the primary purpose of business is to increase the wealth of its proprietors. That, ultimately, means cash wealth, and if it means cash wealth for the proprietors it had better mean cash wealth for the business too. That is the main reason why investment opportunities are usually evaluated primarily in terms of their effect on the cash flow of a business, even if other methods are used as well.

If cash flow is so important, what then of profit? Are business results not reported primarily in terms of profit and loss? Indeed they are, although companies now have to produce a cash flow statement as well as a profit and loss account as part of their annual accounts. However, the key word above is 'reported'. Profit is a reporting device, necessary partly because of the convention, now long enshrined in law, that companies have to report their results to their shareholders at least once a year. However, it is also the best way yet devised of measuring the increase in wealth, or 'net worth', of a business during a period.

The market trader

Ultimately, profit and cash flow are the same thing. It is their timing that differs. The simpler the business, the easier is this idea to understand. Imagine Fred, a market stallholder who buys (for cash) and sells (for cash) tins of beans. Suppose that Fred buys a new supply of beans every day, and that everything he buys is sold the same day, so that there are no unsold stocks; also that there are no other expenses. Suppose that in a year Fred's purchases amount to £80,000 and his sales to £100,000. Table 2.1 shows Fred's cash flow statement and profit and loss account for his first year. From these you will see what common sense tells us to be true – that for Fred, net cash flow and profit are indeed the same thing.

TABLE 2.1 *Comparison of cash flow and profit (Fred)*

	£000
Cash flow statement	
Receipts	100
Payments	−80
Net cash flow	20
Profit and loss account	
Sales	100
Cost of sales	−80
Profit	20

Now imagine Newsoft Limited, a small software house that has just started business in rented premises. They have bought (for cash) IT systems for £60,000, which are estimated to have a useful life of four years and no residual value. They will write off the systems, on a 'straight line' basis, over the four years, so that depreciation charged as an expense will be £15,000 per year. Depreciation is covered in some detail in Chapter 7. Suffice it to say here that it is a way of charging the cost of a long-term or 'fixed' asset as an expense over its expected life. Also assume the following facts concerning the first year of business:

- Sales (all received in cash) are £200,000.

- Expenses (all paid in cash) other than depreciation are £160,000.

Please now look at Table 2.2. It shows Newsoft's cash flow statement and profit and loss account for its first year.

TABLE 2.2 *Comparison of cash flow and profit (Newsoft Limited)*

	£000
Cash flow statement	
Receipts	200
Payment for IT system	−60
Other payments	−160
Net cash flow	−20

Table continues …

TABLE 2.2 *Continued*

	£000
Profit and loss account	
Sales	200
Cost of sales, and expenses other than depreciation	−160
Depreciation ('straight line')	−15
Profit	25

Profit positive, cash flow negative

Newsoft is showing a profit for the year of £25,000, but a negative cash flow of £20,000. The difference of £45,000 is that part of the cash expenditure on the IT systems that has not yet been charged to the profit and loss account as depreciation, as it represents an expense attributable to subsequent years.

At the end of the fourth year, if all other expenses continue to be paid in cash, and all revenues are received in cash, then taking the four-year period as whole, Newsoft's profit, like Fred's, would be equal to its net cash flow.

In the above example of Newsoft (Table 2.2), depreciation was the only reason for the difference between net cash flow and profit. In reality, however, there are many reasons why Newsoft's, or any other company's, net cash flow in any year would rarely if ever equal its profit. They include the following:

- sales made but not yet paid for in cash by the customer (called trade debtors);
- cash expenditure incurred on work not yet completed (work in progress) or sold (finished goods);
- goods and services received from suppliers not yet paid for (trade creditors);
- tax due but not yet paid (non-trade or 'other' creditors).

Accounting standards

If ever you run out of things to read, there is always the bound volume of all the accounting standards that apply in your country. For example, in the UK some of these are called *Statements of Standard Accounting Practice* (SSAP), while others are called *Financial Reporting Standards* (FRS) and the book containing them runs to over three thousand pages. In the USA, standards are published as *Statements by the Financial Accounting Standards Board* (FASB). There is a gradual convergence towards the adoption of international accounting standards (IAS), but at the time of writing (2005) most countries continue to maintain their own. These accounting standards contain the large number of rules that have to be followed in preparing a set of accounts, particularly company accounts. Even these formidable tomes, however, cannot legislate for every single circumstance. Some things are, and probably always will be, left to the judgement of the business person. Among these are some aspects of depreciation.

Depreciation

Over how long a period should assets, IT assets for example, be depreciated? Generally, assets should be depreciated over their expected useful economic lives. However, what is the expected useful economic life of a particular kind of IT asset? For one business it might be two years; for another it might with equal legitimacy be five years. The same kinds of asset might have different expected useful lives at different stages of a business, depending on the speed of its growth. The main thing that the rules require is consistency, within and between accounting periods.

The longer the write-off period, the lower the depreciation per year. Profit is revenue (sales) less expenses. Depreciation is an expense, so the lower the depreciation the higher the profit, and vice versa. It is easy, is it not, to understand the temptation to write off assets over a longer period rather than a shorter period, despite the problems, described in Chapter 7, that this can cause.

Furthermore, there is nothing to say that the 'straight line' method is the only way of calculating depreciation. A method that more closely reflects the decline in market value of an asset would be to write off a percentage of the cost, say 50 per cent, in the first year, then 50 per cent of the remaining cost the following year, and so on until the asset is sold or scrapped. Table 2.3 shows what adopting this approach would do to Newsoft's profit in its first year. Instead of the £25,000 shown in Table 2.2, with the now greater amount of depreciation charged as an expense, the profit has gone down to £10,000. Choose the depreciation period and method for significant assets, and to some extent you have chosen your profit. Finance is an art and not a science.

TABLE 2.3 *Different depreciation method, different profit (Newsoft Limited)*

	£000
Profit and loss account	
Sales	200
Cost of sales, and expenses other than depreciation	− 160
Depreciation (50% per annum on the 'reducing balance')	− 30
Profit	10

Stock valuation

If you need more convincing of this, then think of your local corner shop. The 'cost of sales' of the corner shop in its first year of business is its purchases less the value of its unsold stock at the end of the year. But what is the value of the unsold stock of a shop? Cost price? Perhaps, but the cost of the latest purchases of each line or of the earliest purchases, or the average cost? And what about allowances that should be made for deterioration? And how accurate was the stock count? The valuation of stock has a direct effect on profit. The higher the stock value the lower the cost of sales, and therefore the higher the profit; the lower the stock value the higher the cost of sales, and therefore the lower the profit.

Profit is to some extent a matter of opinion. That is not to deny its importance, or the need to try to calculate it as accurately as possible. If it is important artificially to chop up the continuous process of business into chunks of one year's duration – and it is, for several reasons – then the concept of profit is now universally accepted as the best way of doing so. The reasons why we have to chop business results into one-year chunks include the following:

- reporting results to the proprietors;
- having a basis for assessing tax.

The profit concept is also useful for measuring the performance of divisions or departments within a business, and as a basis for motivating and rewarding employees – with profit-related bonuses, for example.

A BASIS FOR INVESTMENT DECISION-MAKING

The point of all this is to try to determine which of those two most important measures of business activity, cash flow and profit, provides the soundest basis for investment decision-making. Look again at Tables 2.2 and 2.3. By changing the method (and, had we wished, the period) of depreciation, we changed the profit. Did we also change the cash flow? No, we did not. Short of deliberate misrepresentation is there anything that we could do to change the cash flow statement? No, there is not. Our personal bank statement at the end of each month shows our cash position as it is. We may not like it and, in particular, we may not like the colour of the ink in which the final balance is printed, but we are stuck with it. Cash flow is a matter of fact.

Any investment by a company, in IT systems for example, will have an effect on both the company's cash flow and its profit over the following few years. It is of course important to work out the likely effects of an investment on both cash flow and profit, and most businesses do so, as we shall see. But which of the two provides the sounder basis for deciding whether to make the investment or not? For most companies, cash flow is the main basis of financial cases to be used as aids to investment decision-making.

As it happens, the numbers representing the cash flows provide the basis for all the main investment appraisal methods that are commonly used. We have already looked at one of these – net present value. In Chapters 4 and 5 we shall look at them all in some detail. Before doing so, however, we need to look at what it is that we should be evaluating.

When is a benefit not a benefit, and a cost not a cost?

It is often quite difficult to decide what should go into a financial case, and what should be left out. What should go into it is, surely, the benefits and costs attributable to that course of action, were it to be undertaken. In the example of the car project we made a start with trying to establish which costs and benefits are 'attributable' to a proposed investment and which are not. We covered the most fundamental of the principles, but we have to do more in order to complete the picture and to make it relevant in the context of IT decision-making.

We must come up with as complete an answer as possible to the questions 'when is a benefit not a benefit, and a cost not a cost?' This we shall do in the next chapter, using, as the means to achieve understanding, an IT-specific example.

Summary

The main points covered in this chapter, linked to its objectives, have been the following:

- *Companies always have to consider the benefits of a proposed investment as well as the costs. Companies are the custodians of money invested by shareholders, who seek to maximize the return on their investment.*
- *A financial or 'cost–benefit' case in business is a statement of the estimated financial benefits and costs, over a chosen period, of a business opportunity. It is usually part of a business case, in which both financial and non-financial implications of the investment are set out.*
- *In financial cases for discretionary investments, only quantified benefits count. 'So what?' questions, and deliberate understatement, can sometimes help to quantify intangibles.*
- *In business, except for the possible appreciation in value of assets such as land, there are four ways of deriving a financial benefit: increase income, reduce or avoid outgoings, bring income forward, or postpone outgoings.*
- *Cash flow is a matter of fact; profit is a reporting device and, to some extent, a matter of opinion. Cash flow is usually the main basis of financial cases to be used as aids to investment decision-making.*

3 When is a Benefit not a Benefit?

Objectives

The purposes of this chapter are:
- *to allow you to experience, step by step, building an IT financial case in incremental cash flow form;*
- *to show you that it can sometimes be quite difficult to decide whether a particular benefit or cost is really attributable to a proposed IT investment or project;*
- *to derive some rules that will help overcome those difficulties;*
- *to introduce a set of data that will be used for illustration in subsequent chapters.*

When is a benefit not a benefit; when is a cost not a cost, especially in evaluating IT investment? We are now in a position to apply the principles of cash flow-based financial cases to the kind of situation typical in IT decision-making. To do so we shall use an example (Example 3.1). In working through it we shall discover that in practice it is not always easy to answer the above questions.

HOW TO BUILD AN IT FINANCIAL CASE

This is one of the examples in the book from which you might gain by attempting to work through it yourself, before you look at the solution and before you read the explanations that follow it. I shall, quite deliberately, not give you any guidelines in advance, beyond the principles already discussed in earlier chapters. The reason is this. Many people experience difficulty with the task of building IT financial cases. The solution and explanations will have more relevance to you if you have already experienced the difficulty.

You may, of course, not wish to tackle the problem yourself. As I said in the Preface, if you can't stand numbers, then ignore them and just follow the logic in the narrative. Just continue reading, treating the example, its solution and the detailed explanations as a continuous part of the text. For some of the items in the example, alternative answers may be valid, depending on what assumptions you choose to make about the points in question.

The point of the example is to encourage you to think about each item described, and to decide whether or not you think it should be included as a relevant cash flow in the financial case. To some extent, neither the numbers nor the situation as a whole are realistic. For example, with today's technology, whether or not to install a new stock control application would usually be regarded as a separate decision from whether or not to install new equipment on which to run it. I have combined them, and several other things besides, into a single assumed 'project', requiring a single decision. The reason is simply to provide one vehicle for illustrating as many of the problems typically presented by IT financial cases as possible. The next few pages describe the situation.

EXAMPLE 3.1: DESCRIPTION

Assume that a company has some problems in need of solution. Among them are that:

- its expenses are too high;
- it holds too much stock, and knows that it could operate with at least 10 per cent less if only it could be more efficiently organized;
- its customers are taking too long to pay their bills.

All these things are putting an unacceptable strain on the company's cash resources. Parts of the company's existing IT systems need replacing anyway, and the company believes that the benefits from increased efficiency brought about by new systems and new applications would more than justify the costs.

The input data

A short time ago the chief executive officer (CEO) appointed a team led by a senior, non-financial, manager to collect data on the likely benefits and costs of this project over a four-year period. The team was not due to report yet, but assume that this morning the CEO will summon the team leader and ask for a brief statement of what the costs and benefits were looking like in case the matter were to come up at this afternoon's board meeting ('Nothing elaborate – back-of-envelope stuff will do'). The team leader sat down with the file and wrote down the notes that you will find in Table 3.1.

TABLE 3.1 *Example 3.1 – Input data*

	£000
Existing systems	
Purchase price three years ago	760
Depreciation (straight line), per year	190
Book value at the end of this year (Year 0)	190
Maintenance, power and insurance, Year 1	70
then increasing by 10% per year thereafter	
Expected proceeds of sale (Year 0)	30
New systems including software lump sum licence payments	
Purchase price (Year 0)	700
Expected proceeds of sale at end of Year 4	20
Depreciation (straight line), per year	170
Maintenance, power and insurance (Year 1 including warranties)	20
Ditto (Year 2, then increasing by 5% per year thereafter)	40
Supplies and spares for new systems	
Initial cost (Year 0) and will remain at that level throughout the four-year period,	10
but will be run down to zero towards the end of Year 4	
Raw materials and others stocks	
Currently (and will remain at this level if the status quo is maintained)	500
New systems would facilitate a permanent reduction during Year 1 et seq. to	450
However, assume for simplicity that reduction takes place instantaneously at Year 0.	
Stock used will remain constant at £2,000k per year under old systems or new.	
Stock holding costs per year	
10% of stock value	
For this, assume the real situation, namely that stock level will fall evenly during Year 1.	
Trade debtors	
Currently, and will remain at this level if the status quo is maintained	600
New systems would facilitate a permanent reduction during Year 1 et seq. to	530
However, assume for simplicity that reduction takes place instantaneously at Year 0.	
Sales will remain constant at £3,600k per year under old systems or new.	
Finance	
New systems would be financed with 50% debt, 50% new equity	
Consultants' fees	
For work already completed and paid for	30
Contract staff	
If new system not undertaken, then these will be engaged to update existing systems.	

Expected costs during Years 1, 2 and 3:	60	150	80

Table continues ...

TABLE 3.1 *Continued*

	£000

Storekeepers

Cost in Year 1, then increasing by 5% per year thereafter, but see below   20

One storekeeper due to retire at end of Year 2. If new system undertaken, then he
will not be needed beyond the end of Year 1 and is prepared to retire a year early
on payment of lump sum of £15k at end of Year 1 in lieu of his Year 2 wages.
Another storekeeper would also no longer be needed if new systems undertaken.
She has agreed an internal transfer to another job from Day 1 of Year 1. Unknown to her
the new job is currently being advertised externally for £22k, also expected to increase at
5% per year. If new systems decided upon, the advertisement will be immediately withdrawn.

Rent of IT department space

Rent (fixed throughout Years 1 to 4, with an external landlord) per year   120

If new systems installed, then one quarter of this would become vacant from the
beginning of Year 1. The Accounts Payable department would move in to
the vacated space to relieve overcrowding in their current offices. One quarter
of the IT department's rent would be cross-charged to Accounts Payable.

Specialist programmers

The IT department does some external work for which it earns revenue. Each year the
project will require one specialist programmer full-time. There is one existing such
programmer, who will cost £40k in Year 1, expected to increase at an annual compound rate
of 5% thereafter. She is currently doing revenue-earning work. If the project does not proceed,
then she would continue to do so during Year 1, generating £70k of revenue during that year.
If the project does proceed, then during Year 1, because of an expected skills shortage, she
would have to stop revenue-earning work, and instead work on the project. At the beginning
of Year 2 the company expects to be able to hire an additional such specialist at the rate of pay
then applicable to the existing one, who would then resume revenue-earning work for the
remaining three years.

Other non-capital net cash inflows

Years 1, 2, 3 and 4   90   121   117   52

These are simply balancing numbers so that
the eventual totals will be convenient to work with later.

How to approach the task

The team leader now has the task of putting the above data into a suitable form for the board meeting. The question is 'if you had been given the job, what would the financial case look like?' If you have chosen to try this for yourself as an exercise, or if you have to do something like it in real life, then I suggest that you adopt the following approach:

1. Go step by step through the input data (in Table 3.1 for this example). Do not be alarmed by its apparent complexity. In the narrative that follows you will taken step by step through every line.

2. Regarding each item, decide whether it represents a cash flow that is attributable to the proposed investment.

3. Write the numbers representing the cash flows, with plus or minus signs, under the years in which they will occur.

4. Total across and down so that in the bottom right-hand corner you end up with a number representing the total net incremental cash flows attributable to the investment.

Most people who are not financially trained (and some who are, but for whom this kind of thing is not an everyday occurrence) find some difficulty in such tasks. Remember that what we are trying to do is to determine what cash flows representing benefits and costs can properly be attributed to a proposed investment. The purpose, eventually, is to decide whether or not to undertake the investment or, if it were already in progress, to continue with it. Remember also the following points, discussed earlier:

- What we are producing is a cash flow estimate, so it follows that anything that is not a cash flow should be excluded. Later in the book we shall be producing a profit and loss estimate from the same data.

- The cash flow estimate will be used for decision-making. We cannot make decisions that will change the past. Therefore, anything that represents a past cash flow that cannot be reversed (a sunk cost) should be excluded. A past cash inflow that cannot be reversed could, I suppose, be called a 'sunk benefit'. This term is not in common use, but exactly the same principle applies to both costs and benefits.

- Do not confuse decision-making with other business activities. Documents quite similar in some ways to the one we are building here will be produced and maintained for such purposes as pricing (of external contracts) and management accounting. These, however, will include all the costs incurred and revenues earned since the project was first thought of. Such documents are record-keeping documents; ours is intended as an aid to decision-making.

If in doubt, then, about whether a particular item should be included, you should ask the following question: if a decision were to be made to go ahead (or to continue) with the proposed project, would this particular item represent a future cash inflow or outflow that would not have occurred otherwise? If yes, then include the item; if no, then exclude it. By 'the project' I mean, in this case, the proposal to stop doing what we are currently doing and to adopt the alternative that is being proposed.

EXAMPLE 3.1: SOLUTION

With these guidelines in mind, I suggest that you now look at the solution (see Table 3.2). If you attempted the exercise yourself, then compare your answer with mine. With some of the items, the answer depends on what assumptions were made, so my solution may differ from yours. Provided my result follows logically from my assumptions, and yours from your assumptions then there is no problem. If you did not attempt the exercise, then simply read through Table 3.2 point by point and see whether you think that it makes sense.

TABLE 3.2 *Example 3.1 – Solution*

	Yr 0 £000	Yr 1 £000	Yr 2 £000	Yr 3 £000	Yr 4 £000	Total £000
Incremental cash flows arising from changes if new investment is undertaken						
Items listed in sequence given in example						
Sale of old equipment	30					30
'Old' running costs saved		70	77	85	93	325
Cost of new systems	−700					−700
'New' running costs incurred		−20	−40	−42	−44	−146
Eventual sale of new eqpt.					20	20
Stock of supplies	−10				10	0
Raw materials & other stocks	50					50
Trade debtors	70					70
Financing cash flows – ignored						0
Stock holding costs reduced		3	5	5	5	18
Consultants' fee – ignored						0
Contract staff avoided		60	150	80		290
Retm't bonus & wages saved		−15	21			6
Storekeeper redeployed		22	23	24	25	94
Rent of space – ignored						0
Specialist programmers		−70	−42	−44	−46	−202
Other net cash inflows		90	121	117	52	380
Refer also to explanations in the text.						
Net incremental cash flows	−560	140	315	225	115	235

In either case, you should then read through the following paragraphs that explain why I have done what I have done. The only other guidance I would offer is to repeat that while academics, and many practitioners, agree broadly on the principles illustrated by this exercise, individual organizations would differ on points of detail, of format or even on points of principle. They simply do things differently. The best I can hope to do is to offer explanations for the approach I am illustrating that are logical and convincing, to provide a basis for understanding better how your particular organization does things and why.

EXAMPLE 3.1: EXPLANATIONS

The following are explanations for the solution in Table 3.2.

Existing IT equipment

For the purpose of decision-making, the original cost of the existing equipment is irrelevant. It is a past cash outflow that cannot be reversed (a sunk cost), so it is ignored.

The depreciation of the current (and of the proposed new) equipment is undoubtedly important for accounting purposes. However, depreciation is simply an entry in the account books and does not represent a cash flow. Therefore it is excluded from financial cases based on cash flow. Later, it will be taken into account when we come to look at the effect of the proposed investment on profit.

We were told that the book value of the old equipment at the end of the current year will be £190k. The difference between this and the expected proceeds of sale of £30k represents a 'loss on sale' of £160k. This too is important for accounting purposes, and represents inadequate depreciation charged as an expense in the past. However, it does not represent a cash flow, so it is excluded from the cash flow financial case.

One piece of information about the old equipment that is relevant to our cash flow estimate is the expected proceeds of sale of £30k. It is shown as a cash inflow in Year 0.

The only other relevant information about the old equipment is its running costs, which we shall no longer incur if it is sold. Avoiding a cash outflow that would otherwise be incurred, is a benefit attributable to the investment, so the relevant amounts are included as positive numbers in the appropriate years. Even though this is an incremental financial case, I have chosen to show the old running costs and the new as separate items, simply to illustrate that point. Showing them separately is also a way of highlighting the difference between the 'old' and 'new' numbers, if to do so is an important argument in selling the case, internally or externally. Instead, I could of course have shown a single incremental line entitled 'system running costs'. I adopt this approach later in Table 3.6.

New systems

The purchase cost (£700k) of the new systems is clearly a cash outflow that will occur if the proposed project is undertaken but would not occur if it is not. Therefore it is included.

Depreciation does not represent a cash flow, so it is excluded. Once again, however, if we wished to consider the effect of the proposed investment on profit, as distinct from cash flow, as we shall do later, then of course depreciation would be taken into account.

The eventual proceeds of sale represent a cash inflow that will only occur if the new systems are acquired, so the amount is included. In the case of equipment that is subject to regular replacement, we might produce several versions of the financial case. Each would assume different replacement times, at which the equipment would have different estimated market values. In this way it is possible to work out the optimum replacement cycle for such equipment.

Is it right to include in our financial case the sale proceeds of both the old equipment and the new? The answer is yes, because whichever course of action is decided upon, stay as we are or make the change, we shall end up in four years' time in the same situation (with no equipment, just as in our earlier example of the two cars).

The running costs and maintenance of the new systems are cash outflows obviously attributable to them, so they are included.

Supplies and spares for new systems

The inclusion of this item, although the amount is quite trivial, was to illustrate the fact that with many investments in major assets there are two quite separate and different kinds of 'capital' expenditures. There is the cost of the asset itself. In addition, there usually has to be an initial investment in stocks of supplies and spares. For this also, a cash outflow will be incurred. At this point, it is appropriate to digress in order to compare and contrast the terms 'fixed capital' and 'working capital'.

Characteristics of 'fixed capital' items

Major assets, such as significant items of IT hardware, are relatively long-term investments, by which I mean that they have expected useful lives of more than one year. They are usually called 'fixed assets', and the money used to acquire them is therefore sometimes called 'fixed capital'. Significant one-time charges for software, whether for ownership or for rights of use, are now treated for most accounting and tax purposes, in the UK at least, just like hardware. For a summary of the accounting and tax rules for software, please see Appendix 4.

The main characteristic of most fixed assets is that during their useful lives their value is used up and not replenished. This is what 'depreciation' means. Therefore the value of the capital invested in them is also used up.

When the old car finally goes to the breakers, it is not just the car that has been used up but the money that you spent on it. Both these things are represented in accounting terms by charging depreciation as an expense. Doing so reduces the 'book value' of the asset; it also reduces the profit, because the higher the expenses the lower the profit. Profit is simply the amount by which the capital of a business is increased by trading, so reducing the profit also reduces the capital.

Characteristics of 'working capital' items

By contrast, things like stocks, whether of supplies and spares, raw materials, work in progress or finished goods, are short-term assets. By this I mean that they are typically used up in less than a year. Such assets are usually called 'current assets' or 'circulating assets', and the money used to acquire them is usually called 'working capital' or 'circulating capital'.

The main characteristic of stocks of things like supplies and spares is that as they are used up they are replenished, so the level of the stocks tends to remain the same. Therefore the amount of money (working capital) invested in them tends to remain much the same throughout the life of the asset that they exist to support. In preparing a financial case, the assumption is often made that shortly before the end of that asset's life, the stocks of its associated supplies and spares will be run down to zero. At this point, what would have been a cash outflow to replenish the stock does not occur. The avoidance of a cash outflow is just as much a benefit as is an increase in cash inflow.

Suppose, however, the probability that the system now being proposed will eventually be replaced by a similar one for which it is believed that the supplies and spares will be equally suitable. In that case, the assumption would probably be that the stock of supplies and spares would not be run down. If that were so, then there would not be a corresponding avoidance of the final cash outflow for replenishment. Here is one example of the evaluation of a project being influenced by what may be known, or reasonably assumed, about its eventual successor. We shall meet others.

Raw materials and other stocks

That was rather a long explanation, but this particular topic is one that many people have difficulty with. Also, what is true of movements in one kind of stock (supplies and spares) is also true of other kinds. The argument is therefore equally valid for the general stocks of the business (raw materials, work in progress and finished goods).

Stock reduction is an important purpose of many IT applications. Stocks on a shelf waiting to be processed or sold have had to be paid for – with cash. So have the materials and labour expended on partially finished products or services, usually known as work in progress. The greater the quantity of stock, the more cash has had to be paid. We have either had to borrow this money and are paying interest on it, or we are losing interest on money that could otherwise have been invested.

How to handle a decrease in stock levels

If stocks have to be increased, for seasonal reasons or because of an expansion of business, those stocks will have to be paid for. That will represent a cash outflow to bring them up to their new higher level. On the other hand, if, as a result of new systems, stocks are reduced in any year (usage remaining constant), it must mean that cash that would have been paid out for replenishment has not had to be paid. There will thus have been a decrease in cash outflow that year equal to the decrease in stocks. Since we are assuming that this decrease in cash outflow would not have occurred but for the new system, it is therefore a benefit attributable to the investment, and should be included in our cash flow financial case.

Table 3.3 shows in detail how the numbers are arrived at. Notice that it is the amount by which stocks have decreased between the end of one year and the end of the next that represents the decrease in cash outflow during the year. Once stocks have stabilized at a new level there is no further change to the annual cash outflow until the stock level changes again. The numbers in Table 3.3 are trivial, but you may find it a useful template for more complex situations.

TABLE 3.3 *How reducing stock levels reduces cash outflow*

	Ref	Yr 0 £000	Yr 1 £000	Yr 2 £000	Yr 3 £000	Yr 4 £000
Stock at end of year if project implemented *	a	450	450	450	450	450
Stock used during year	b	2000	2000	2000	2000	2000
Total of stock used and in hand $(a+b)$	c	2450	2450	2450	2450	2450
Stock at beginning of year	d	500	450	450	450	450
Stock bought during year (cash outflow) $(c-d)$	e	1950	2000	2000	2000	2000
Stock bought during the year if no new project	f	2000	2000	2000	2000	2000
Reduction in cash outflow due to project $(f-e)$		50	0	0	0	0

* *Recall that in this example it is actually during Year 1 that the reduction in stock level takes place. Treating it as happening at the end of Year 0 is a simplifying assumption, adopted to make later parts of the evaluation process easier to handle. Also, and for illustration only, Year 0 is treated as though it were a full year.*

Now we revert to the point alluded to earlier. At the beginning of the project we had to spend cash on an initial stock. Therefore, an equivalent amount of cash will be 'liberated' when that stock is run down to zero at the project's end. The initial cash outflow is balanced by a corresponding cash inflow at the end. Unless, that is, we believe that the stocks can and will continue to be useful to the successor project.

The influence of a successor project

Where, as in this example and in many IT applications, an expected benefit of a project is a reduction in stocks, then the reverse process must be considered. As stock is reduced, cash that would otherwise have to be spent replenishing it no longer has to be spent (the avoidance of a cash outflow). However, to evaluate a project at all it has to be assigned, however artificially, an 'end'. If the benefit of the project were indeed to end, then in theory there would be an increase back to the earlier level of stock, and a consequent cash outflow corresponding to the earlier inflow represented by the reduction. Unless, that is, we believe that the effects of this project (lower stock levels) will continue under its successors. In this case, we would be justified in not burdening the presently proposed project with such a cash outflow.

For example, imagine a project to install a computer-integrated manufacturing system. Once installed and working, it would be most artificial to imagine that the whole system would be dismantled in a few years just because the technology on which it was first installed needed replacing. At that time, the proposal to replace the technology should be evaluated for what it would then be: a technology replacement proposal, not a 'new application' proposal. In practice, therefore, it is unlikely that an increase in stock at the end of a project would need to be considered.

Trade debtors

Trade debtors are customers who have not yet paid for goods or services that they have bought from us. Money that belongs to us is in their bank accounts rather than in ours. That means that, as with money tied up in stocks, we are either having to borrow money and are paying interest on it, or we are losing interest on money that could otherwise be invested. If, as a result of the new system, debtors are reduced in any year (sales remaining constant) it must mean that there has been a cash inflow that year equal to the decrease in debtors. Since we are assuming that this cash inflow would not have occurred but for the new system, it is attributable to the project. It should therefore be included in our cash flow financial case.

Table 3.4 shows in detail how the numbers are arrived at. As with the reduction in stocks, it is the amount by which debtors have decreased between the end of one year and the end of the next that represents the increase in cash inflow during that year. Once debtors have stabilized at a new level there is no further change to the annual cash inflow.

TABLE 3.4 *How reducing debtors increases cash inflow*

	Ref	Yr 0 £000	Yr 1 £000	Yr 2 £000	Yr 3 £000	Yr 4 £000
Debtors at start of year if project implemented *	a	600	530	530	530	530
Sales during year	b	3600	3600	3600	3600	3600
Total of initial debtors and sales during year (a + b)	c	4200	4130	4130	4130	4130
Debtors at end of year	d	530	530	530	530	530
Debts paid during year (cash inflow) (c − d)	e	3670	3600	3600	3600	3600
Debts paid during year if no new project	f	3600	3600	3600	3600	3600
Increase in cash inflow due to project (e − f)		70	0	0	0	0

* Recall that in this example it is actually during Year 1 that the reduction in debtors takes
place. Treating it as happening at the end of Year 0 is a simplifying assumption, adopted to
make later parts of the evaluation process easier to handle. Also, and for illustration only,
Year 0 is treated as though it were a full year.

As with stock, if it is believed that the effects of a credit control application
will continue after its initial evaluation period, then the benefit
represented by the initial reduction in debtors need not be reversed in
the financial case.

Financing

As discussed in Chapter 1, there is certainly a sense in which receipt of a
bank loan is a cash inflow. Its eventual repayment is a cash outflow, as are
the periodic payments of interest. However, as also demonstrated (see
Table 1.13), the discounting process has the effect of cancelling out these
'financial' cash flows, so to include them would be a waste of time and
space. Also, it starts to get a bit silly if a financial case were to include
'financial cash flows' if the project happened to need borrowed money, but
did not include them if the company happened to have sufficient cash of
its own. For both these reasons, 'financial cash flows' are ignored.

Stock holding costs

The assumption made in this case is that stock holding costs (for example
warehousing, insurance, deterioration, theft and obsolescence) vary with
the average levels of stock. So the benefit each year attributable to the new
system is an avoidance of cash outflow equal to 10 per cent of the difference
between the average stock level under the old system and the average stock
level under the new. As you may imagine, we shall eventually be
discounting the cash flow estimates that we have compiled. The discounting process will take care of the cost of the money 'tied up' in the stock, so
only the 'non-financial' costs of holding stock should be taken into account.

Table 3.5 shows in detail how the numbers are arrived at. It was only in
recording the reduction of stock itself that we made the simplifying

assumption of an instantaneous occurrence at the end of Year 0. For the purpose of calculating stock holding costs, I have assumed that the reduction in stocks occurs gradually and evenly throughout Year 1.

TABLE 3.5 *How reducing stock levels reduces stock holding costs*

	Ref	Yr 0 £000	Yr 1 £000	Yr 2 £000	Yr 3 £000	Yr 4 £000
Assumptions:						
1 Holding costs vary with average stock levels						
2 Stock level is reduced evenly throughout Year 1, i.e. the simplifying assumption no longer applies						
3 For illustration only, Year 0 is treated as though it were a full year.						
The 'do nothing' case						
Stock at end of each year		500	500	500	500	500
Average stock during year	*a*	500	500	500	500	500
If new project implemented						
Stock at end of each year		500	450	450	450	450
Average stock during year	*b*	500	475	450	450	450
Reduction in average stock held (*a* − *b*)	*c*	0	25	50	50	50
Reduction in stock holding costs (10% × *c*)		0	3	5	5	5

Consultants' fee

'Dear Bloggs and Co, as we have decided not to go ahead with the project, we request the return of your consultancy fee.' Unless they are an unusually generous firm of consultants, their fee is unlikely to be returnable, whatever decision is made about the project. The fee is a sunk cost and should therefore be excluded from the financial case.

Contract staff

This is another example of costs avoided: an avoidance of cash outflows that, but for the proposed investment, would occur. Therefore the amounts are included as attributable benefits.

Storekeepers

Here, some thought is needed to ascertain what cash flows are actually attributable. If the new project does not happen, the older storekeeper will continue to be paid wages until the end of Year 2. If it does, then, as a direct result, his Year 2 wages will not be payable: the avoidance of a cash outflow and therefore a benefit attributable to the project. However, also as a direct result of the project, the lump sum of £15k will be payable, in addition to his Year 1 wages. This is an attributable cash outflow.

With regard to the second storekeeper, since she is staying with the firm, at the same wages, her wages are an equal expense under either option and should therefore be ignored. However, but for the proposed investment, the firm clearly intends to employ an additional person and it is the expense of that additional person that will be avoided if the investment is undertaken. Therefore, it is the wages for the job externally advertised that represent the avoidance of a cash outflow attributable to the project. The fact that the new job arises in a part of the firm remote from the project is not relevant. It is the company as a whole that will avoid the cash outflow.

Rent of IT department space

Cross-charges, sometimes called allocations, are 'book' transfers from one departmental budget to another. They represent the value of goods or services provided by one department to another within an organization. The rent of IT department space is an example.

An analogy with depreciation may be helpful. Depreciation can be thought of as a way of allocating amounts of money spent at a particular time to the future periods that benefit from the expenditure. Cross-charges can be thought of as a way of allocating amounts of money, spent by one part of a business, to other parts of it that benefit from the expenditure. Both are consequences, precise or approximate, of money having been spent, but both are simply entries in account books. They are not themselves cash flows.

The question remains 'if a decision were to be made to go ahead with the proposed project would this particular cross-charge represent a cash flow that would not have occurred otherwise?' In this case the answer is no. There would be no change to the amount paid externally for the space occupied by the IT department.

Suppose, however, that things were really bad in accounts payable, so bad that a decision to rent additional external space had already been taken. Then suppose that the opportunity to move into the IT department's space would allow that decision to be rescinded. Then, the (real) money that would no longer have to be spent on external space becomes a benefit (the avoidance of a cash outflow) attributable to the project. It would therefore be included in the financial case.

Can 'funny' money be treated as if it were real money?

Are there then any circumstances in which it might be possible to regard a cross-charge as a 'cash flow' in investment evaluation? The answer has to be that so long as we choose to use cash flow analysis as a basis for the evaluation, then we should stick to its rules. The most obvious of these is that only changes to cash flows should be included.

However, cross-charges may provide clues to the real cash flows that lie behind them. In a perfect world, a cross-charge to a departmental budget would always represent precisely a real cash flow that had occurred or would occur elsewhere in the company. In that perfect world the 'receiving' manager could treat cross-charges as though they were real cash flows, because the amounts would correspond to real cash flows.

In practice, a 'receiving' manager will know where a past cross-charge has come from. It may therefore be possible, by enquiry, to determine the amount of any real cash flows that gave rise to it. Similarly, it may be possible, by enquiry, to determine the estimated amount of future changes to a cross-charge if an investment being evaluated goes ahead. If so, it may be possible to discover the amount of the estimated real cash flows, if any, that lie behind it. If truly 'attributable' according to the rules, then those cash flows should be included in the evaluation. However, what would be included would indeed be the attributable cash flows, not the cross-charges that provided the clue to their existence.

Estimating the effects of a decision on budgets

Budget-holding managers will of course be interested in the effects that investments, if undertaken, will have on their budgets, and on how their department's performance will be measured. For that reason, and because cross-charges are usually a fact of life for budget-holders, documents that look very like cash flow estimates will often be produced that include cross-charges. Such documents may indeed show the effects of proposed projects on budgets.

Analyses that contain both cash and non-cash items are not 'cash flow financial cases' as we have come to understand them. It follows that it would seem to be invalid to apply to them evaluation techniques, such as discounted cash flow, designed to evaluate only cash flows. However, as already acknowledged, organizations have their particular ways of doing things. Nevertheless, if variations on the standard theme are used, it is important to try to work out exactly what 'advice' is being offered by the results.

Specialist programmers

The attributable cost in Year 1 is the opportunity cost represented by the revenue forgone. Thereafter, the attributable cost is that of hiring an additional specialist specifically for the project.

Other cash outflows avoided

As stated in the problem, all significant cash flows would usually be itemized. In this example, these are just balancing numbers, designed to ensure that the totals are numbers that it will be easy for us to work with later.

WHAT CASH FLOWS ARE RELEVANT?

That concludes the explanations of the solution to Example 3.1. The bottom line of Table 3.2 shows the total net incremental cash flows attributable to the proposed investment and the years in which they would occur. Figure 3.1 shows these cash flows diagrammatically, while Figure 3.2 is a similar diagram, but of the cumulative cash flows. The example should have reinforced the rules that we formulated in Chapter 1 about which items should, and which should not, be included in cash flow financial cases. It has also suggested a few additional rules. The following, for convenience, is a now a slightly enlarged summary of the rules.

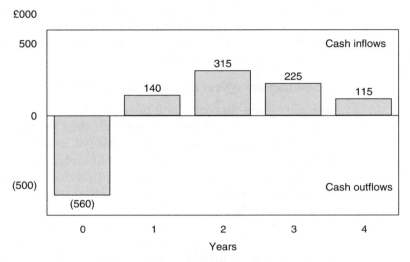

FIGURE 3.1 *Example 3.1 – Cash flows*

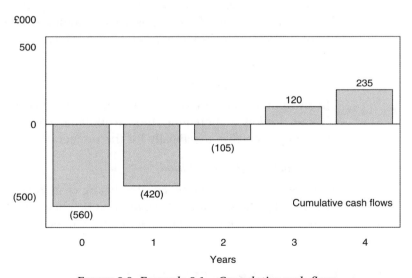

FIGURE 3.2 *Example 3.1 – Cumulative cash flows*

The following should be included in cash flow financial cases:

- Cash flows that will occur if the proposed investment goes ahead, but will not occur if it does not.

In consequence, the following should be excluded from cash flow financial cases:

- Past cash flows that cannot be reversed (sunk costs, and indeed 'sunk benefits').
- Cash flows that do not differ between the alternatives.
- Depreciation and losses (or profits) on the sale of assets.
- Cross-charges or allocations from one departmental budget to another. However, cross-charges may provide clues to real cash flows that will occur elsewhere in the business that may themselves be attributable to the investment.
- Anything else that is not a cash flow.

In addition, we have already discussed the fact that financial cash flows, including receipt and repayment of loans, and payments of interest, should also be excluded because they are cancelled out by the discounting process.

Categories of cash flow

The cash flows in Table 3.2 are in the sequence in which the items in the example were originally presented. This was deliberate to facilitate reference between the problem, the solution and the explanations. However, as already discussed in the explanations, different cash flows are subject to different accounting (and tax) treatment and these differences will be significant for some of the analyses that we shall do later. For this reason, it makes sense to group like items together and to subtotal them as in Table 3.6. Three categories are appropriate. These are cash flows arising from changes to, respectively:

- fixed capital;
- working capital;
- operating income and outgoings.

The terms 'fixed capital' and 'working capital' refer to things that affect the balance sheet. Their characteristics were described earlier in this chapter. 'Operating income and outgoings' refers to things that affect the profit and loss account as well as affecting cash flows.

TABLE 3.6 *Example 3.1 – Categorized solution*

	Yr 0 £000	Yr 1 £000	Yr 2 £000	Yr 3 £000	Yr 4 £000	Total £000
Incremental cash flows arising from changes to fixed capital items						
Sale of old equipment	30					30
Cost of new systems	−700					−700
Eventual sale of new eqpt.					20	20
Subtotals	−670	0	0	0	20	−650
Incremental cash flows arising from changes to working capital items						
Stock of supplies	−10				10	0
Raw materials & other stocks	50					50
Trade debtors	70					70
Subtotals	110	0	0	0	10	120
Incremental cash flows arising from changes to operating income and outgoings						
System running costs (incremental)		50	37	43	49	179
Stock holding costs reduced		3	5	5	5	18
Consultants' fee – ignored						0
Contract staff avoided		60	150	80		290
Retirement bonus & wages saved		−15	21			6
Storekeeper redeployed		22	23	24	25	94
Rent of space – ignored						0
Specialist programmers		−70	−42	−44	−46	−202
Other net cash inflows		90	121	117	52	380
Subtotals	0	140	315	225	85	765
Financing cash flows – ignored						0
Refer also to explanations in the text.						
Net incremental cash flows	−560	140	315	225	115	235

IS IT A WORTHWHILE INVESTMENT?

What is the sign of the number in the bottom right-hand corner of Table 3.6? It is positive, which means that in cash terms the benefits of undertaking the proposed investment exceed the costs. If the sign were negative, it would mean that, even in cash terms, we should be worse off making the change than staying as we are. The evaluation methods we shall be considering in the next two chapters have the effect, at best, of leaving that total number unchanged, and at worst, of making it smaller or even negative. So, a financial case that showed a negative total at this point would need to be substantially revised to make it worthy of further consideration.

The positive total in Table 3.6 tells us that in cash terms we should be £235k better off by undertaking the investment than by not doing so. However, even though the number is indeed positive, is it big enough to make the investment worthwhile? What the whole bottom line tells us is that if we invest net cash of £560k, over a four-year period, we should get our money back plus £235k. Even before doing any calculating, gut-feel probably tells us that that seems like a reasonable investment. Not spectacular, but reasonable – at least worth exploring a little further. The various investment appraisal methods, to be discussed in the following two chapters, allow us to undertake this exploration.

Summary

The main points covered in this chapter, linked to its objectives, have been the following:

- *We have made decisions about the cash flows to go into a financial case, in incremental cash flow form, containing as many as possible of the elements typical of a proposed IT investment.*
- *We have experienced the difficulties that can arise in making those decisions. The difficulties can be minimized by adherence to the rules summarized in the next bullet point.*
- *It is usual to include in an incremental cash flow financial case only cash flows that will occur if the proposed investment is undertaken, or continues, but will not occur if it does not. Consequently, the following are usually excluded: sunk costs (and 'sunk benefits'), depreciation and losses on sale, and cross-charges. 'Financial' cash flows are also excluded.*
- *We have built up a set of data to which we shall refer in subsequent chapters.*

4 How Financial Cases are Evaluated: Part 1

This chapter and the one that follows it both cover what is really a single topic: how IT and other investment proposals are evaluated. The reason why the topic has been spread over two chapters is to keep chapters to a reasonable length.

Objectives

When you have studied this chapter you should be able to:

- *describe and contrast, in a business context, the two discounted cash flow (DCF) methods of investment evaluation:*
  - *net present value (NPV)*
  - *internal rate of return (IRR);*
- *apply the above methods to an IT financial case and explain the significance and limitations of the results;*
- *explain how 'profitability index' (PI) can be used to compare the profitability of projects from their NPV results;*
- *explain what 'cost of capital' means and why it is the basis for the discount rates used in NPV calculations;*
- *distinguish between 'systematic risk' and 'project risk' and describe how they may be taken into account in using DCF methods.*

You will no doubt recall the simple car example in Chapter 1. One of its purposes, which, in Chapter 3, we applied in building an IT financial case, was to make clear the need to ensure that only relevant cash flows are attributed to an investment. Another purpose was to show that determining the relevant cash flows is not the end of the financial case but the beginning. The reason, as we discovered, is that the cash numbers by themselves do not tell us the real value of the proposed investment. To find that, we explored the use of discounted cash flow, and specifically net present value (NPV).

PRESENT VALUE REVISITED

In this chapter, we shall extend our understanding of discounted cash flow and apply its principles to the IT financial case that we built in Example 3.1. We shall try to determine which, financially, is the better of the two possible options in that example: to stay as we are or to adopt the proposed change. As with the car example, we shall only need to work with the total cash numbers. For what we shall discuss in this chapter, although not in the next one, the detail that led to the totals is irrelevant.

Discounted cash flow, you will recall, allows us to calculate the real values, the 'present values', of cash flows occurring at different times, by taking into account the 'time value of money'. The way it worked in the car example in Chapter 1 was to discount the cash flows at a rate equal to the 'cost of money' of the individual concerned. In that example, we assumed that our only source of money was an overdraft and that the cost of the overdraft, our personal cost of money, was 13 per cent per annum. Thirteen per cent was also, of course, the return expected by the bank, so we could say that our cost of money is equal to the return expected by the provider of that money. This particular way of expressing it will be helpful in what follows. You will also recall that the reason why an overdraft was assumed in the car example was that it gave us the closest parallel with a business situation, because, in a sense, all of a company's, or any other organization's, money is 'borrowed'.

THE COST OF CAPITAL

The term 'cost of money' is also used in business. However, 'cost of capital' is a more commonly used term, although it means the same thing. Our personal 'cost of money' was fundamental in determining the real costs to us of the two car options. It was the basis of the discount rate that we used in discounting the cash flows, and it was easy to work out. For the same reasons, a company's cost of capital is fundamental in determining the real costs and benefits to the company of any investment, in IT or anything else, that it may make.

So, the cost of capital is also the basis of the discount rate used by a company in discounted cash flow calculations. The difference is that working out a company's cost of capital can be rather more complicated. Furthermore, the detailed arguments to support the calculations are lengthy. For these reasons, this is one thing in the book that I will concede as belonging in 'deep finance' territory. In practice, the finance department or finance person in a company would be expected to provide guidance on what discount rate to use in NPV calculations. However, the following paragraphs give a summary of the main principles.

In order to work out a company's cost of capital, it is first necessary to know what its capital consists of. In most companies it consists of two elements: money belonging to shareholders ('equity', which is share capital plus reserves) and money lent by lenders ('loan capital' or 'debt'). The cost of a loan, the 'return required by the lender', is known. It is the periodic rate of interest charged. The complicated part is the cost of equity, the 'return required by shareholders', but a starting point is to ask why people invest in shares and how they get their 'return'.

Cost of equity

Shareholders, at least those in companies quoted on a stock exchange, get their return in one or both of two ways: by dividends or capital growth. Capital growth means an increase in the market price of the share; dividends are periodic payments, usually made once or twice a year, out of net profit. Dividends, however, are not compulsory, and capital growth is not certain; indeed, it may be negative. It depends on market expectations of the company's future performance, but that in turn depends on unpredictable 'systematic risk' factors in the economy, such as interest and taxation rates and consumer demand. So, shares in general are a more risky investment than, say, Government bonds, on which the return is certain.

Business, and investment in business, is about risk and reward. The greater the risk, the higher the expected reward. So, investors expect a higher return from shares in general than from Government bonds. They also expect a higher return from shares in volatile industries than from those in more stable ones.

Cost of debt

Lenders to a company will usually be prepared to accept a lower return than shareholders, because lending is less risky. There are two reasons for this. First, payment of interest on a loan is compulsory, while dividends are not. Second, lenders have more security than do shareholders. They have a higher priority for getting paid when a company is wound up, so they stand more chance of getting their money back should it fail.

WEIGHTED AVERAGE COST OF CAPITAL (WACC)

So, what is a particular company's cost of capital? It is a combination of its cost of equity and its cost of debt. If there were equal quantities of equity and debt, then the cost of capital would be the average of the two. Because the respective quantities are usually unequal, a weighted average is required. So, a company's cost of capital is the weighted average of its costs of equity and debt. The following example illustrates the calculation and introduces the effect of tax.

Assume that a company has £3 million of share capital and £1 million of loan capital. The total capital is therefore £4 million. Suppose that the 'cost of equity' is 12 per cent per annum and the cost of debt eight per cent. What is the company's current 'cost of capital'? The calculation is as follows:

$$(3/4 \times 12) + (1/4 \times 8) = 9 + 2 = 11\%$$

Therefore the basis of the discount rate used by this particular company in discounted cash flow calculations would be 11 per cent, but only if the company ignores tax in such calculations. Dividends are paid out of already-taxed profit. Interest on business loans, however, unlike interest on personal loans, is an expense deductible in arriving at profit. Therefore, the true cost of loan interest is not its gross cost but its net-of-tax cost. If the tax rate paid by the above company is 30 per cent, then the net-of-tax cost is not eight per cent but 5.6 per cent. To arrive at the after-tax cost of capital, the above calculation would be restated as follows:

$$(3/4 \times 12) + (1/4 \times 5.6) = 9 + 1.4 = 10.4\%$$

Not all organizations are taxable and not all businesses take tax into account in investment evaluations. However, many do, and that is why a chapter on tax (Chapter 6) is included in the book. Until we reach that point, all our evaluations will be done on a before-tax basis. That means that we shall be evaluating before-tax cash flows using before-tax discount rates. In the above example, that would mean using 11 per cent as the discount rate, not 10.4 per cent.

A company's weighted average cost of capital, whether before or after tax, represents the average return expected by all the providers of that capital. It follows that any discretionary investment (in for example an IT investment) had better provide a return at least slightly greater than the cost of capital if it is to be worthwhile. That is why cost of capital is the basis of the discount rate used in business NPV calculations. I say 'the basis of the discount rate' because, as we shall see later in this chapter, some companies make adjustments to it as one way of reflecting the different risk of different investments. This 'project risk' is quite different from the risk inherent in shares, discussed above. The latter, sometimes called 'systematic risk', is taken into account in working out the cost of the equity component in the cost of capital.

The effects of time

The cost of capital will change over time. Old loans will be paid off and new ones taken out. More shares may be issued or shares may be bought back by companies with surplus cash. Market expectations of the return required from shares generally will change in line with changes to market interest rates and other economic factors. Expectations of the return required from particular shares may change as views of their risk change.

Should these expected variations not be taken into account in evaluations (such as NPV evaluations) that involve the cost of capital? In theory, yes. In practice, however, especially over the relatively short evaluation periods chosen for most IT projects, they are nearly always ignored. Today's cost of capital, and the discount rate derived from it, is usually deemed to apply for the whole period of the evaluation.

APPLYING PRESENT VALUES

We are now in a position to work out the net present value (NPV) of the investment whose cash flows we estimated in Example 3.1. In doing so, we shall assume that the before-tax discount rate to be applied to the cash flows is 10 per cent. This is chosen purely to be a convenient number to work with. Table 4.1 shows the answer. If you wish to work it out for yourself, then use the discount table called Table A1.1 in Appendix 1. Referring to the discount table, simply look up the 10 per cent discount factors for one, two, three and four years respectively. Enter them in the appropriate columns and then multiply the cash flows by the discount factors to arrive at the present values for each year. Finally, add all the present values to arrive at the 'net present value' to go into the total column. Figure 4.1 shows the discounted cash flows diagrammatically.

TABLE 4.1 *Example 3.1 – Net present value*

	Ref	Yr 0 £000	Yr 1 £000	Yr 2 £000	Yr 3 £000	Yr 4 £000	Total £000
Assumption: All cash flows occur on the last day of each year							
Net cash flows	a	−560	140	315	225	115	235
Discount factors (10%)	b	1.0000	0.9091	0.8264	0.7513	0.6830	
Present values ($a \times b$)		−560.00	127.27	260.32	169.04	78.55	75.18

The term 'present values' refers to the per-year amounts. The total of those amounts, £75.18k in this case, is usually referred to as the 'net present value' because it is the sum of a series of present values, some of which are positive and some negative.

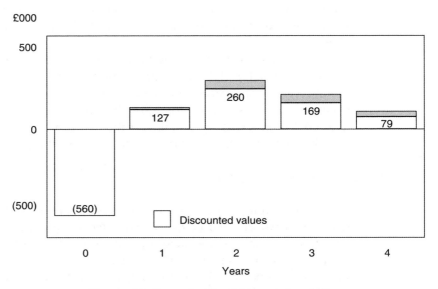

FIGURE 4.1 *Example 3.1 – Discounted cash flows*

A common mistake in doing these calculations is to forget that 'Year 0' is taken as meaning 'today', in respect of which the discount factor is of course 1.0. It is only future cash flows that are discounted. Remember that the term 'net present value' (NPV) is used because it refers to the sum of a series of individual present values, some of which are positive and some negative.

What does the answer mean?

As with the car example, we need to ask what the NPV of £75,180 actually means. Remember that in the car example we had produced a 'cost case'. We were only considering the net costs of the alternative courses of action. In the 'whole project' approach, therefore, we were looking for the alternative that yielded the smallest negative NPV. This told us which alternative had the lowest cost in real terms. Using the incremental approach, a positive incremental NPV meant that, by comparison with continuing as we were, the proposed alternative was cheaper in real terms.

When looking at business investments, however, as distinct from personal ones, we have already discussed the need to take into account not just costs but benefits also. So, rather than looking for the alternative that yields the smallest negative NPV we should be looking for the one that yields the largest positive NPV. Using the incremental approach, a positive NPV, as in Table 4.1, means that, compared with continuing as we are, the proposed alternative is more beneficial in real terms. In fact, in using the incremental approach, a positive NPV, however small, always indicates that in real terms the proposed change is preferable, at least in theory, to the 'stay as we are' option.

Another way of expressing the answer in Table 4.1 is to say that by undertaking the proposed project we should be better off by £75,180 after taking into account the cost of the money invested in it. Here is yet another way of expressing the answer: if, as in this example, a positive value remains after discounting the cash flows at the cost of capital, it must mean that the percentage return yielded by the investment must be greater than the cost of the capital invested. If the NPV had been negative, then it would mean that the percentage return is less than the cost of capital, and the business would be worse off as a result. How to establish exactly what that percentage 'rate of return' is will be considered later in this chapter.

Finally, suppose that there is one other investment (Project B) under consideration besides ours (Project A), of roughly similar amount, size and risk to ours. Suppose also that the two investments are mutually exclusive, that is they are both competing for the same limited funds. As an IT example in real life, this situation might represent proposals for a required solution being tendered by different suppliers. Suppose Project B, when compared incrementally to 'staying as we are', yields a positive NPV of £130k. If we are otherwise indifferent to which approach to adopt, then the numbers suggest that Project B should be undertaken rather than Project A (NPV £75,180). This is because for a roughly similar investment it yields a higher positive NPV.

Decisions are made by people, not by financial models. In making decisions, people take into account many things, including, but not limited to, the 'advice' suggested by financial models. Nevertheless, in IT decisions the financial numbers are often an important factor in the decision-making and may sometimes be decisive. Therefore, we need to be sure that we understand exactly what it is that a particular result is telling us. From what has just been discussed it is possible to formulate what we might call the 'NPV decision rule'. It is as follows.

THE NPV DECISION RULE

If the estimated cash flows of an investment are discounted at the weighted average cost of capital, then:

- if the resulting NPV is positive, by however small an amount, then the proposed investment is, in theory, worthwhile, because it would yield in real terms more than the money invested in it;
- if the resulting NPV is negative, by however small an amount, then the proposed investment is not worthwhile, because it would yield in real terms less than the money invested in it;
- if several mutually exclusive investments of similar kind, size and level of risk are competing for the same funds then the best option from a purely financial viewpoint is the one that yields the largest positive NPV.

PROFITABILITY INDEX

Now suppose that we are evaluating two or more mutually exclusive projects of dissimilar size, exclusive either because of limited funds or because of the nature of the situation. An example would be the typical IT situation in which two or more suppliers are responding to a request to provide quotations for a particular IT solution. Suppose that 'our' project (Example 3.1), with its NPV of approximately £75k, represents one such project, and that a competing one, when all of its estimated cash flows are taken into account, gives an expected NPV of £80k. If all non-financial considerations between the two situations were regarded as equal, then which of the two should be accepted? The answer, at first glance, is the one that has the highest positive NPV. However, suppose that the initial investments required by the two alternatives, and their expected returns, were substantially different. Would it not be better to use a measure that indicated which project would generate most money from each pound spent? Such a 'profitability index' is sometimes used. The profitability index (PI) is usually taken as the total present value of the future net cash flows of a project (all the PVs except Year 0), divided by the present value of the net initial (Year 0) investment.

Table 4.2 shows our project as Project A, with its NPV of £75.18k and its net initial investment of £560k. The present value of its future net cash flows is £635.18k. Its profitability index would be (635/560 =) 113 per cent, or 1.13 if you prefer. Suppose the figures for Project B to be as stated in Table 4.2. Although its NPV of £80k is indeed higher than that of Project A, its profitability index is lower, at 110, or 1.10, so it yields slightly less in terms of return per pound invested. Since Project A has, marginally, the higher profitability index, it should, other things being the same, be accepted rather than the alternative. Profitability index is a way of using the powerful NPV concept to compare the real values of projects of different magnitudes.

TABLE 4.2 *Profitability index (PI) or excess present value index*

	Ref	Project A (Our project) £000	Project B (Competing project) £000
Project A data taken from Table 4.1			
Present value of future net cash flows	*a*	635.18	850.00
Present value of net initial investment	*b*	−560.00	−770.00
Net present value (NPV)		75.18	80.00
Profitability index (PI) (*a/b*)		113% or 1.13	110% or 1.10

> **Checkpoint**
>
> So far in this chapter, we have covered the following factors relating to its first three objectives:
>
> - We have looked in more detail at the concept of net present value (NPV), first considered in Chapter 1.
> - We have defined 'cost of capital' and discussed its significance in investment evaluations.
> - We have discussed risk and reward, and why investors require a higher return from shares than from, say, Government bonds.
> - We have derived an 'NPV decision rule' to help interpret NPV results.
> - We have discussed 'profitability index' as a way of deriving a measure of profitability from NPV results.

INTERNAL RATE OF RETURN

Net present value (NPV) is only one side of the coin called 'discounted cash flow'. We can now look at the other side of that coin.

We have just noted that if a positive value remains after discounting the cash flows of an investment at the cost of the capital invested, then it must mean that the percentage 'return' yielded by the cash flows must be greater than that cost of capital. However, we left open the question of exactly what that percentage return is and how it is calculated. It is called 'internal rate of return (IRR)'. We shall look at the question of how it is calculated shortly, but before doing so we shall look at a very simple example that illustrates the concept of IRR.

Suppose that you deposit £100 in a bank today. Suppose also that you have no idea what rate of interest the bank is paying. A year from today you discover that the balance of your account is £105, at which point you withdraw all the money and close the account. What is the rate of interest earned by your investment during the year? The answer is obviously five per cent. If the balance on the account were £107 the rate of interest earned would have been seven per cent; if the balance were £115 the rate of interest would have been 15 per cent, and so on.

A miniature 'project'

Let us now think of that example as though it were a miniature 'project'. The only 'cost' is the investment of the £100; the only 'benefit' is the receipt of the £105 exactly one year later. If the £100 is your only supply of money, and if (despite your apparent indifference) the rate of interest of five per cent were in fact the best rate obtainable at that time, then the opportunity cost of money invested in the bank was five per cent per annum. (Recall, from Chapter 1, that for a cash-rich individual, it is that person's opportunity cost of money that is the appropriate discount rate to use in NPV calculations – the cost of the best alternative forgone in order to make the investment.) Let us now set out a statement of the cash flows of the 'project' and then discount them at the opportunity cost of money in order to work out their net present value. Table 4.3 gives the answer.

TABLE 4.3 *A miniature 'project'*

	Ref	Yr 0 (£)	Yr 1 (£)	Total (£)
Cash flows arising from bank investment:				
Cash outflow – money invested		−100.00		−100.00
Cash inflow – money withdrawn			105.00	105.00
Net cash flows	a	−100.00	105.00	5.00
Discount factors (5%)	b	1.0000	0.9524	
Present values (a × b)		−100.00	100.00	0.00

You will not, I think, be surprised to find that the NPV of the 'project' is zero. Discounted at the cost of money, the cash outflow exactly equals the cash inflow. Furthermore, I think you will agree that, whatever the interest rate assumed, if the cash flows of the above project are discounted at that same rate, then its net present will always be zero.

An NPV of zero means that the discounted value of the benefits of an investment is exactly equal and opposite to the discounted value of its costs. However, we have, I think, agreed that the discount rate that gives that NPV of zero represents the rate of interest earned by the investment. Let us now shorten that last phrase. If we change 'rate of interest earned by the investment' to 'internal rate of return' then we have an explanation of what that commonly used term actually means.

The above 'project' was trivial. However, what is true for one investment is true for others, even though the cash flows would be more varied. We are now able to state a definition of internal rate of return (IRR) as follows: the internal rate of return of a series of positive and negative cash flows is represented by the discount rate that, when applied to them, yields an NPV of zero. Note that the concept of IRR requires at least one negative initial cash flow – an 'investment'. If there is no investment, it means that any percentage 'return' is infinite. Thus, not all IT investments are suitable for IRR analysis, as we shall see later in Chapter 9 when considering a typical outsourcing decision. This is a limitation of IRR that does not apply to NPV.

Earlier in this chapter I conceded that one particular topic – how to calculate a company's cost of capital – is a matter that can justifiably be left to people in deep finance. I shall now concede that one other topic – how to calculate internal rate of return mathematically – is a matter that can justifiably be left to people in deep mathematics. Such people tell me, and I am happy to believe them, that it is all a question of solving polynomial equations. I think that most readers will not feel unduly insulted if I continue the explanation of IRR as though you, like me, are not entirely at home with polynomial equations.

Fortunately, it does not matter much, for two reasons. One is that modern spreadsheets, which most people use for tasks such as investment evaluation, have IRR and NPV functions built in. So do many financial calculators. The second reason is that, with a knowledge of NPV it is, as we shall see, a simple matter to derive a reasonable approximation to the IRR of any given set of cash flows.

How to derive IRR

Please refer back to Table 4.1. Discounting the cash flows at 10 per cent gave us an NPV of roughly £75k. What do you think would happen to the NPV of the cash flows if we were to apply a much higher discount rate, say 24 per cent? Table 4.4 shows the answer.

TABLE 4.4 *Effect of higher discount rate on NPV*

	Ref	Yr 0 £000	Yr 1 £000	Yr 2 £000	Yr 3 £000	Yr 4 £000	Total £000
Assumption: All cash flows occur on the last day of each year							
Net cash flows	*a*	− 560	140	315	225	115	235
Discount factors (24%)	*b*	1.0000	0.8065	0.6504	0.5245	0.4230	
Present values (*a* × *b*)		− 560.00	112.91	204.88	118.01	48.65	− 75.55

Even without looking at the answer, the clue lies in the word 'discount'. In everyday life discount implies something – a price – getting smaller. The higher the discount the lower the price. For our current purpose discount also implies something – the real value of cash flows – getting smaller. The higher the discount rate, the smaller the NPV; so much smaller in this case that it has gone negative. It is now roughly − £75k. This suggests the method that we might use to work out a reasonable approximation of IRR. Although the relationship of discount rate to NPV is not a straight-line one, it is nearly so at normally encountered discount rates.

Remember that the internal rate of return (IRR) is the discount rate that gives an NPV of exactly zero. So the question is 'if a discount rate of 10 per cent gives an NPV of + £75k and a rate of 24 per cent gives an NPV of − £75k, what discount rate, approximately, will give an NPV of zero?' If we were to assume a linear relationship, then the answer would be approximately 17 per cent (the rate that lies midway between 10 per cent and 24 per cent). In Figure 4.2 the true NPVs of our cash flows for all discount rates between 10 per cent and 24 per cent are plotted against the straight-line approximation. From this graph you can see that the true IRR is actually 16.2 per cent. The approximation of 17 per cent would usually be regarded as accurate enough.

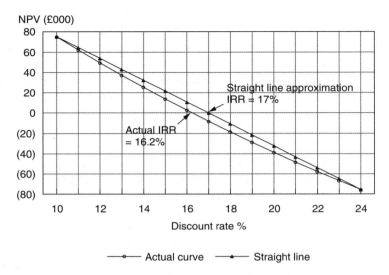

FIGURE 4.2 *Example 3.1 – Internal rate of return*

How is IRR used?

The first question is 'is the IRR greater than the "required return", represented by the discount rate that would be applied to NPV calculations?' If it is not, then this would mean that the return from the investment would be less than the cost of the capital invested in it. If it is, as in this case, then another test will usually be applied.

Organizations will, over time, accumulate experience of the IRR typical of investments of a particular kind, size and level of risk that they have undertaken. They will regard this as a yardstick or 'hurdle rate' for future investments. If the current hurdle rate for investments like ours is, say, 26 per cent, then ours, with its IRR of approximately 16 per cent, may not stand much of a chance, unless there are important factors of a non-financial nature to be taken into account. We should have to try to find ways of improving it. An IRR less than the hurdle rate may cause an investment to be rejected, even though the IRR is greater than the cost of capital.

Which is better: a bank account that pays interest at five per cent (has an 'internal rate of return' of five per cent) or one that pays interest at seven per cent? The one that pays the higher interest rate, of course – the one that has the higher 'internal rate of return'. The same principle applies to any investment, including one in IT. In comparing two similarly sized investments, the one more likely to be chosen would be the one that shows the higher IRR. However, the restriction to 'similarly sized investments' was deliberate. Compare the following two proposals:

Project A   IRR 20%
Project B   IRR 1943%

From a comparison of the IRRs, Project B would appear to be the more attractive by an overwhelming margin. However, a percentage by itself gives no indication of the relative sizes of the projects being compared. Remembering that NPVs are absolute numbers, suppose for example that the NPVs of the above projects are as follows:

Project A   NPV £2.59 million
Project B   NPV £18.5k

Project A is a proposal for a major network to improve the company's countrywide distribution system, while Project B is a proposal to reorganize the IT supplies store. Which is now the more worthwhile?

That was a ridiculously exaggerated example to make the point that reliance on percentage returns can be misleading. But therein lies what some people regard as the weakness of IRR: that it is a percentage. Others regard IRR as useful precisely because it gives a percentage result. Business people are used to results expressed as percentages. However, it would usually be wise to look at NPVs as well as IRRs as part of the decision-making process.

It is now possible to formulate what we can call the 'IRR decision rule', which is as follows.

THE IRR DECISION RULE

The internal rate of return (IRR) of a proposed investment is the discount rate that, applied to its estimated cash flows, yields an NPV of exactly zero.

- If the IRR is greater than the company's cost of capital, by however small a margin, then the proposed investment is, in theory, worthwhile because it would yield in real terms more than the required return on the money invested in it.

- If the IRR is less than the company's cost of capital, by however small a margin, then the proposed investment is not worthwhile, because it would yield in real terms less than the required return on the money invested in it.

- If several mutually exclusive investments of roughly similar size are competing for the same funds, then, other things being equal, the best option financially is the one that yields the largest positive IRR.

NPV and IRR contrasted

It was asserted earlier that NPV and IRR are the two sides of one coin: discounted cash flow. It should now be clear that this is indeed the case. Here is a summary that highlights the contrast between the two:

- Net present value (NPV) is the absolute number obtained by applying a discount rate, usually equal to, or based on, the weighted average cost of capital, to a series of cash flows.
- Internal rate of return (IRR) is the discount rate that, when applied to a series of cash flows, both positive and negative, yields an NPV of exactly zero.

While they are indeed two sides of the same coin, IRR has some practical limitations that NPV does not. These are as follows:

- IRR requires an initial cash outflow (an 'investment') in order to give a meaningful result; NPV does not.
- IRR gives a percentage result that, if not considered in the context of the size of an investment, can lead to misinterpretation; NPV is expressed as an absolute number, so the problem does not arise.
- Not so far considered is the fact that if, in a series of cash flows, the sign of the cumulative sum changes more than once, IRR will give multiple answers. This is because of the mathematics on which it is based. There is no such problem with NPV.

NPV, IRR AND RISK

Earlier, we discussed why the discount rate used in NPV calculations for investment evaluation is usually the company's weighted average cost of capital, or at least a value based on it. You will no doubt recall the fundamental reason for this. If the investment is the only one being considered, then a positive NPV means that we should be better off undertaking it than not doing so. A negative NPV says the reverse and the investment should not be undertaken. If we are comparing several mutually exclusive investments, then the one that yields the largest positive NPV is the most desirable from a financial viewpoint. However, it may be that some investments being proposed are more risky, and therefore more uncertain in their outcome, than others. They would no doubt be subjected to sensitivity analysis and possibly other risk assessment methods. Dixon (1994) gives good descriptions, with examples, of the many methods of dealing with risk and uncertainty. The question is how, if at all, can discounted cash flow be used to take into account the relatively greater risk and uncertainty of one investment over another?

Please look again at Figure 4.2. It shows how, for investments whose cash inflows exceed their cash outflows, the NPV decreases, and eventually goes negative, as the discount rate increases. This should provide a clue as to how a variation on the discounted cash flow theme is sometimes used to take project risk into account. Another clue is to remind ourselves that with most projects it is the benefits that get discounted most, because they usually occur later in time than the costs. The answer is that, in using NPV to evaluate investments, some companies apply a discount rate higher than the weighted average cost of capital. How much higher depends upon the perceived level of project risk.

Levels of risk

Suppose that a company has defined three categories of IT investment depending on their perceived level of risk, as shown in Table 4.5.

TABLE 4.5 *Example risk categories of IT investment*

Category	Type of investment	Risk category
1	Technology replacement	Low risk
2	Old hat, but new for us	Medium risk
3	Pushing the frontiers	High risk

Assessing this kind of risk can, of course, only be arbitrary. Table 4.6 shows examples of the kind of discount rates that might be used in working out the NPVs of investment cash flows.

TABLE 4.6 *Example discount rates*

Category	Discount rate
1	10% (cost of capital)
2	15% (cost of capital + 5%)
3	20% (cost of capital + 10%)

Suppose that this kind of approach were to be adopted in the case of our proposed investment in Example 3.1. If this were indeed the case then, by reading from the graph in Figure 4.2, the NPV of that proposed investment would be one of those in Table 4.7, depending upon which risk category it had been placed in.

TABLE 4.7 *Risk-adjusted NPVs for Example 3.1*

Category	NPV (approx)
1	+£75k
2	+£14k
3	−£39k

You will probably agree that only if classified as 'Category 1' would our particular proposal stand any chance of being undertaken. Note that the IRR would remain the same in all categories; that is decided once and for all by the arithmetic of the cash flows. The way IRR is sometimes used to reflect project risk is to impose higher hurdle rates for riskier investments. The higher the risk, the higher the required return.

Disadvantages of inflated discount rates

Inflating discount rates is certainly a simple way of adapting the NPV method to reflect the perceived project risk of a proposed investment, and it is quite often done. However, the approach is open to some fairly serious objections. You might find it worthwhile to pause at this point to think what they might be.

First, using the same inflated discount rate for all the cash flows assumes that they are all equally risky. This is most unlikely to be the case. Second, recall that for convenience we usually perform the calculations on net total cash flows. This means that the numbers we are using are in fact net totals of benefits and costs. Discounting means making numbers smaller. Making the benefits smaller by using a higher discount rate may make sense: that is precisely why we are using the inflated discount rate. But does it make sense also to make the costs smaller? It does not. The risk with costs is of an overrun, so if we want to reflect this we should be inflating the costs, not discounting them.

These are serious criticisms. However, it remains true that the method is quite widely used. As with most things in finance, the important thing is to be consistent. It is also important that people producing and interpreting the results should understand clearly what the numbers are telling them.

'Certainty equivalents'

Rather than using risk-adjusted discount rates, some companies approach the matter of project risk by applying 'certainty equivalents' or 'confidence factors' to the benefits (the cash inflows) before doing the NPV calculation. The cash flows having been individually 'risk-adjusted', the NPV calculations are then done using as a discount rate the unadjusted weighted average cost of capital.

In the previous example, all cash inflows in Category 1 investments might be reduced by, say, five per cent; those in Category 2 by 15 per cent and those in Category 3 by 25 per cent. The percentages applied are purely subjective, but then so are most of the cash flow estimates themselves. While it has the merit of simplicity, the method is rather a blunt instrument. Also, a predictable action of the sponsor of a proposal might be to try to inflate the cash inflows, knowing that they are subsequently going to be reduced.

Slightly less blunt is to apply different factors to the cash inflows in different years. For example, in a Category 2 investment (see above) the reduction applied to cash inflows in Years 1 to 4 might be, respectively, zero per cent, five per cent, 12 per cent and 20 per cent. Less blunt still might be to examine each significant cash flow and apply an individual factor to it.

The resulting reduction in benefits, by whatever method achieved, would of course produce a lower NPV and a lower IRR and would make the investment less attractive. To the perfectly reasonable argument that this is all purely subjective, I would respond that so is the inflation of the discount rate to an arbitrary figure that is then applied to all the cash flows. At least the idea of 'certainty equivalents' makes some attempt at assessing the risks associated with particular cash flows occurring at particular times.

More art than science

Finally, let us remind ourselves that every single number in a cash flow estimate is exactly that: an estimate. As somebody said, forecasting is notoriously difficult, especially when it concerns the future. Furthermore, all the evaluation tools described here and in the next chapter have imperfections and require certain assumptions to be made. As with much of finance, the whole of this subject is more art than science. I repeat that in order to achieve something that is in any way helpful to decision-making the two main requirements are consistency and a clear under-standing of what the results of any particular method, imperfect though it may be, are telling us.

The assertion that what we are considering is more art than science is in fact unfair to one of the techniques that we have considered, namely NPV. NPV is strictly mathematical and unambiguous. Any wrongness can only arise either from non-cash flows or non-relevant cash flows having been included in the numbers to be analysed. IRR, as we discussed earlier, although also mathematical, can nevertheless be ambiguous by, for example, giving multiple results.

The other evaluation methods, to be considered in the next chapter, are both useful and widely used. However, with the exception of 'shareholder value added'(SVA) they do not have the mathematical rigour of discounted cash flow. In the case of one of them ('payback') the method does not necessarily consider all the cash flows involved; in the case of another ('return on investment' or 'accounting rate of return') the method uses accounting numbers that are usually not exclusively cash flows.

There is a lot of number work in this chapter and in the next one. To help you keep track of it, at the end of the next chapter you will find a summary of all the evaluation methods (Table 5.10), a summary of relevant totals and other extracts from the various tables of Example 3.1 (Table 5.11) and a summary of all the evaluation results from Example 3.1 (Table 5.12). You may find it useful to glance at those three tables now to the extent that they summarise what has already been covered in this chapter.

Summary

The main points covered in this chapter, linked to its objectives, have been the following:

- *The two 'discounted cash flow' methods of investment evaluation are net present value (NPV) and internal rate of return (IRR).*

- *NPV is the absolute number obtained by discounting a series of cash flows at a rate equal to or based on a company's weighted average cost of capital. A positive NPV suggests that, in theory at least, a proposed investment is worth making; a negative NPV suggests the converse.*

- *IRR is the percentage rate of return implicit in an investment. It is the discount rate that, applied to the investment cash flows, yields an NPV of zero. An IRR greater than the cost of capital suggests that, in theory at least, the proposed investment is worth undertaking; an IRR less than the cost of capital suggests the converse. An investment with an IRR greater than the cost of capital may still have to meet a company-imposed 'hurdle rate'.*

- *'Profitability index' is a way of deriving a measure of profitability from NPV results.*

- *A company's cost of capital is the return required by the providers of the capital. It is usually the weighted average of the cost of equity and the cost of debt. Using it in NPV calculations gives a result that shows whether the investment yields an amount greater or less than the cost of the capital invested.*

- *'Systematic risk' is a term used to describe those unpredictable aspects of the economy as a whole, such as interest rates, tax rates and consumer demand, that make shares a more risky investment than, say, Government bonds. It is taken into account in calculating the cost of equity.*

- *'Project risk' refers to the fact that some investments or projects are more risky than others. It is sometimes taken into account by adjusting the cash flows or by applying an inflated discount rate in the NPV calculation. The latter approach can, however, give misleading results.*

5 How Financial Cases are Evaluated: Part 2

Objectives

When you have studied this chapter, a continuation of the previous one, you should be able to:

- *Describe the following methods of evaluating financial cases:*
  - *payback;*
  - *discounted payback;*
  - *return on investment (ROI);*
  - *shareholder value added (SVA);*
- *Apply all the above methods to an IT financial case, and explain the significance and limitations of the results.*

In the previous chapter we explored the application of discounted cash flow methods to the evaluation of IT, and other, financial cases. At the end of this one we shall look at a method (SVA) that at its simplest can be thought of as a variation of NPV. However, before doing so we shall discuss some other widely-used methods. The methods are payback and return on investment (ROI), also known as 'accounting rate of return' (ARR) or 'return on capital employed' (ROCE). We shall continue in this chapter to use the output from Example 3.1 for the purpose of illustration, in particular Table 3.6 on page 50.

PAYBACK

Payback is an almost universally used evaluation method. This is because it is both simple and rooted in common sense. It is also known as 'break-even', and the question it seeks to answer is very simple: how soon would we get our money back if we put it into this particular investment?

What is the payback of the financial case in Example 3.1? While not the most demanding of the things that I invite you to do in this book, you may nevertheless like to work it out for yourself. The usual assumptions are that the initial investment is made on the last day of Year 0 and that benefits accrue evenly throughout each year. The answer is shown in Table 5.1.

Figure 5.1 shows the now familiar diagram of this investment, with the break-even point marked on it.

TABLE 5.1 *Example 3.1 – Payback*

	Ref	Yr 0 £000	Yr 1 £000	Yr 2 £000	Yr 3 £000	Yr 4 £000	Total £000
Assumption: Cash flows occur on last day of Year 0, and then evenly within Years 1 to 4							
Net cash flows		−560	140	315	225	115	235
Cumulative net cash flows			−420	−105	120	235	

Break-even occurs during Year 3, when the cum. cash flow changes from negative to positive.

Net cash flow in Year 3	*a*	225
Net cash flow per month during Year 3 (*a*/12)	*b*	18.8
Positive cash flows in Year 3	*c*	120
Months from break-even to end of Year 3 (*c*/*b*)	*d*	6.4
Months in Years 1 to 3	*e*	36
Break-even occurs after (months) (*e* − *d*)		29.6

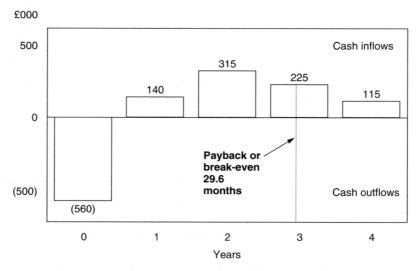

FIGURE 5.1 *Example 3.1 – Payback or break-even*

Some organizations use payback as a filter in order to weed out investments not regarded as worthy of further consideration. This is often done where more investment proposals are put forward than there are funds with which to undertake them. If a proposal passes the payback test by breaking even within the company's current 'hurdle period', then it may be subjected to some or all of the other evaluation methods. If not, it may be rejected out of hand. As an example, if investments of similar type, size and risk have typically paid back within 15 months, then ours, with a payback of nearly 30 months would not stand much of a chance unless the payback could be substantially improved. The simple expedient of using leasing to spread the payments can often bring forward the payback of an investment.

PAYBACK AND RISK

The payback question – how soon will we get our money back? – is one that we as individuals would ask almost instinctively if invited by a friend to put money into some 'little earner' that they had in mind, such as (perhaps) producing and selling the new jelly-slicer that the world has been waiting for. Why is this? The reason is associated with the idea of risk and uncertainty. Most of us, if we have any spare cash, put it into something that we believe to be reasonably safe. Most of us are, as the jargon has it, risk-averse.

In the previous chapter we looked at an example that categorized IT investments into three levels of project risk. A straight technology replacement proposal, with new but proven technology from the same trusted supplier, and with no change to existing applications, might be regarded as low risk. Undertaking a new application, one that is new for us but that has been available for years and used successfully by many organizations like ours, might be regarded as medium risk but still reasonably safe. However, what about being one of the first organizations to invest in a completely new application, using new technology and never before tried in our industry? That is perhaps rather closer to the jelly-slicer in terms of risk.

Suppose the jelly-slicing friend managed to convince you that after six months you would get your money back and that from then on it would be pure profit all the way? You might think that not too much could go wrong in six months. You might also think that for the prospect of returns from the investment for many years into the future, such risks as there are would be worth taking. Furthermore, until the promised profits start pouring in you would only be losing six months' worth of interest on your money.

However, suppose the payback estimate is not six months, but five years? A lot more can go wrong in five years than can go wrong in six months, and you would be losing five years' worth of interest meanwhile, not six months', so the eventual returns would have to be greater to compensate for that. In an unscientific but common sense way, payback gives an indication of the risk and uncertainty associated with a proposed investment.

Criticisms of payback

However, this example highlights one of the more obvious dangers of the payback method. If used slavishly, substantial cash inflows after the break-even point may be ignored. Suppose that our investment's estimated cash flows were not as in Figure 5.1 but as in Figure 5.2. The payback period of the two investments is the same. However, the latter is obviously a more attractive investment. Slavish use of payback could cause the difference to be ignored.

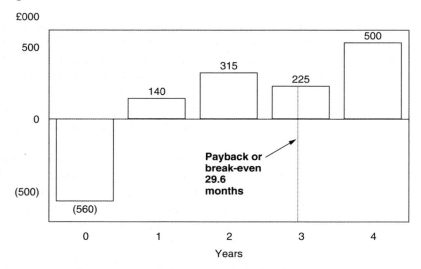

FIGURE 5.2 *Cash flows beyond the break-even point*

A more serious criticism of the payback method, at least in its basic form, is that it ignores what, in earlier chapters, we have come to know as the 'time value of money'. From those earlier examples we know that, while the initial net cash outflows can be taken at face value because they are paid 'today', the subsequent benefits cannot. They are worth less than face value, and the later they are received the less, proportionally, are they worth in real terms. Figure 4.1 on page 58 illustrated the point.

DISCOUNTED PAYBACK

In the light of the last-mentioned weakness, it may have occurred to you that payback is just as capable of being applied to discounted as to undiscounted cash flows. Try it yourself, using the present values that we derived in the last chapter (Table 4.1). Table 5.2 gives the answer, using exactly the same approach that was used earlier in Table 5.1. Figure 5.3 shows the answer diagrammatically.

TABLE 5.2 *Example 3.1 – Discounted payback*

	Ref	Yr 0 £000	Yr 1 £000	Yr 2 £000	Yr 3 £000	Yr 4 £000	Total £000
Assumption: Cash flows occur on last day of Year 0, and then evenly within Years 1 to 4							
Discounted cash flows		−560	127	260	169	79	75
Cumulative discounted cash flows			−433	−173	−4	75	
Break-even occurs during Yr 4, when the cum. disc't'd cash flow changes from neg. to positive.							
Net cash flow in Year 4	a					79	
Net cash flow per month during Year 4 (a/12)	b					6.6	
Positive cash flows in Year 4	c					75	
Months from break-even to end of Year 4 (c/b)	d					11.4	
Months in Years 1 to 4	e					48	
Break-even occurs after (months) (e − d)						36.6	

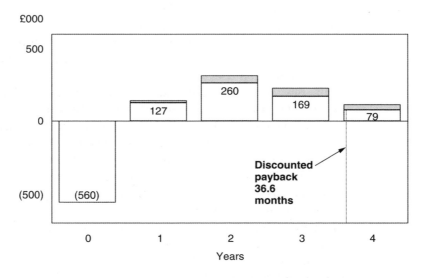

FIGURE 5.3 *Example 3.1 – Discounted payback*

Checkpoint

So far in this chapter we have discussed payback. Most companies use payback. Its advantages are:
- it is simple;

- it gives a common sense indication of the risk associated with a proposed investment;
- it can provide a yardstick or 'hurdle', based on experience, against which investments of similar type can be evaluated;
- it can be a useful filter for weeding out unsuitable investments with relatively little effort.

The disadvantages of payback are:
- used slavishly, it may cause substantial cash flows, positive or negative, beyond the break-even point to be ignored in the evaluation process;
- in its basic form, payback ignores the time value of money. This drawback can be mitigated by applying the payback method to discounted cash flows.

RETURN ON INVESTMENT (ROI)

In discussing ROI one thing is almost certain. That is that the particular methods that I describe will not be exactly the same as the one used by your organization. This is because, unlike discounted cash flow and payback, there are many different possible ways of doing ROI calculations; there are no textbook rules. The explanations of ROI offered here should, however, be sufficient to help you understand the particular approach that your organization uses.

All the evaluation methods so far considered have been based exclusively on cash flow. Many of the numbers used in ROI calculations are also usually cash flows – but not all of them. The reason why most of them are the same is that, for the sake of simplicity, timing differences are usually ignored. By this I mean mainly the timing differences that occur between selling goods or services and getting paid; also between receiving goods or services and paying for them.

The reason why not all the numbers in ROI calculations are necessarily the same as cash flows is that ROI deals with accounting profit, which explains one of its alternative names: 'accounting rate of return' (ARR). We have already, in Chapter 2, considered the fact that, by contrast with cash flow, profit is to some extent a matter of opinion. We looked at two examples that illustrated the point: depreciation and the valuation of stock.

Opinion it may be, but profit is an important opinion. It is the main basis for reporting business results and being assessed for tax. It is often also the basis for determining department, division or branch performance and for calculating performance-related bonuses. Therefore, it is desirable to know the effect on profit if a particular investment decision is to be taken. For this purpose, return on investment (ROI) is still the most widely used method. As we shall discover, however, it can be more complicated than the cash flow-based methods considered so far.

What is ROI?

ROI expresses the profit generated by an investment (in IT, for example) as a percentage of the capital (the financial resources) employed in it. What are we putting into the investment, and what will we get out of it? This is an identical question to the one implied by the financial ratio 'return on capital employed' (ROCE), regarded as a key measure of business activity. The only difference is that ROCE applies to the business as a whole, whereas ROI as we are now discussing it applies to an investment that is a subset of the business.

A business can indeed be viewed as a continuing series of investments, some large, some small, each of which uses a part of the business's capital. If the business as a whole is to be profitable, then these individual investments had better be profitable too. It is the profitability of an investment that ROI sets out to measure. It is the similarity of approach to measuring the profitability of a business and of an investment that no doubt led to the term 'return on capital employed' being sometimes used synonymously with ROI. As already noted, its other alternative name, 'accounting rate of return', reflects the fact that the method uses accounting numbers rather than exclusively cash flows. For the rest of this chapter we shall use the term ROI to embrace all three names.

Which profit, what capital employed?

So, the questions are 'what capital will be employed in the investment?' and 'what profit will it make?' Simple questions, but immediately they cause a problem and lead to two more questions: 'what do we mean by capital employed?' and 'what do we mean by profit?'

In using return on capital employed (ROCE) to measure the profitability of a business the problem does not arise. This is because business results are reported annually, and business people are used to thinking in annual terms. There may be debate about which of the various 'profit' numbers to use (for example, operating profit or profit after tax). Whichever is chosen, however, it is readily available in the profit and loss account of the year under review. We may argue about whether, for 'capital employed', we should use the capital at the beginning of the year or at the end of the year, or the average capital during the year. However, whichever number is chosen can be easily found in the balance sheet. But how many business investments run for exactly one year? The answer is few, if any. IT investments usually have a life of several years.

How, then, can we adapt a method that originated as a means of measuring the annual profitability of a business, to the measurement of non-annual investments? Opinions vary, but the way most businesses do it is to express the average annual operating profit generated by the investment as a percentage of the average capital employed in it. An alternative approach is to compare the average annual profit not with the average but with the initial capital employed. There is one possible danger in this latter approach that will become apparent. That excepted, most of what is done with ROI is a matter of opinion and preference; it does not actually matter very much which approach is adopted. Consistency is the important thing.

How to calculate average annual profit

We shall continue to use Example 3.1. Refer again to Table 3.6 on page 50 as necessary. The first stage is to work out the average profit to be generated by the investment. Table 5.3 shows the method. Here, as in most real situations, there are two things to be done, and it will now be apparent why Table 3.6 separated the cash flows into three different categories: fixed capital, working capital and operating cash flows. This separation was not necessary for using the cash flow-based methods so far considered, but it will be needed also for the next method to be discussed: shareholder value added (SVA).

TABLE 5.3 *Example 3.1 – ROI 'average annual profit' calculation*

	Ref	Yr 0 £000	Yr 1 £000	Yr 2 £000	Yr 3 £000	Yr 4 £000	Total £000
Fixed capital calculations							
Fixed capital invested in Yr 0							−700
Expected proceeds in Yr 4							20
Net fixed cap. invested		*(depreciated over Yrs 1 to 4)*					−680
Calculation of annual profits							
Depreciation of new equipmt.			−170	−170	−170	−170	−680
Net changes to operating income and outgoings*			140	315	225	85	765
Annual operating profit	a		−30	145	55	−85	85
Calculation of average annual profit							
Average annual profit (= total of (a) /4)							21.25

* The same as net operating cash flows, because timing differences are ignored.

Of the above-mentioned three categories of cash flow, only two affect operating profit: the fixed capital and the operating cash flows. Changes to working capital usually involve the conversion of one kind of asset to another. For example, the cash inflow arising when customers pay their bills more quickly is exactly that: the conversion of part of one asset called 'debtors' into another asset called 'cash'. Such changes affect the balance sheet but not the profit and loss account, at least not directly.

What incremental fixed capital cash flows will be generated by the acquisition and eventual disposal of the new systems? There are two: the initial cost of £700k at the end of Year 0 and the eventual expected proceeds of sale of £20k at the end of Year 4. However, now that we are dealing with profit and loss rather than cash flows the question is rather 'how will these cash flows be represented in the profit and loss accounts of Years 1 to 4?' The answer is 'through the mechanism of depreciation'. As already discussed, the 'straight line' method is the one most often used in practice and we shall assume it here. What is it that should be depreciated? The answer is 'the original cost less the eventual expected proceeds of sale'. So, in this case the total depreciation to be charged over the four-year period will be (700 – 20) = £680k (or £170k per annum).

What incremental operating cash flows will be generated by the investment if it is undertaken? We know from Table 3.6 that these come to a total of £765k. How will these affect the profit and loss accounts of Years 1 to 4? It has already been said that, in practice, timing differences between making sales and receiving payment, and between incurring costs and making payment, are usually ignored. The reason for this is that it makes at least one part of a quite complicated process much simpler for what is usually a relatively trivial sacrifice of accuracy. If the timing differences are ignored then 'sales' becomes the same as 'cash received from sales', and 'costs' becomes the same as 'cash paid for costs'. This means that the numbers in the line in Table 3.6 called 'incremental cash flows arising from changes to operating income and outgoings' can be used to represent simply 'incremental changes to operating revenues and costs'. This being so, the numbers can be used without change in the ROI calculation.

We now have what are usually the only two components necessary for the determination of 'profit' (usually operating profit) for ROI calculations. Still referring to Table 5.3, subtracting the total depreciation (£680k) from the incremental net revenues (£765k) gives the incremental profit (£85k). Finally, dividing by the number of years gives us what we are looking for: the average annual incremental profit (£21.25k). Notice that for the purpose of working out the ROI, it is only necessary to work with the total numbers. However, it is usually a simple matter to fill in the year-by-year details, which I have done in Table 5.3. It is often desirable to see the likely effect of the investment on profit year by year, not just in total, especially if operating profit is a basis for paying bonuses or measuring departmental performance.

How to calculate average capital employed

As already discussed, there are two kinds of asset: long-term ('fixed') assets and short-term ('current') assets. The financial resources used to acquire and replenish them are usually called respectively 'fixed capital' and 'working capital'. Depreciation reflects the fact that fixed assets are usually used up over their useful economic lives, as is the capital invested in them. Current assets, on the other hand, are used up or 'turned over' quite quickly (in weeks or even days) but are constantly being replenished out of the cash generated by trading. The total of the incremental fixed capital invested and the incremental working capital required by, or liberated by, a project represents the total 'capital employed' in it.

So, referring again to Table 3.6, we need to find out two things. First, how much incremental fixed capital is employed in the investment; second, how much incremental working capital is employed in it, or liberated by it? Table 5.4 shows the answers to these questions.

TABLE 5.4 *Example 3.1 – ROI 'average capital employed' calculation*

	Ref		Total £000
Fixed capital invested in Yr 0			−700
Expected proceeds in Yr 4	*a*		20
Net fixed capital invested	*b*	*(depreciated over Yrs 1 to 4)*	−680
Average fixed capital employed [(*b*/2) − *a*]			−360
Working capital liberated in Yr 0 and remaining so throughout Yrs 1 to 4			120
Working capital invested in Yr 0 and remaining so throughout Yrs 1 to 4			−10
Working capital £10k liberated at end of Yr 4 *(ignored)*			
Average capital employed			−250

Average fixed capital

What incremental fixed capital is employed in the investment? The answer (£680k) is given by the first three lines of the table. The next stage is to work out the average fixed capital employed. Left to their own devices, most people do this by dividing the initial capital employed by the number of years (in this case, 700 / 4 = £175k). Or, they might do it by dividing the net capital employed by the number of years (680 / 4 = £170k). Wrong. Please think of the last time you had a bowl of soup. At the beginning of the meal the bowl was full. By the time you had finished the soup, however long you took to consume it, it was empty. What was the average contents of the bowl? The answer is one-half of the original contents.

At the beginning of the project the fixed capital invested in it was £700k. At the end, just before the equipment is sold, £20k remains invested, the remainder of £680k having been used up. However long the project (four years or four hundred years) the average capital employed is therefore one-half of the £680k that has been used up, plus the £20k that has been employed until the very last day. The calculation in this case is therefore [(680 / 2) + 20] = £360k.

Average working capital

What incremental working capital is employed in the investment? In this case, one of the main purposes of the investment is to reduce the working capital employed on things like stock and debtors. So, after taking into account the stock of supplies and spares for the new systems, £110k less of working capital will be required each year. Because it happens only right at the end of the project, the recovery of £10k invested in the stock of supplies has been ignored. Deducting from the average fixed capital invested (£360k) the average working capital liberated (£110k) gives the answer we are looking for: the average capital employed (£250k).

How is ROI used?

There is now the quite trivial task of calculating the ROI from the two components just derived, by expressing the average operating profit generated by the investment as a percentage of the average capital employed in it. Table 5.5 gives us the final answer. The ROI given in Table 5.5 is 8.5 per cent. But so what? The answer to this is the same as the answer to the similar question asked earlier with respect to payback and to IRR. What is this company's accumulated experience of the ROI, calculated in this particular way, of investments of similar type, size and risk? If the answer to that question is, say 15 per cent, then our proposal does not appear in a very good light. If this company's ROI 'hurdle rate' for investments of this kind were to be only eight per cent then we may just have scraped home. In fact, our proposal that originally looked quite promising is probably in pretty bad shape by this particular measure.

TABLE 5.5 *Example 3.1 – ROI average annual profit as percentage of average capital employed*

	Ref	Total £000
Average annual profit generated by the project (from Table 5.3)	*a*	21.25
Average capital employed in the project (from Table 5.4)	*b*	250.00
Return on investment (ROI)#	(*a* / *b*)%	8.50 %

 # Also sometimes known as Return on Capital Employed (ROCE) or Accounting Rate of Return (ARR)

ROI AND RISK

If ROI is applied to numbers derived from cash flow estimates that have themselves been adjusted for project risk, then that risk has already been taken into account. If not, then a way of differentiating between investments with different perceived levels of project risk is to apply higher ROI hurdle rates to riskier investments.

ROI as average profit over initial capital employed

Remember that there are no 'official' rules for calculating ROI. Instead of average capital, some people use 'initial capital employed' in ROI calculations. Table 5.6 shows the calculation. If you wondered why, in Example 3.1, we made the simplifying assumption that the reduction in working capital occurs instantaneously at the end of Year 0 rather than during Year 1, when it would actually occur, then a glance back at Table 5.4 will provide one answer. It was so that all the attributable changes to capital employed, the effects of which would remain throughout the project, could be calculated easily.

TABLE 5.6 *Example 3.1 – ROI average annual profit as percentage of initial capital employed*

	Ref	Total
Average annual profit generated by the project (from Table 5.3)	*a*	21.25
Initial capital employed in the project (from Table 5.4)	*b*	590.00 *
* Fixed capital invested 700, less net working capital liberated 110		
Return on investment (ROI)#	(*a / b*)%	3.60 %

 # Also sometimes known as Return on Capital Employed (ROCE) or Accounting Rate of Return (ARR)

There is another reason, however, which applies both to the 'initial capital' approach to ROI and to the discussion of 'shareholder value added' (SVA) that follows. If this simplifying assumption is not made, then the (in this case substantial) benefits of reducing the working capital would be ignored in the calculations. This is not a danger with the approach based on 'average capital employed', because all changes to working capital throughout the evaluation can be taken into account through the averaging process. The small sacrifice of accuracy inflicted by putting changes to working capital into Year 0 is a reasonable price to pay for having a set of data that can be applied consistently to all the evaluation methods.

Some loose ends

In the example we have just worked through, what happened to the proceeds of sale of the old equipment and to the loss on sale that resulted? Why were these numbers not included in the ROI calculations? If it is indeed incremental capital employed that we are concerned with then it could certainly be argued that the net initial capital employed is the cost of the new systems (£700k) less the sale proceeds of the old (£30k). Some people might argue that it is this net number (£670k) that should be used in the 'average capital' calculations. I have ignored the 'old' proceeds on the grounds that it is only the cost of the new systems that, via depreciation, will affect the profit during Years 1 to 4, the chosen evaluation period.

I have ignored the loss on disposal for the same reason, but for another also. What is called loss on disposal is the difference between the book value and the market value of a disposed asset. It only arises because of inadequate depreciation in the past. Should a new investment be burdened with a 'loss' that arose out of what proved to be inaccurate accounting for its predecessor? I think not. However, because ROI has no firm 'textbook' rules, this aspect too can be regarded as a matter of personal preference.

Finally, a criticism of the particular ROI method that I have illustrated might be that it does not take into account the cost of capital. Fortunately, help is at hand with the next evaluation method to be explained: shareholder value added (SVA). SVA, which does take into account the cost of capital, might be regarded by some as a substitute for ROI. Alternatively, if wished, the annual cost of capital, calculated by the method illustrated in Table 5.8, could simply be deducted from the annual operating profit numbers shown in Table 5.3 before doing the ROI calculation.

Checkpoint

The purpose of ROI is to measure the return from an investment in terms of accounting profit (usually, but not necessarily, operating profit) as a percentage of capital employed (usually, but not necessarily, average capital employed). The main reasons why ROI is used are:

- it expresses the profitability of a project in a form that is familiar to business people: an annualized percentage;
- it can be used to show the effect of a proposed investment on company or departmental profitability;
- when used in a consistent way, it can provide a yardstick by which to compare the profitability of a proposed project with ones of similar type, size and risk undertaken in the past.

Its disadvantages are:

- there is no general agreement on how it should be calculated;
- in calculating ROI, unlike NPV and IRR, it is necessary to take into account the different characteristics of three different kinds of income and outgoings: fixed capital, working capital and operational;
- ROI, at least in its base form, does not take into account the time value of money.

SHAREHOLDER VALUE ADDED

Somewhere between NPV and ROI, but closer to the former, is the idea of shareholder value added (SVA). At the end of Chapter 13 the fundamental idea of SVA is introduced in the context of its original purpose. This was to determine whether, during an accounting year, a company has 'added value' to its shareholders by producing an after-tax profit that is greater than the return expected by them. That section includes an example of the SVA calculation, which, at its simplest and when applied to a company as a whole, is to deduct the return expected by the shareholders from the profit after tax. The example is shown in Table 13.3 on page 264.

Some companies have taken this essentially simple idea and adopted it as a way of managing the business. Thus used, it is sometimes applied as part of a 'value-based management' framework. The point is that if the purpose of a company as a whole is to 'add value' to its shareholders, then each part of the company's business can and should be managed to contribute towards that end. That can mean setting SVA targets for divisions and departments, and motivating people to achieve them. It can also mean using SVA to evaluate investment opportunities, including proposed investments in IT.

Here we shall confine ourselves to the use of SVA in investment decision-making. But what is new? We have already considered and used the idea of evaluating an investment opportunity by reference to the return required by the company's providers of capital. The method was called net present value (NPV), and it consists of discounting the cash flows of the proposed investment at the company's weighted average cost of capital or at a rate based on it. SVA is also based on cash flow and at its simplest can be used to obtain a result that is identical to NPV. We have also noted earlier (page 54) that 'cost of capital' is an alternative and shorter way of saying 'return required by the providers of capital'.

Consider the following IT proposal.

EXAMPLE 5.1

TABLE 5.7 *Example 5.1 – A simple IT proposal*

Year		£000
0	Investment in assets	−100
1	Operating cash flow	30
2	,, ,, ,,	56
3	,, ,, ,,	50
4	,, ,, ,,	26

Assumptions

- The investment in assets is made on the last day of Year 0, will be depreciated straight-line over Years 1 to 4 and will have no residual value.

- The company's current weighted average cost of capital, used in NPV calculations, is 10 per cent.

Table 5.8 shows both the NPV and the basic SVA calculations. The NPV of the amounts of 'shareholder value added' is the same as the NPV of the cash flows from which they were derived. In view of earlier advice against including depreciation of assets in cash flow estimates, it may seem odd that here we appear, in effect, to be doing just that. First, the word 'depreciation' in this context is used as a shorthand for the using up of the capital over the life of the investment. Second, the purpose of Table 5.8 is to show that at its most fundamental, SVA is just another way of setting out present values. However, part of its usefulness is that it gives year-by-year results, whereas NPV only gives a single figure. It is useful to know when the value added by an investment occurs. A step-by-step explanation of what is happening in the SVA calculations in Table 5.8 follows the table.

TABLE 5.8 *Example 5.1 – Similarity of NPV and SVA calculations at a simple level*

	Ref	Yr 0 £000	Yr 1 £000	Yr 2 £000	Yr 3 £000	Yr 4 £000	Total £000
NPV calculations							
Investment (capital)		−100					−100
Net operating cash flows	*a*		30	56	50	26	162
Discount factors (10%)		1.0000	0.9091	0.8264	0.7513	0.6830	
Present values and NPV		−100	27.27	46.28	37.57	17.76	28.88
SVA calculations							
Capital at beginning of year	*b*		100	75	50	25	
'Depreciation'	*c*		25	25	25	25	
Capital at end of year			75	50	25	0	
Net operating cash flows	*a*		30	56	50	26	162
Cost of capital (10% × *b*)			−10	−7.5	−5	−2.5	−25
'Depreciation'	*c*		−25	−25	−25	−25	−100
Shareholder value added	*d*		−5	23.5	20	−1.5	37
Discount factors (10%)	*e*		0.9091	0.8264	0.7513	0.6830	
PVs and NPV of SVA (*d* × *e*)			−4.55	19.42	15.03	−1.02	28.88

The first stage of the SVA calculations is to calculate the amount of capital (money) invested at the beginning of each year. If, as we are told, the assets acquired will be depreciated 'straight-line' over four years, then it follows that the capital used to acquire them could also be said to be used up or 'depreciated' at the same rate. Remember, it was not just your old car that ended up worth nothing; so did the money with which you bought it.

The next stage is to show the operating cash flows and the cost of capital. What rate did we choose as the basis for discounting cash flows in NPV calculations? The answer is the rate representing the average return required by the providers of the capital, shortened to 'cost of capital', and in this case 10 per cent. The cost of capital each year is worked out by multiplying the capital at the beginning of the year by the percentage cost of capital.

The final stage is to show the quasi 'cash flows' represented by the 'depreciation' of the capital. The sum of these three elements is the 'shareholder value added' (SVA): the value that has been created for the shareholders each year by the investment after deducting the cost of capital, the return expected by the providers of the capital invested in it.

Table 5.9 applies the same approach to Example 3.1.

TABLE 5.9 *Example 3.1 – An SVA calculation that equates SVA to NPV*

	Ref	Yr 0 £000	Yr 1 £000	Yr 2 £000	Yr 3 £000	Yr 4 £000	Total £000
See Table 3.6 on page 50 for the data in this table							
Net fixed capital invested in Yr 0							−670
Net working capital liberated in Yr 0 and remaining so throughout Yrs 1 to 4							110
Net capital invested							−560
SVA calculations							
Capital at beginning of year	*a*		560	420	280	140	
(Numbers on line above are shown as positive only for convenience)							
'Depreciation'	*b*		−140	−140	−140	−140	
Capital at end of year			420	280	140	0	
Net operating cash flows	*c*		140	315	225	85	765
Cost of capital (10% × *a*)			−56	−42	−28	−14	−140
'Depreciation'	*b*		−140	−140	−140	−140	−560
Proceeds of sale						20	20
Working capital liberated						10	10
Shareholder value added	*d*		−56	133	57	−39	95
Discount factors (10%)	*e*		0.9091	0.8264	0.7513	0.6830	
PVs and NPV of SVA (*d* × *e*)			−50.91	109.91	42.82	−26.64	75.18

Note that the NPV of £75.18k is the same as that shown in Table 4.1 on page 57.

This is more complicated than Example 5.1 (Table 5.8). However the principles used are the same, and once again the NPV of the amounts of SVA is the same as the NPV of the cash flows from which they were derived. Notice that the effect of the permanent reduction in working capital is to reduce the total amount of capital invested, so there is less capital to be used up or 'depreciated'. Excluding the proceeds of sale (£20k) and the liberated working capital (£10k) from the cost of capital calculation is necessary because these events would happen at the end of Year 4.

I said above that SVA, like NPV, is based on cash flow. When applied to an individual investment opportunity, the cash flow numbers are readily available, as in the above examples. When applied to the performance of a company as a whole (see Chapter 13), the relevant cash flow numbers can usually be found in the cash flow statement. In the examples so far, for the sake of simplicity, tax has been ignored. Its effect on SVA and other evaluation methods will be considered in the next chapter.

THE METHODS COMPARED

All the investment evaluation methods described in both this chapter and the preceding one provide different insights into the desirability of a proposed investment. As we have seen, their results can all be derived from the same base data. For convenience, Table 5.10 summarizes all the methods discussed and their main characteristics. Table 5.11 summarizes relevant totals and other extracts from the various tables of Example 3.1, while Table 5.12 summarizes all the evaluation results so far from Example 3.1. At the end of the next chapter, the results of all the evaluation methods that we have applied to Example 3.1 will be summarized, both before and after tax.

TABLE 5.10 *Summary of investment evaluation methods*

Method	Basis	Usual calculation	Result expressed as
Net present value (NPV)	Cash flow	Net cash flows discounted at cost of capital	Number
Shareholder value added (SVA)	Cash flow	Basic calculation is operating cash flows per year, less cost of capital, less 'depreciation' of fixed capital invested; answer discounted at cost of capital	Number
Internal rate of return (IRR)	Cash flow	Discount rate that yields NPV of zero	Percentage
Payback	Cash flow	Months after which cash benefits equal initial costs	Period
Discounted payback	Cash flow	Months after which discounted cash benefits equal initial costs	Period
Return on investment (ROI)	Profit	Average operating profit over average capital employed or over initial capital employed, but many possible variations	Percentage

TABLE 5.11 *Example 3.1 – Summary of relevant totals*

	Yr 0 £000	Yr 1 £000	Yr 2 £000	Yr 3 £000	Yr 4 £000	Total £000
Cash flow totals from Table 3.6 on page 50						
Sale of old equipment	30	0	0	0	0	30
Cost of new systems	−700	0	0	0	20	−680
Fixed capital cash flows	−670	0	0	0	20	−650
Working capital cash flows	110	0	0	0	10	120
Operating cash flows	0	140	315	225	85	765
Net incremental cash flows	−560	140	315	225	115	235
Present values from Table 4.1 on page 57						
PVs and NPV of above	−560	127.27	260.32	169.04	78.55	75.18
Shareholder value added totals from Table 5.9 on page 86						
Shareholder value added		−56	133	57	−39	95
Present values from Table 5.9						
PVs and NPV of above		−50.91	109.91	42.82	−26.64	75.18
Profit totals and other extracts from Tables 5.3, 5.4 and 5.6						
Annual operating profit		−30	145	55	−85	85
Average annual profit						21.25
Average capital employed						250
Initial capital employed						590

TABLE 5.12 *Example 3.1 – Summary of evaluation results*

Method	Table ref.	Page ref.	Results
Cash flow-based methods			
Net present value (NPV) of cash flows	4.1	57	£75,180
Profitability index (PI)	4.2	60	113%
Shareholder value added (SVA)	5.9	86	£95,000
Net present value of SVA	5.9	86	£75,180
Internal rate of return (IRR)	Fig. 4.2	64	16.2%
Payback	5.1	72	30 months
Discounted payback	5.2	75	37 months
Profit-based methods			
Return on investment (ROI):			
• average annual profit / av. capital employed	5.5	81	8.5%
• average annual profit / initial cap. employed	5.6	82	3.6%

Summary

The main points covered in this chapter, all linked to both its objectives, have been the following:
- Payback or break-even is a method that seeks an answer to the question in respect of the cash flows of a proposed investment: 'when do we get our money back?'
- Discounted payback is the payback method applied to discounted cash flows.
- Return on investment (ROI) uses accounting numbers to express the profit, usually operating profit, generated by an investment as a percentage of the capital, average or initial, employed in it. ROI is usually compared with a 'hurdle rate' that represents, based on experience, the required accounting rate of return from investments of this kind.
- At its simplest and when applied to the evaluation of individual investment opportunities, shareholder value added (SVA) is another way of setting out present values. However, part of its usefulness is that it gives year-by-year results, whereas NPV only gives a single figure.

6 The Effects of Taxation

Objectives

When you have studied this chapter you should be able to:
- *explain why it is important to understand the effects of taxation on IT and other investments undertaken by tax-paying organizations;*
- *describe the main principles of business tax, and particularly company (corporation) tax;*
- *work out the effects of corporation tax on the profit and cash flows of a proposed IT, or other, investment;*
- *work out the after-tax value added to shareholders by the investment, and its after-tax NPV, IRR, payback and ROI.*

Why bother with taxation when evaluating an investment opportunity? The answer is that tax affects both profit and cash flow. If the investment is profitable, then extra tax will be payable as a result. It is the after-tax profit of the company that finally belongs to the shareholders. After-tax profit is thus the ultimate measure of value that has been added to the shareholders by the business as a whole. It is also, therefore, the measure of what the investment being evaluated will contribute to that result.

Taxation is different in every country, although the broad principles are much the same. The above objectives will be achieved using examples from UK taxation. Representative tax rates will be used because precise rates, current at the time of writing, would no doubt soon be out of date.

'Income tax,' said judge Lord Macnaghten during a legal case in 1901, 'is a tax on income.' We may give the judge full marks for brevity, and two cheers for wit, but some amplification of this profound statement may be helpful if we are to understand the effects of tax on IT investments and why decision makers often take them into account. We shall start by comparing the principles of personal tax, with which we are only too familiar, with business tax, with which we may not be.

PERSONAL TAX

Employees are taxed on their earnings less any deductible expenses. The category of deductible expenses is very small and excludes any expenses that are reimbursed by the employer. For people in the IT world it typically includes subscriptions to professional bodies relevant to the employee's work, but not much else. Employees are also taxed on benefits not received directly in cash, such as company cars and interest-free loans. However, individuals are given a 'personal allowance' of income that is tax-free.

So, the earnings of employed individuals have to be adjusted in order to arrive at their 'taxable income', the amount on which they are actually taxed. For example, if annual salary is £20k, benefits in kind come to £1k, allowable expenses are £200 and the personal allowance is £5k, then taxable income is (20,000 + 1,000 − 200 − 5,000) = £15,800. Assuming a tax rate of 20 per cent, and ignoring the possible impact of higher rate tax, the tax payable by the individual would be (20% × £15,800) = £3,160.

BUSINESS TAX

The main principles of business taxation are generally much the same for both incorporated businesses (companies) and unincorporated businesses (sole traders and partnerships), although there are some important differences. In the UK, for example, one difference concerns the particular sets of rules under which tax due from different kinds of business is assessed and collected. The rules are as follows:

- The profits of sole traders, whether the profits are withdrawn from the business or not, are regarded as part of the personal income of the proprietor and are taxed under income tax rules.
- In the case of partnerships, it is each partner's share of the profits, whether withdrawn or not, that is treated as that partner's personal income and taxed under income tax rules.
- Company profits, whether or not distributed as dividends, are taxed under a system known as corporation tax.

The explanations of business taxation that follow are based on companies and corporation tax. If the examples used were applied to an unincorporated business the only significant differences would be the tax rates and the times at which tax is payable.

What is taxed?

Businesses are taxed on their profits. This usually means their earnings (revenues, whether received in cash or not), less the expenses (whether paid in cash or not) incurred in achieving those earnings. Unlike the expenses of employed individuals, nearly all the expenses incurred by a business are 'tax-allowable', including interest. Business expenses not tax-allowable are typically 'entertaining', political donations, expenditure on capital (long-term) assets and depreciation. To compensate for the disallowance of depreciation of fixed assets, businesses can claim 'capital allowances' (see below) at legislated standard rates.

If a business's expenses and capital allowances together exceed its revenue it is said to have made a 'tax loss'. UK tax losses can be carried forward to be set against future profits, or carried back and set against the profits of the immediately preceding year, resulting in a refund of tax paid. In the case of a group of companies, a loss in one company can be set against the profits of other companies in the same group. Figure 6.1 illustrates what is meant by 'taxable profit' and 'tax loss'.

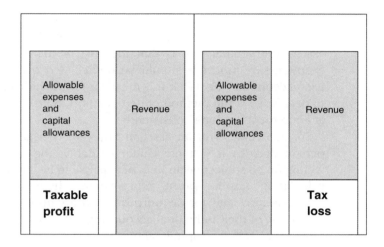

FIGURE 6.1 *Taxable profit and tax loss*

So, the profits of businesses, like the income of individuals, have to be adjusted in order to arrive at the 'taxable profit', the amount on which they are actually taxed. For example, assume the summary of a company's results as shown in Table 6.1.

TABLE 6.1 *How to calculate taxable profit*

	£million
Revenue	100
Expenses, including depreciation £3 million	80
Profit before tax	20
Capital allowance claimable	2
The company's taxable profit would be worked out as follows:	
Profit before tax	20
Add disallowed expense (depreciation)	3
	23
Less capital allowance	2
Taxable profit	21

In this example, assuming a corporation tax rate of 30 per cent, the tax payable by the company would be 30 per cent of its taxable profit of £21 million (= £6.3 million). In the examples that follow, it will be assumed that tax is payable in the year following that to which it relates.

CAPITAL ALLOWANCES

Why is depreciation not a 'tax-allowable' expense? The clue to the answer lies in the earlier discussion of depreciation in Chapter 2. Concerning fixed assets, the general rule is that the cost of the asset less any expected eventual sale proceeds should be depreciated over the asset's expected useful economic life. What this means is for the individual business person to decide; so is the method of depreciation to be used, although whatever is done must be done consistently.

So, depreciation of an asset in any year is what a particular business person decides it will be. Understandably, the tax authorities are not willing for so subjective an item of expense to be allowed as a deduction in calculating taxable profit. Government therefore legislates standard 'depreciation' rates for tax purposes that are applicable to all businesses, regardless of their individual accounting policies. These fixed depreciation rates are called 'capital allowances' or sometimes 'writing down allowances'. There are different rates for different kinds of asset. IT equipment (including, since 1992, most lump sum payments for IT software – see Appendix 4) belongs in the broad category of 'plant and machinery'.

Capital allowance rates

In the examples that follow, it will be assumed that the capital allowance rate for IT equipment and software licences is 25 per cent of cost in the year of acquisition, followed by 25 per cent of the remaining balance (the 'tax book value' (TBV)) in subsequent years until disposal. It will also be assumed that the capital allowance given in the year of disposal, called a 'balancing allowance', is the tax book value (cost less capital allowances so far), less any proceeds of sale. As an example of the above assumptions, which are based on current UK practice, Figure 6.2 shows, in percentage terms, the capital allowances on an asset purchased in Year 0 and scrapped in Year 3.

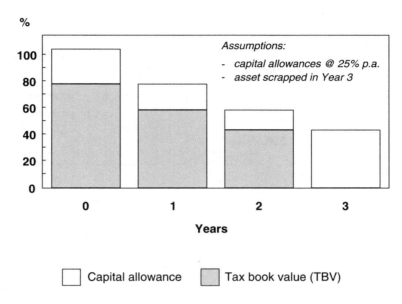

FIGURE 6.2 *Capital allowances*

An example

A numeric example should help to make all this clear. Assume an IT asset purchased for £1000 in Year 0 and eventually sold for £100 in Year 3. Table 6.2 shows the capital allowances and the resulting decrease in corporation tax payable, assuming that the company pays corporation tax at 30 per cent. You have all the information you need in order to work it out for yourself. Figure 6.3 shows the answer diagrammatically.

TABLE 6.2 *How to calculate capital allowances (CAs) (1)*

	Ref	Yr 0 £000	Yr 1 £000	Yr 2 £000	Yr 3 £000	Total £000
Tax rate % $\boxed{30}$	a					
Cost of new equipment		−1000				−1000.00
Cap. allowance rate % $\boxed{25}$	b					
Capital allowance and tax book value (TBV) calculation						
TBV $[c − d \,(\text{Yr} − 1)]$	c	−1000	−750.00	−562.50	−421.88	
Eventual sale proceeds					100.00	100.00
CA $(b \times c)$ except in yr sold	d	−250	−187.50	−140.62	−321.88	
Tax reduced by $(−d \times a)$		75	56.25	42.19	96.56	270.00
Net-of-tax cost of asset						−630.00

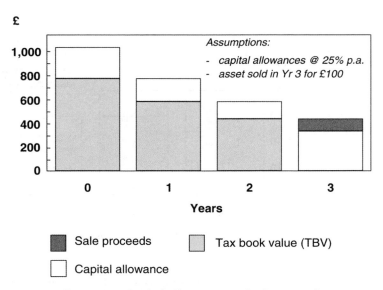

FIGURE 6.3 *Capital allowances and sale proceeds*

The final amount of −£630 in the total column of Table 6.2 represents the net-of-tax cost of the asset over its life from Years 0 to 3. It is the net total of the cost, less the proceeds of sale and less the 'tax relief'. Notice that the total tax relief given (£270) is 30 per cent of the net cost (£900) of the asset (that is, its cost less the proceeds of sale). This reflects the intention of the rules: that over an asset's life its net cost will, through the mechanism of capital allowances, be deducted from taxable profit.

What would happen if, in Year 3, the asset were sold, not for £100 but for £500, more than the tax book value? The answer is that instead of a balancing allowance that reduces tax payable that year, there would be a 'balancing charge' (of £78.12) that would increase the tax payable. The balancing charge is the difference between the tax book value of £421.88 and the proceeds of sale of £500. This is all set out in Table 6.3. The net tax relief given (£150) is still 30 per cent of what is now the net cost (£500) of the asset.

An important feature of UK capital allowances is that there is no apportionment based on time. An asset acquired even on the last day of a business's accounting year qualifies for the full capital allowance that year, resulting in a reduction of taxable profit equal to 25 per cent of the asset's cost, or such other first year allowance percentage rate as may be in force. This is unlike other business expenses deducted from revenue to arrive at taxable profit, which are apportioned over the period(s) to which they relate.

TABLE 6.3 *How to calculate capital allowances (CAs) (2)*

	Ref	Yr 0 £000	Yr 1 £000	Yr 2 £000	Yr 3 £000	Total £000
Tax rate % [30]	a					
Cost of new equipment		−1000				−1000.00
Cap. allowance rate % [25]	b					
Capital allowance and tax book value (TBV) calculation						
TBV [c − d (Yr − 1)]	c	−1000	−750.00	−562.50	−421.88	
Eventual sale proceeds					500.00	500.00
CA (b × c) except in yr sold	d	−250	−187.50	−140.62	78.12	
Tax reduced by (−d × a)		75	56.25	42.19	−23.44	150.00
Net-of-tax cost of asset						−350.00

Who claims capital allowances?

Capital allowances are always claimed by the legal owner of an asset, except in the case of hire purchase. In this case, the hirer is deemed to be the owner from the beginning of the agreement, even though title does not actually pass until the last payment has been made.

So, where an asset is either purchased or hire-purchased by the intending user company, it is that company that claims the capital allowances. If an asset is leased, capital allowances are claimed by the head lessor (the legal owner).

> **Checkpoint**
> So far in this chapter we have covered the first two of its objectives. In particular:
> - we have discussed why it is desirable for companies to take tax into account in evaluating IT and other investment opportunities;
> - we have learned the main principles of business taxation, especially corporation tax, in general terms, using UK taxation as an example;
> - we have seen why accounting depreciation is not allowed as a 'tax-deductible' expense, and used examples to illustrate the rules governing capital allowances.

HOW DOES TAX AFFECT AN IT FINANCIAL CASE?

We can now return to Example 3.1 and see how our proposed investment is affected by tax. Please turn again to Table 3.6 on page 50. In the previous chapter, under the subheading *How to calculate average annual profit*, we noted that of the three categories of cash flow shown in Table 3.6 (fixed capital, working capital and operating cash flows) only the first- and last-named affect operating profit. Changes to working capital usually represent simply the conversion of one kind of asset to another; for example, debtors into cash, or cash into stock. Such changes affect the balance sheet but not the profit and loss account, at least not directly.

The two categories that do affect operating profit were fixed capital and operating cash flows. Since businesses are taxed on the basis of profit, it follows that those same two categories will also affect tax. We shall examine the tax effects of each of them in turn, starting with operating cash flows.

Tax effect of operating cash flows

You will recall that by the expedient of ignoring timing differences we have been able to treat changes to operating cash inflows and outflows as though they were the same as changes to operating revenues and costs. The operating cash flows in each of the years 1 to 4 are positive, and come to a total of £765k. That means that they all, in their guise of net revenues, have the effect of increasing profit by £765k. If something causes a company's profit to increase, what happens to the amount of tax that it has to pay? It too increases.

Assuming a rate of corporation tax of 30 per cent, how much extra tax is therefore payable as a result of the increased profit? The answer is given in Table 6.4. Not, I think you will agree, a very complicated calculation. The increase in tax payable caused by the investment would be the increased profit multiplied by the tax rate.

TABLE 6.4 *Example 3.1 – Increase in tax due to increase in net revenues*

	Ref	Yr 0 £000	Yr 1 £000	Yr 2 £000	Yr 3 £000	Yr 4 £000	Total £000
Tax rate %	$\boxed{30}$ a						
Increases in net revenues	b		140.00	315.00	225.00	85.00	765.00
(from Table 3.6 on page 50)							
Tax payable increased by ($b \times a$)			42.00	94.50	67.50	25.50	229.50

Tax effect of fixed capital cash flows

How, in the previous chapter, did the fixed capital cash flows affect the profit? The answer, you will recall, was through the mechanism of depreciation. But we now know that depreciation is not a tax-allowable expense. Instead, we are able to deduct capital allowances. We have already worked through a couple of examples of capital allowances, so for this part of the exercise we just need to repeat the calculations but with different numbers, plus one additional consideration, just to keep it interesting.

Assuming, as above, a tax rate of 30 per cent and a capital allowance rate of 25 per cent, how much less tax is payable as a result of the capital allowances? Table 6.5 shows the answer. The reduction in tax payable caused by the investment would be the capital allowances multiplied by the tax rate.

TABLE 6.5 *Example 3.1 – Decrease in tax due to capital allowances (CAs)*

	Ref	Yr 0 £000	Yr 1 £000	Yr 2 £000	Yr 3 £000	Yr 4 £000	Total £000
Tax rate %	30 a						
Cost of new equipment		−700					
Cap. allowance rate %	25 b						
Capital allowance and tax book value (TBV) calculation							
TBV [$c − d$ (Yr − 1)]	c	−700	−525.00	−393.75	−295.31	−221.48	
Eventual sale proceeds						20.00	
CA ($b \times c$) except in yr sold	d	−175	−131.25	−98.44	−73.83	−201.48	
Sale of old equipment *		30					
* Final CA on old equipment is usually reduced by full amount of sale proceeds							
Net CA	e	−145	−131.25	−98.44	−73.83	−201.48	
Tax reduced by ($-e \times a$)		43.50	39.38	29.53	22.15	60.44	195.00

Remember that we are seeking all the relevant incremental cash flows that would result from the investment. These include the tax cash flows. We have seen that capital allowances in the year of disposal of an asset are reduced by any proceeds of sale. The treatment of the proceeds of the old equipment in Table 6.5 is based on the assumption that any sale value this year would diminish to zero by the following year if the project to replace it were not undertaken. If we include the sale proceeds as a benefit attributable to the project (which we have done), then we should include the reduction in capital allowance as an attributable cost.

For the sake of simplicity I have ignored what would in reality be different timings of the capital allowances and put the whole reduction in Year 0. The resulting slight sacrifice of accuracy is trivial.

The tax cash flows

We have now worked out both the increase in tax payable resulting from the increased profit, and the reduction in tax payable resulting from the capital allowances. It is now only necessary to combine these two results in order to establish the net tax cash flows attributable to the investment. These are shown in Table 6.6. In the bottom line of Table 6.6, positive numbers represent reductions in tax payable; negative numbers represent increases. If you did the workings for yourself, did you remember the 'tax delay' of a year? It means that corporation tax cash flows usually occur in the year following that to which they relate. There can, however, be exceptions to this rule.

TABLE 6.6 *Example 3.1 – Net tax cash flows*

	Ref	Yr 0 £000	Yr 1 £000	Yr 2 £000	Yr 3 £000	Yr 4 £000	Yr 5 £000	Total £000
Increases in tax payable due to increases in net revenues								
From Table 6.4			−42.00	−94.50	−67.50	−25.50		−229.50
(Shown as negatives, as representing increases in cash outflow)								
Decreases in tax payable due to capital allowances								
From Table 6.5		43.50	39.38	29.53	22.15	60.44		195.00
Net changes	a	43.50	−2.62	−64.97	−45.35	34.94		−34.50
Net tax cash flows *			43.50	−2.62	−64.97	−45.35	34.94	−34.50

* *(a) assume delayed by one year*

As a result of the tax delay, 'Year 5' has crept into Table 6.6. There is an endless debate about whether tax cash flows occurring after the chosen end date of an investment evaluation should be included or excluded. On the one hand, they are undeniably cash flows attributable to the investment. On the other hand, if you include tax cash flows, then why not also include other cash flows that occur outside the evaluation period? These would in turn give rise to further tax effects. The fact is that some people do it one way, others do it the other way. I have included Year 5 only to raise the point.

The deciding factor is often the purely practical one that a spreadsheet designed to evaluate a four-year evaluation will usually be given six columns: one each for Years 0 to 4 and one for the totals. Anything, including a tax cash flow, that doesn't belong in Years 0 to 4 is simply ignored. Because of capital allowances, the tax cash flow in the last year of a typical IT evaluation is often positive. It might be regarded as a pity that a positive cash flow should be lost solely because of the vagaries of spreadsheet design. You may find here echoes of the earlier debate about whether to include the effects of benefits that will outlast the technology on which an application is initially implemented. Total accuracy is not achievable. As always, consistency is the important thing.

We worked through the tax effects in the above particular way because the step-by-step approach made them easier to understand. We could instead have deducted the capital allowances from the increases in net revenues and then worked out tax at 30 per cent on the resulting net numbers. Arithmetically, this would have given the same answer that we arrived at in Table 6.6.

AFTER TAX EVALUATION OF AN INVESTMENT

We established at the beginning of this chapter that incremental tax cash flows are just as relevant to an investment, and therefore attributable to it, as any other cash flows. It follows that they are usually, but not always, taken into account in evaluating an investment proposal.

After-tax cost of capital

In Chapters 1 and 4 we discussed the concepts of cost of money (capital) and 'opportunity cost of money'. We noted that the opportunity cost of using our own personal money is not the gross interest rate that we should otherwise have received on it if invested, but the net-of-tax interest rate. By contrast, if we are using borrowed money, our personal 'cost of money' is the gross interest rate that we are paying. This is because, in general, interest on personal borrowings is not 'tax-deductible'.

In Chapter 4 we noted one of the main differences between personal tax and business tax: namely that business interest is tax-deductible. Dividend payments to shareholders, however, are not. These facts should be taken into account in doing any after-tax evaluation. We need to compare like with like. In order to determine the real value of after-tax cash flows, we should measure them against the after-tax cost of capital. To see how this is done we shall revisit the example that we used in Chapter 4.

In that example, which assumed unequal quantities of equity and debt, the cost of equity was assumed to be 12 per cent; the cost of debt eight per cent. We shall now, just for a change, assume equal quantities of equity and debt. What are now the before- and after-tax costs of capital, assuming a tax rate of 30 per cent? Table 6.7 shows the answer. The before-tax cost is, of course, 10 per cent, the after-tax cost is 8.8 per cent. This will be the discount rate for working out the after-tax NPV of our example, except that to facilitate use of the discount table we shall use the nearest whole-number figure of nine per cent. I repeat my earlier suggestion that, in practice, you find out from your finance department or finance person what discount rate to use, and whether it is before-tax or after-tax.

TABLE 6.7 *After-tax cost of capital*

	Ref	Before tax	After tax @ 30%
Assumptions: Interest is tax-deductible, dividends are not.			
The company has equal quantities of debt and equity.			
Costs of equity and debt are as stated.			
Cost of equity %	*a*	12.00%	12.00%
Cost of debt %	*b*	8.00%	5.60%
Cost of capital [(*a* + *b*) / 2]		10.00%	8.80%

After-tax NPV and IRR

We now have all that we need in order to work out the after-tax evaluations of our proposed investment: the before-tax cash flows, the tax cash flows and the after-tax cost of capital (nine per cent). We shall start with the NPV. The answer (£66,900) is given in Table 6.8.

TABLE 6.8 *Example 3.1 – After-tax NPV and IRR*

	Yr 0 £000	Yr 1 £000	Yr 2 £000	Yr 3 £000	Yr 4 £000	Yr 5 £000	Total £000
Before-tax cash flows (Table 3.6)	−560.00	140.00	315.00	225.00	115.00		235.00
Tax cash flows (Table 6.6)		43.50	−2.62	−64.97	−45.35	34.94	−34.50
After-tax cash flows	−560.00	183.50	312.38	160.03	69.65	34.94	200.50
Discount factors (9%) *	1.0000	0.9174	0.8417	0.7722	0.7084	0.6499	
After tax PVs and NPV	−560.00	168.34	262.93	123.58	49.34	22.71	66.90
After tax IRR							14.8%

* *For the purpose of illustration 9% has been used as the nearest whole-number rate to 8.8%.*

The after-tax internal rate of return (IRR) is worked out by exactly the same method used earlier to obtain the before-tax value, referred to in Chapter 4, and illustrated in Figure 4.2. You could try it for yourself using the same method. I shall not use space by simply repeating Figure 4.2 with different numbers. Suffice it to say that the precise answer, given by financial calculator or spreadsheet function, is 14.8 per cent. Using the 'trial and error' approach, the discount rate of nine per cent used above gave an NPV of £67k; a discount rate of 22 per cent gives an NPV of −£67k. The rate midway between nine per cent and 22 per cent is 15.5 per cent, which could be taken as a reasonable approximation of the after-tax IRR.

After-tax SVA

The after-tax SVA (£74,500) is shown in Table 6.9. Its NPV of £66,900 is of course the same as the NPV of the project cash flows in Table 6.8.

TABLE 6.9 *Example 3.1 – SVA calculation that equates SVA to NPV, after tax*

	Ref	Yr 0 £000	Yr 1 £000	Yr 2 £000	Yr 3 £000	Yr 4 £000	Yr 5 £000	Total £000
Sources of data in this table are Tables 3.6 (page 50) and 6.6 (page 100).								
Net fixed capital invested in Yr 0								−670
Net working capital liberated in Yr 0 and remaining so throughout Yrs 1 to 4								110
Net capital invested								−560
SVA calculations								
Capital at beginning of year	*a*		560	420	280	140		
(Positive numbers on line above are being used only for convenience)								

Table continues ...

TABLE 6.9 *Continued*

	Ref	Yr 0 £000	Yr 1 £000	Yr 2 £000	Yr 3 £000	Yr 4 £000	Yr 5 £000	Total £000
'Depreciation'	b		−140	−140	−140	−140		
Capital at end of year			420	280	140	0		
Net operating cash flows	c		140	315	225	85		
Cost of capital (9% × a)			−50.4	−37.8	−25.2	−12.6		
'Depreciation'	b		−140	−140	−140	−140		
Proceeds of sale						20		
Working capital liberated						10		
Net tax cash flows			43.50	−2.62	−64.97	−45.35	34.94	
Shareholder value added	d		−6.9	134.58	−5.17	−82.95	34.94	74.50
Discount factors (9%)	e		0.9174	0.8417	0.7722	0.7084	0.6499	
PVs and NPV of SVA (d × e)			−6.33	113.27	−3.99	−58.76	22.71	66.90

Note that the NPV of £66.9k is the same as that shown in Table 6.8 on page 102.

After-tax payback and ROI

The after-tax payback and discounted payback can also be worked out using the methods used earlier to obtain the before-tax results. The answers are 28.8 months and 37.2 months respectively. ROI is sometimes, but not necessarily, confined to being used as a before-tax evaluation tool. This is probably because a major use of ROI is to determine the effect of a proposed investment on a departmental budget. Departmental budgets do not usually get charged with tax. I have, however, done the ROI after-tax calculations and they are shown in Tables 6.10–6.12.

TABLE 6.10 *Example 3.1 – ROI 'average annual profit' calculation, after tax*

	Ref	Total £000
Total operating profit from Table 5.3 on page 78		85.0
Total net extra tax arising from project from Table 6.6 on page 100		−34.5
After-tax profit from project	a	50.5
Calculation of average annual after-tax profit		
Average annual after-tax profit (a / 4)		12.63

The fact that the tax cash flows are spread over five years is ignored. The average annual after-tax profit is the total after-tax profit divided by the number of years (four) of the project.

TABLE 6.11 *Example 3.1 – ROI average annual after-tax profit as percentage of average capital employed*

	Ref	Total £000
Average annual after-tax profit (from Table 6.10)	*a*	12.63
Average capital employed in the project (from Table 5.4)	*b*	250.00
After-tax ROI	(*a* / *b*)%	5.05

TABLE 6.12 *Example 3.1 – ROI average annual after-tax profit as percentage of initial capital employed*

	Ref	Total
Average annual after-tax profit (from Table 6.10)	*a*	12.63
Initial capital employed in the project (from Table 5.6)*	*b*	590.00
* *Fixed capital invested 700, less net working capital liberated 110*		
After-tax ROI	(*a* / *b*)%	2.14

THE RESULTS COMPARED

Table 6.13 summarizes the results of all the evaluations we have done on Example 3.1 before tax and, where appropriate, after tax.

TABLE 6.13 *Example 3.1 – Summary of evaluation results, before and after tax*

Method	Results before tax	Results after tax	Table ref. (after tax)
Cash flow-based methods			
Net present value (NPV) of cash flows	£75,180	£66,900	6.8
Profitability index (before tax only)	113%		
Shareholder value added (SVA)	£95,000	£74,500	6.9
Net present value of SVA	£75,180	£66,900	6.9
Internal rate of return (IRR)	16.2%	14.8%	6.8
Payback (after-tax result is given – no table provided)	30 months	29 months	
Discounted payback (ditto)	37 months	37 months	
Profit-based methods			
Return on investment (ROI):			
• average annual profit / av. capital employed	8.5%	5.1%	6.11
• average annual profit / initial cap. employed	3.6%	2.1%	6.12

TAXATION AND LEASING

Earlier in this chapter, leasing was mentioned in the context of capital allowances. When assets are leased, capital allowances are claimable by the owner, the 'head lessor', which deducts them, together with its allowable expenses, from its revenues to determine its taxable profit.

In Chapter 8, we shall be looking at the subject of leasing, and specifically IT leasing. One benefit of leasing to lessees (user companies) is that it makes tax accounting easier. This is because, for tax purposes, payments under leases generally are treated as tax-deductible expenses in computing taxable profit. Some adjustments may have to be made, but despite that, expenses are generally regarded as easier to handle than capital allowances. A summary of the UK accounting rules for leasing appears in Appendix 2.

Summary

The main points covered in this chapter, linked to its objectives, have been the following:

- *After-tax profit is what ultimately belongs to the shareholders. Therefore the effects of taxation are usually included in any evaluation of IT or other investment opportunities that will contribute towards that profit.*
- *Tax is payable on business profits, adjusted for disallowed expenses (including depreciation) and capital allowances.*
- *IT and other investments typically have two significant effects on business profits, and therefore on tax. Increased net revenues result in more tax being payable; capital allowances cause less tax to be payable.*
- *In using discounted cash flow to evaluate investment opportunities, after-tax evaluations should be done using the organization's after-tax cost of capital, so that like is being compared with like.*

7 IT Aspects of Depreciation

Objectives

When you have studied this chapter you should be able to:
- *explain what depreciation is and what problems can be caused by the particular characteristics of IT assets;*
- *describe what is meant by 'loss on disposal' and explain what accounting and IT policies might help to avoid or minimize it;*
- *recommend an appropriate method for the depreciation of upgradable IT assets.*

DEPRECIATION OF IT ASSETS

Take any dozen organizations and you will find as many different approaches to the depreciation of IT assets. Some methods cause an artificially high or low charge to the profit and loss account and to budgets in the year of acquisition. Some approaches to the depreciation of upgrades have the effect of causing depreciation 'peaks', either in the middle or at the end of life of the upgradable range.

Depreciation is an accounting technique for charging the cost of a fixed asset as an expense to the profit and loss accounts of the years that benefit from its use. The expense reduces the profit, and the book value of the asset on the balance sheet is correspondingly reduced. When the asset is eventually sold, the proceeds of sale are deducted from its book value. Any remaining amount is charged to the profit and loss account as 'loss on disposal'.

The term 'depreciation' is usually restricted to the decline in value of tangible assets, such as IT hardware. 'Amortization' is usually used to describe the decline in value of intangible assets. This is especially true of leaseholds, but it is also applied to IT assets such as licences to use software. For more information on the accounting and tax treatment of software, refer to Appendix 4.

Depreciation is governed by accounting standards. The current international standard is International Accounting Standard 16 (IAS 16); the current UK standard is Financial Reporting Standard 15 (FRS 15) – Tangible Fixed Assets. The gist of the rules is that the cost of an asset, less its expected residual value, should be depreciated over its expected useful economic life. The standards do not require any particular method of depreciation to be adopted. This, and the estimated life of the asset, are left to be determined by the business person. There are a number of possible depreciation methods, the most important of which are described below.

STRAIGHT-LINE DEPRECIATION

As its name implies, this method charges the cost of the asset, less any expected proceeds of sale, in equal amounts over the asset's expected useful economic life. It is easy to use and reflects the fact that the usefulness of most assets is much the same for each year of their economic lives. Its main disadvantage arises from the fact that it does not usually reflect the true decline in market value of an asset over its life. We know that the most expensive journey made by a new car is the drive from the showroom. The market value curve of most IT hardware assets behaves in much the same way.

Although the book value of assets does not have slavishly to reflect their market value, any significant difference between the two leads to a 'loss on disposal' when the asset is disposed of (see below). The straight-line method, combined with a frequent tendency to overestimate asset life, makes this a common problem. However, despite its drawbacks, the majority of businesses, at least in the UK, use straight-line depreciation.

REDUCING BALANCE DEPRECIATION

Using this approach, a fixed percentage rate of decline, for example 40 per cent, is charged as depreciation each year. This method reflects more closely the decline in market value of most assets and is also easy enough to use. Its main problem is the fact that it results in a higher charge in the first year than the straight-line method. A higher charge to the profit and loss account means less profit, and a higher charge against a departmental budget means less money for other things. However, the higher the depreciation charge early in an asset's life, the less likely is a substantial loss on eventual disposal.

LOSS ON DISPOSAL

When an asset is disposed of (for example, when it is traded in for a replacement), any remaining book value, less any trade-in value, is charged to the profit and loss account, and often to a departmental budget, as an expense. This is a common reason for delaying the replacement of old IT technology with new.

Avoiding the problem

A longer-term solution is to take a more realistic view of the useful life of the assets concerned and depreciate accordingly, or to use an alternative method of depreciation.

A way to avoid the immediate problem, where the option is available, is to upgrade the asset rather than replace it. The advantage of this is that with an upgrade the original asset remains *in situ* and continues to be depreciated in the usual way, so that a loss on disposal does not arise. However, if the same problem but with bigger numbers is to be avoided in the future, then the useful life of that asset, or of assets of that class, should be reassessed and the depreciation period shortened. Also, depending on the company's depreciation policy for upgrades, this approach could bring its own problems (see below).

Another approach, applicable to IT hardware, is to avoid the balance sheet altogether and use operating leases. However, if such a lease were to be terminated early, any termination charge may have a similarly undesirable effect on the profit and loss account to 'loss on disposal'. The shorter the lease, the less likely this would be, but then the higher would be the periodic lease payments.

Scraping the barrel

Much IT equipment is sold at a discounted price. Where the upgrade option is not available, it has been known for some companies to try to postpone the 'loss on disposal' problem by getting the supplier to invoice new equipment at a higher price, with a correspondingly higher value shown for trade-in of the old. The higher the trade-in value, the lower the immediate 'loss on disposal'. However, without also taking a more realistic view on asset life, the problem has merely been postponed. It will reoccur, with bigger numbers, when the new asset itself comes to be replaced. Any such manipulation of values will have accounting, corporation tax, value added tax and legal implications for the customer, the supplier and any finance company involved. The safest course is not to do it, but if it is contemplated, then professional advice should be sought. This subject is also covered in Chapter 9 in the context of outsourcing.

An even more desperate approach, sometimes adopted, is to install the new asset, while keeping the old one and simply switching it off, continuing to depreciate it in the normal way until it is fully 'written off', when it is then disposed of. Running costs of the old asset are saved and a loss on disposal is avoided. However, possibly substantial proceeds of sale are forgone and depreciation will have to be charged on the new asset as well as the old. Given that budgets are not legal requirements but matters of administrative convenience, it is surprising the contortions that are sometimes gone through in order to stay within such self-imposed rules.

These attempts to postpone reality are simply that. The cost of an asset, less any eventual proceeds of sale, will always eventually hit the profit and loss account as an expense and, if applicable, be charged against a budget in one way or another. This will either be as depreciation during the asset's life or as loss on disposal at the end of it.

FREQUENCY OF DEPRECIATION CHARGE

Most organizations charge depreciation monthly from the date of acquisition of an asset or sometimes from the date of first productive use. Some, however, still adopt the approach of charging a full year's depreciation in the accounting year of acquisition, regardless of when in that year it is acquired. This may be fine for assets having a long life of, say, 20 years or more, but many of today's IT assets have very short lives in some companies.

It is true that where large numbers of assets are acquired on a regular basis the effect averages out. It may also, in an arbitrary way, sometimes help to alleviate the loss on disposal problem. However, with major assets, charging depreciation monthly reflects more accurately the contribution made to revenue-earning by the asset during its useful economic life.

DEPRECIATION OF UPGRADABLE ASSETS

Upgradability is a particular feature of some IT assets. In general, organizations use one of three methods, described and illustrated below (see Figure 7.1). The first two can cause serious distortion to the accounts and to budgets if the amounts are significant, and are not recommended. The third is to be preferred. The methods are as follows.

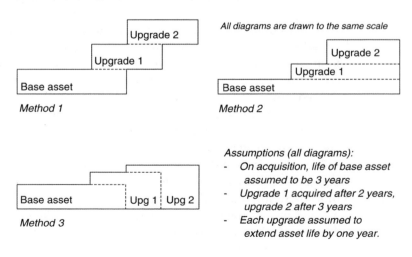

FIGURE 7.1 *Depreciation of upgradable assets*

Method 1: Treat each upgrade as though it were a separate new asset

In this example, the base asset is assumed to have a three-year life, so is depreciated over three years. Each upgrade is assumed to have a two-year life, so is depreciated over two years from when it was acquired. A glance at Figure 7.1 shows how this approach can cause a 'depreciation peak' in the mid-life of the asset, quite unrelated to its contribution to earning revenue.

Method 2: Depreciate to the expected end of life of the range

When companies that adopt this approach buy a base asset that they know to be upgradable they take as its 'expected useful life' the estimated life of the range as a whole, including upgrades. For example, suppose this to be five years. It follows, so the theory goes, that subsequently acquired upgrades must have the same expected end of life. Consequently the periods over which successive upgrades can be depreciated are progressively shorter and the per annum depreciation of the upgraded asset becomes higher and higher. Figure 7.1 shows that this approach also results in a depreciation peak, this time at the end of life rather than in the middle. The approach demands the almost impossible task of estimating the end of life of a range of equipment. However, an obvious attraction of it is the low charge for depreciation in the early years.

Method 3: Reassess remaining useful economic life after each upgrade

This method reflects the fact that the effect of an upgrade is to prolong the useful economic life of the base asset. It requires that on acquiring a base asset, the expected useful life of that asset be assessed, ignoring possible upgrades. On acquiring each upgrade a fresh assessment should be made of the remaining useful life and the remaining book value depreciated over that period. As Figure 7.1 shows, this method avoids depreciation peaks and comes closest to representing what has actually happened. It also allows for an indefinite number of upgrades, an increasingly common phenomenon with IT hardware and software.

Summary

The main points covered in this chapter, linked to its objectives, have been the following:

- *Depreciation is an accounting method for spreading the cost of fixed assets over their expected useful economic lives. Characteristics of most IT assets (short and unpredictable lives, uncertain residual values and upgradability) all represent challenges to customary depreciation methods.*

- *'Loss on disposal' is the difference between the book value and market value of an asset. Its cause is inadequate depreciation during the asset's life. By being charged as an expense, its effect is to reduce profit. Short-term, it can be avoided by upgrading rather than exchanging. Ultimately, it can only be avoided by depreciating over realistic periods, by using more 'front-loaded' methods or by writing operating leases.*
- *The recommended way to depreciate upgradable assets is to reassess useful economic life at the time of each upgrade and to reschedule the remaining book value over that remaining life.*

8 IT Financing and Leasing

Objectives

When you have studied this chapter you should be able to:
- *distinguish between 'financing' and 'leasing', define what a lease is and state what, in IT terms, can be leased;*
- *explain how IT leasing developed and what kinds of companies provide it;*
- *describe and define the main characteristics of the following kinds of lease:*
  - *finance lease*
  - *hire purchase*
  - *operating lease;*
- *explain what, in leasing terms, is meant by 'residual value';*
- *explain, concerning each of the above kinds of lease, who owns the asset and whose balance sheet it appears on;*
- *name the currently relevant UK, EU, US and international rules and accounting standards that have an impact on IT leasing.*

INTRODUCTION

'Financing' is the process of obtaining the money for something that it is wished to acquire or have the use of. 'Leasing' is a narrower term that means paying to use an asset that belongs to someone else. Financing and leasing are heavily regulated activities. At the time of writing (December 2005), in most countries the accounting rules, on leasing (and most other things), are in a state of transition towards the eventual adoption of International Accounting Standards, although it is likely to be some years before full international standardization is achieved. The following three specific matters are, however, of immediate relevance to companies in countries that are members of the European Union, including of course the UK. From accounting periods beginning on or after 1 January 2005:

- Publicly traded companies ('PLCs' in the UK) governed by the law of a Member State of the European Union are required to prepare their *consolidated (or group) accounts* using International Accounting Standards (IASs), instead of national accounting standards.

- Publicly traded companies in the UK are permitted to use IASs in their *individual accounts* or to continue using UK accounting standards.

- Non-publicly traded companies (non-PLCs) in the UK are permitted to use IASs in both their individual and consolidated accounts, or to continue using UK accounting standards.

However, in respect of the second and third items above, once a company has prepared its accounts using IASs for a financial year, it cannot switch back to UK standards in subsequent financial years. The above rules will be slightly amplified in Appendix 2 of this book, together with details of the UK and EU legislation that gave rise to them.

It happens that the main UK accounting standard for leasing (SSAP 21, referred to later in this chapter) is very close to the international standard (IAS 17, also referred to) and contains the words '... compliance with SSAP 21 will ensure compliance with IAS 17 in all material respects'. Therefore, the above objectives of this chapter will be achieved by discussing the subject primarily from a UK perspective. Leasing will also be handled primarily from the viewpoint of the customer (the lessee). With only occasional exceptions demanded by the sense, I shall continue to use the word 'customer' rather than 'lessee' to refer to the user of a leased asset. This is to avoid confusion with the similar word 'lessor', which I shall use to refer to the owner of the asset.

Most of this chapter is in fact about IT leasing, which is still, in my observation, one of the least understood aspects of the whole subject of finance, despite its widespread use. The term 'leasing' is usually associated with hardware but can also be applied to the financing of lump sum payments for licences to use software. It is usually not associated with a service, but you can use financing, normally a loan, to rearrange the timing and amounts of payments due to the service provider, a matter also discussed in the context of outsourcing in Chapter 9.

WHAT IS A LEASE?

A lease is a contract under which the owner of an asset (the lessor) permits someone else (the lessee or customer) to use it during a defined period in return for agreed payments. Depending on the kind of lease, the IT lessor assumes some or all of the following risks:

- the creditworthiness of the customer;
- obsolescence and the decline in market value of the leased asset;
- changes in interest rates, if the lease is at a fixed rate;
- changes in tax rates, although this risk is usually passed on to the customer by means of a 'tax variation clause'.

It follows that during the life of a leased asset the lessor must recover, from one or more customers:

- the cost of the asset;
- interest paid or forgone on the money used to acquire it;

- a proportion of the lessor's overheads;
- a reasonable reward (profit) for services provided and risks assumed.

Who offers IT leasing?

There are three quite different kinds of company that offer IT leasing. They are:

- banks;
- independent leasing companies;
- IT manufacturers.

Definitions and explanations of the different kinds of lease are given later in the chapter. They also appear in the list of definitions at the end of the book. Meanwhile, suffice it to say that, in general:

- Banks usually offer only full payout finance leases and hire purchase. They do not deal in the equipment that they finance. They may, however, offer operating leases through subsidiary companies.
- Independent leasing companies usually offer only operating leases or variations on the operating lease theme. They are usually dealers in equipment as well as being lessors.
- Some IT manufacturers offer leasing facilities, as a sales aid, as a service to their customers and as a business in its own right. They may offer all the kinds of financing mentioned in this chapter.

Why lease IT?

Organizations lease IT for one or more of three main reasons:

- cash management;
- asset management;
- financial management.

Cash management

This may mean finding cash that is not otherwise available, or conserving cash for more productive uses, or conserving existing lines of credit. It may also mean the attempt to match payments for an asset against the revenues and cash inflows that the asset will help to generate.

Asset management

Even in some quite small organizations IT often means a network of many individual machines, and the cabling, software and services that make them work and keep them working. For some organizations, help in acquiring, upgrading and eventually disposing of these assets is a major benefit of leasing. Furthermore, some leases – operating leases – provide protection against obsolescence of hardware by incorporating guaranteed 'residual values'. For an explanation of residual value see page 128. Furthermore, assets that are owned, and therefore 'on the books' of an organization have to be accounted for, which means several things:

- maintaining an asset register containing the financial details of every asset, where it is located and who is responsible for it;
- financial accounting;
- tax accounting;
- management accounting, especially in an organization that is divisionalized.

The greater the number of assets, the bigger the accounting task. Making one single quarterly or annual payment to a finance company rather than having to account for perhaps thousands of individual assets can be a major benefit for many organizations. As we shall see, however, only one kind of lease – the 'operating lease' – has the effect of taking the leased assets 'off the books' of the customer organization.

Financial management

Aspects of financial management for which leasing may be used include the following:

- off balance sheet financing and the optimization of key financial ratios;
- international financing;
- low interest rates (leasing may sometimes be cheaper than ordinary borrowing).

Leasing used to have major tax advantages for lessors, which good lessors would pass on to their customers. However, these have been eroded by successive governments to the point where tax is now largely a neutral factor in leasing so far as the customer is concerned.

HOW IT LEASING DEVELOPED

In order to understand the current state of IT leasing and some of its more confusing aspects, it helps to understand something of its history. General-purpose computers have been widely available since about 1960. Until the appearance of the personal computer (PC) in about 1980, 'computer' meant 'large or medium-sized computer'. The large ones were usually called 'mainframes' (as they still are), the medium-sized ones 'minis'. There were also some specialist 'scientific' machines.

All the major manufacturers rented their equipment to their customers. Ownership of equipment remained with the manufacturer, to whom machines were returned at the end of the contract or earlier if an agreed period of notice had been given. In typical rental contracts, hardware, software and services such as maintenance were all 'bundled' together and were not separable. There were few computer manufacturers. Those that there were tended each to concentrate on a particular segment of the market, corresponding more or less with the types of equipment described above.

There was little real competition, prices were high and, by today's standards, the pace of development was relatively slow. Each manufacturer's customer base was therefore fairly stable and rental was a relatively low-risk business.

What killed rental?

In the middle of the 1970s, three things happened to bring this rather cosy state of affairs to an end. First, as knowledge of computer technology developed, new companies began to challenge the existing suppliers. Most of them could not afford the massive investment necessary to develop new control software, or operating systems, needed to make them work. But they could and did build cheaper machines that could run the software already developed by the established suppliers. The term 'plug-compatible' was sometimes used to describe these look-alike machines.

Second, a number of cases brought under US law resulted in the established suppliers being required to 'un-bundle' their contracts. They had to make their hardware, software and services separately available and each had to be separately priced. This enabled the new competitors to sell their machines in the knowledge that their customers could acquire the necessary control software from the established suppliers. Other new companies began developing application software. Yet others started challenging the established suppliers in the field of services.

The effect of competition

The third thing that happened was a consequence of the other two. There was an increase in the pace of development of all aspects of 'computing': hardware, software and services.

What happened to the rental base of the established suppliers when credible, cheaper competition started to become a reality? What happened when customers could return their hardware at a few weeks' notice in favour of a cheaper alternative, while continuing to use the same software? The answer is that, quite suddenly, from being stable and reasonably assured, the rental base became volatile and uncertain.

What was the response of the established suppliers? Could they increase the price of rental to compensate them for the increased business risk? Hardly, because the reason for the increased risk was precisely the availability to their customers of alternatives that were already cheaper. They did the only thing that they could have done. Up to this point, their customers could pay for their IT in any way they liked: provided it was rental. A subtle change in the rules meant that they could still pay in any way they liked: provided now that their IT was acquired by outright purchase. Software was now separately acquired under licence and services were also charged for separately. The new hardware suppliers were themselves subject to the rules of the brave new world that they had helped to create. So they too sold their products outright.

A cash mountain and a cash flow problem

What did this sudden conversion from rental to outright sale do to the cash flows of the established suppliers? The answer is that suddenly receiving all the cash from product sales on Day 1, rather than over four or five years, produced a large once-and-for-all cash windfall. This was used to pay for the massive research and development programmes that produced the systems for the mid-1980s, 1990s and beyond. By contrast, what did the withdrawal of rental and the requirement to purchase do to the cash flows of customer organizations? It meant that they suddenly had to find a great deal of money in order to finance their rapidly growing IT requirements. Many of them did not have it.

All this happened quite soon after the four-fold increase in the price of oil in the mid-1970s. Much of this 'oil money' had found its way to the banks. Their profits showed a marked increase, and in some ways, no doubt, the banks could hardly believe their good fortune. However, with increasing profits came the privilege of paying increased tax, at rates substantially higher than those of today. Although the tax rates were higher, so were capital allowance rates. This, you may recall, is the name given in the UK to the method whereby businesses obtain tax relief from capital investment. For some years these allowances were 100 per cent, which meant that taxable profit could be reduced by the full cost of an asset in the year in which it was acquired. Capital allowances, and other aspects of tax, were explained in Chapter 6. If only the banks could invest in a lot of capital equipment, then they would pay a lot less tax.

Tax incentives

On the one hand, then, much of industry, commerce and the public sector needed expensive equipment that it could not afford to buy. On the other hand, the banks wanted to invest in expensive equipment, because by doing so they would pay less tax. The obvious solution was for the banks to buy the equipment, claiming the tax allowances in the process, and make it available to the organizations that needed it, in return for regular payments. Leasing was a phenomenon waiting to happen. Happen it did, and the story of IT leasing since then can best be told by describing the various leasing facilities that have become available from then until now. Before we do so, however, a pertinent question is whether IT customers were, in general, happy with the idea of rental. Did they deplore the enforced change to outright purchase or did they welcome it?

The rebirth of 'rental'

While computer users would no doubt have liked prices to be lower, they were, in general, happy with the idea of rental. They liked the idea of paying to use, rather than to own, IT assets. The thought of owning a lot of expensive and rapidly depreciating equipment that was nothing to do with their core business would probably never have occurred to many of them. If asked, many would also have replied, 'Why would we wish to pay at the outset for the whole cost of IT and other assets before they have contributed one penny to the earning of revenue in our business?'

Banks as lessors

We have now seen how banks came to be IT lessors. Leasing was simply a 'tax-efficient' variation on their main business of lending money on the security of assets. In the case of leasing, the security was pretty strong because, in order to obtain the desired tax allowances, banks had to actually own the leased assets. However, as with all bank lending, the banks had no interest whatever in handling or dealing in the assets themselves. This fact determined the kind of IT lease that they were prepared to write. Because it was purely a financial transaction it came to be called a 'finance lease' (in the USA, a 'capital lease'). This will be the first kind of lease that we shall look at in detail.

Real security only lies in tangible equipment that could be sold if the customer defaulted. That is one reason why in the early days only IT hardware was leased, but not software. The other reason was that hardware was then much the biggest element in IT expenditure. Lessors are now willing to lease the lump sum amounts paid for software licences, although it provides no more security now than it did then, and to finance services. The reason is that software and services now represent a large and growing proportion of total expenditure on IT. Another reason, relevant in the UK, is that the Finance (No.2) Act of 1992 simplified the tax rules on software, making it easier to lease. Appendix 4 summarizes these rules.

IT manufacturers as lessors

It was, as we have seen, a combination of tax benefits and customer demand that brought the banks into leasing. However, its availability was a considerable benefit to IT manufacturers. Their customers used leasing from the banks and from the emerging independent leasing companies as a way of affording the otherwise unaffordable. Later, some of the manufacturers themselves set up their own leasing operations, usually through specialist subsidiary companies.

The manufacturers started by offering finance leases, in direct competition with the banks. This gave them a sales aid under their direct control and allowed them to develop features that matched the specific needs of their customers. It also gave them the same tax advantages that the banks enjoyed. Furthermore, the increased competition tended to produce keener lease rates and better terms and conditions generally for customers. For the first time, customers could choose where they obtained all the non-personnel components of their IT requirements (hardware, software, services) and the money with which to acquire them.

We shall now look at particular types of lease and some particular aspects of leasing, This will be a convenient way of discussing the main principles. However, it is becoming less common for leases to be written in their simple generic forms. As organizations' IT requirements are becoming more complex, and as services and software feature ever more prominently, so the boundaries between one kind of lease and another are becoming blurred. Increasingly, financing arrangements are being devised that contain elements of different kinds of lease. For things such as services and termination charges that cannot be leased, loan finance can be built into the overall financing arrangement as well.

> ### Checkpoint
>
> So far in this chapter we have covered the first two of its six objectives. In particular:
>
> - we have defined what a lease is and what, in IT terms, can be leased;
> - we have looked at how IT leasing developed and at what kinds of companies provide it.

TYPES OF LEASE

We shall consider types of lease under the following headings:

- finance leases;
- hire purchase;
- operating leases, and their variations:
  - non-full payout finance leases
  - composite leases
  - exchange leases.

We shall also briefly consider rental.

FINANCE LEASES

The finance lease ('capital lease' in the USA) was, as we have seen, the answer to the requirement of organizations for cash with which to pay for assets, and to the wish of banks to minimize their tax liabilities. They are offered mainly by banks and manufacturers' leasing companies. Out of the circumstances that gave rise to the finance lease grew its main features, described in the following paragraphs.

A finance lease is initially written for a fixed 'primary' period. For most IT assets this is usually between two and five years. The lessor pays the supplier for the asset. Ownership, that would normally have passed to the customer under the agreement for sale of the goods, is diverted to the lessor by a legal process known usually as 'novation'. During the primary period of most finance leases the customer (the lessee) pays by instalments the full purchase price of the asset plus interest on the money borrowed. Finance leases of which this is true are called 'full payout finance leases'. Although the asset is owned by the lessor, the customer, rather confusingly, is described as having 'full economic ownership'. Except when otherwise stated, it is full payout finance leases that we shall be considering here. 'Non-full payout finance leases' we shall consider later.

Most IT leases of all kinds, including finance leases, are at fixed rates, although a variable rate option is usually available. Most leases involve regular payments of equal amount. However, irregular payment streams can usually be arranged. These may include 'holidays' (install now, start paying later) or steps (smaller payments now, larger payments later). Payments are usually quarterly, but can be annually or at other intervals and may be either in advance or in arrears.

Options at the end of the primary period

A finance-leased asset is not returnable to the lessor. Remember that banks were the originators of finance leases and banks are not usually interested in handling the assets that they finance. At the end of the lease, when all payments have been made, the customer is responsible for disposal. If the finance-leased asset is sold, it is sold by the customer, acting as agent of the lessor, who is the legal owner, although the lessor may provide help for the customer in finding a buyer. The proceeds of sale belong to the customer (who has paid the full purchase price, remember), less a nominal percentage, typically one or two per cent, payable to the lessor. In the UK, but not in many other countries, there are legal restrictions that usually have the effect of preventing a leased asset from being sold by the lessor directly to the customer. In the UK, usually only under hire purchase, which is a lease with a purchase option and is described later, can the customer (the 'hirer') acquire title to a leased asset directly from the lessor.

All IT leases have to allow for the likelihood that they will not run exactly for their full term. Customers may wish either to terminate a lease early or to extend it into a 'secondary period'. On early termination of a finance lease, all outstanding amounts become payable, usually discounted to reflect the fact that the lessor is getting its money earlier. The customer organization then exercises its right of sale, retaining most of the proceeds of sale as described above. Because the customer has paid the full purchase price of the asset, extension of a finance lease, if required, is usually granted for a nominal 'peppercorn' amount, typically one or two per cent per annum of the original purchase price of the leased asset.

Upgrades

IT finance leases had to be able to accommodate the particular features of IT assets, of which upgradability is one. An upgrade is usually the subject of a new lease, written at the time the upgrade is acquired, at the rate then on offer by the lessor. Alternatively, the original lease may be amended. In either case, the 'new' lease will reflect the fact that the effect of an upgrade is to extend the life of the base asset. The practical effect will usually be for the lessor to charge for the cost of the upgrade by an extension of the primary period and (usually) an increase in the periodic payments. An alternative approach is to extend the lease, within reason, by whatever period is necessary to ensure no increase in periodic payments. This can be particularly attractive to customers with tight budgets.

It is possible for an upgrade to a purchased asset to be leased and for an upgrade to a leased asset to be purchased. However, neither is done very often. If it is, then both parties have to agree on the respective shares of any eventual sale proceeds that will belong to them. Also, an upgrade to a leased asset can be leased with a different lessor, subject to the agreement of the first. In this case, all three parties have to agree on their shares of any eventual proceeds. This, too, is not done very often.

Whose balance sheet?

If the customer had purchased the asset instead of finance-leasing it, whose balance sheet would it have appeared on? The customer's, of course. The asset is being used exclusively in the customer's business to earn revenue. Under a finance lease, there is certainly a difference in legal ownership; the lessor owns the asset. But is there any difference in who has exclusive use of it or in how it is used? The answer is that there is no practical difference. Furthermore, the customer still pays 100 per cent of the asset's cost, albeit spread over time.

Whose balance sheet, therefore, should a finance-leased asset appear on: the customer's or the lessor's? This question is one that leaders of the accounting profession, in most countries, wrestled with for a long time. The conclusion they came to, in the mid-1980s, was that the economic substance of the lease should take precedence over its legal form and that finance-leased assets should appear on the balance sheet of the customer.

How are finance leases accounted for?

I repeat, a finance-leased asset has to appear on the balance sheet of the customer. On Day 1 of the lease, the asset is recorded in the customer's books at its purchase price. A corresponding liability represents the obligation of the customer to pay for it. Over time the asset is depreciated, just as it would have been if purchased. When payments are made, the liability is diminished by the capital element of the payments; the interest element is charged to the profit and loss account in proportion to the size of the outstanding debt.

If you would like an example that illustrates the reason for the seemingly odd idea of showing as an asset something that is not owned, then the airline industry may provide it. Previously, all lease payments were treated as expenses and charged straight to the profit and loss account of the customer, just like rental. The leased asset did not appear on the customer's balance sheet. Many aeroplanes are leased. Suppose that you had wished to analyse the accounts of an airline, all of whose aeroplanes were leased under finance leases. On the balance sheet you would look for the assets. You might see a few buildings, some delivery vehicles, stocks of fuel, some office furniture and some IT systems, but... no aeroplanes (the airline's main revenue-earning assets).

With the growth of leasing as a financing method, it was decided that that situation made nonsense of any serious attempt at financial analysis. The rule-makers therefore decided that where a lease transfers 'substantially all the risks and rewards of ownership' to the lessee (the customer), then the leased asset should appear on the customer's balance sheet, not the lessor's. A finance lease is such a lease. The full definition of a finance lease, compared and contrasted with that of an operating lease, is given later in this chapter, in the section on operating leases. The definitions also appear in Appendix 2, together with summaries of other relevant UK and US accounting standards concerning leasing.

Finance leases and tax

Even though a finance-leased asset appears on the customer's balance sheet and not the lessor's, you will recall that it is owned by the lessor, who therefore claims the capital allowances. So, tax relief is given to the customer by allowing the lease payments as a tax-deductible expense. In practice, adjustments are made to reflect the fact that, as with a repayment mortgage, the interest element in a finance lease is higher in early payments than in later ones.

SALE AND LEASE-BACK

An asset that a company has purchased can at any time be sold to a bank or other lessor and then leased back. Such an arrangement is known, not surprisingly, as 'sale and lease-back'. Subject to complying with certain tax rules, it involves the sale of the asset, for cash, to the lessor and the simultaneous writing of a lease, the asset itself remaining *in situ*. This is most often done when an upgrade is required. The base asset is sold to a lessor and the (now upgraded) asset is leased back. By this means a company that is short of cash may obtain the use of a needed upgrade for little or no immediate cash outlay. It also avoids the awkward issue of joint ownership, discussed earlier. Lease-back under a finance lease is not a way of taking the asset off the customer's balance sheet. It remains there, for the obvious reason that a finance-leased asset has, as just described, to be 'on balance sheet'.

Points to look out for in a finance lease

There are usually few unknowns in a finance lease. The lessor assumes the risks of customer creditworthiness and, if the lease is at a fixed rate, interest rates. However, its financial interest in the eventual market value, if any, of the leased asset is small, being limited to the typical one or two per cent of sale proceeds to which it is entitled. There are, nevertheless, differences between finance lessors' contracts, apart from interest rates. For example, some lessors may be less willing than others to permit non-standard payment patterns.

When is a finance lease appropriate?

Since the tax advantages that used to be a feature of leasing are no more, finance leasing is, in its practical effect, now much like hire purchase. It will continue to be used, especially for assets, such as software licences, which have no residual value, and where title cannot pass to the customer because of licensing considerations, thus making hire purchase unsuitable. Finance leasing will also continue to be used to finance assets for which operating leases (see later in this chapter) cannot be used, because the assets have little or no residual value, or because they are second-hand.

HIRE PURCHASE

We are perhaps most familiar with hire purchase in domestic life, but it is also used as a way of financing business assets. In this context it is sometimes called lease purchase. Hire purchase, like finance leasing, is offered mainly by banks, through specialist subsidiaries. It is also offered by some IT manufacturers through their specialist leasing companies.

Hire purchase is a lease with a purchase option. It is a way of paying by instalments for an asset that is ultimately to be owned. In the UK, unlike many other countries, it is the only kind of lease under which ownership can pass directly from lessor to customer. Transfer of legal title to the customer actually occurs only when the last payment is made. Although the 'purchase option' is only an option, it is invariably exercised by the hirer (the customer). Indeed, in certain key respects (accounting and taxation) eventual exercise of the option is assumed from the outset. For example, a hire-purchased asset appears on the customer's balance sheet from Day 1 of the agreement at its full purchase cost, as with the finance lease already discussed. Also as with a finance lease, the corresponding obligation to make payments appears as a liability on the customer's balance sheet.

Hire purchase and tax

Because the hired asset is deemed to be owned by the customer from Day 1, tax capital allowances are claimed by the customer from Day 1. So, in every practical respect, 'hire purchase' means 'purchase', but paid for by instalments. The interest element of each payment is treated as an expense, apportioned to reflect the fact that the interest element in early payments is higher than in later ones. The capital element is treated as what it is: a partial repayment of the 'loan'.

A simple approximation often used for this apportionment of interest is called, rather clumsily, 'sum of the years' digits' (SOYD). For example, assume that the total interest payable under a three-year hire purchase or finance lease agreement is £6000. The SOYD (1 + 2 + 3) equals 6. The SOYD apportionment of interest would be as follows:

Year 1	3/6ths of 6000	=	3000
2	2/6ths	=	2000
3	1/6th	=	1000

For four- and five-year agreements the SOYD apportionment would be done respectively in tenths and fifteenths, and so on.

Why bother to have two different financing methods (hire purchase and finance lease) that, in every respect except legal ownership of the asset, appear to be much the same in their practical effect? The answer lies in our brief excursion into the history of leasing and the origin of the finance lease. Hire purchase had been in existence for a long time. Historically, legal ownership was and is deemed, for tax purposes, to be vested in the customer from Day 1. However, the crucial requirement for the banks was that they should have access to the capital allowances and for that they needed ownership. Hence the invention of the finance lease. The two financing methods have coexisted ever since and will no doubt continue to do so.

LEASING AND FINANCIAL CASES

Whether to invest some of an organization's limited resources in new or replacement IT systems, and how to pay for the investment, are two quite different decisions. The first is usually called an 'investment decision', the second a 'financing decision'. Purists would say that they should always be kept separate, and they often are, although sometimes they are merged, lease cash flows being simply substituted for capital values in the financial case supporting the investment decision. However, there are some very practical reasons for keeping these two decisions separate, associated with the investment evaluation methods already discussed in Chapters 4 and 5.

For example, the net present value method certainly 'works' with leasing cash flows, simply because it 'works' with any cash flows. However, the mere names of some of the other investment evaluation methods, such as 'internal rate of return' (IRR) and 'return on investment' (ROI) imply, and indeed require, that there should be an 'investment' (an upfront commitment of money) upon which a 'return' is to be calculated. Taking an extreme case, if the upfront 'investment' is zero, because it has been replaced by a lease payment stream that includes an initial holiday, then the answer to the calculations – the 'return' – yielded by these two evaluation methods is infinitely great. However, those particular arithmetic results should not be taken as suggesting an infinitely desirable investment and would be best ignored.

The effect of leasing is usually to remove or greatly decrease that large initial investment by spreading the payments. However, leasing does not of itself convert what is in reality an investment decision to something else just because it has the effect of removing the large upfront payment. What it does is oblige the customer to make an additional and separate 'financing decision' to determine the real value of leasing compared with paying the lump sum upfront. The main aid to making this kind of decision is a present value (PV) calculation that compares the present value of a proposed lease payment stream with the present value of the alternative upfront payment.

What discount rate do you think should be used in present value calculations of this particular kind? In the calculations that we have done so far, we have used the organization's weighted average cost of capital (WACC) as the discount rate. That was because the WACC was our point of reference: what we wanted to know was whether the return from the investment was greater than the weighted average cost of the capital (money) to be invested, and by how much. What is our point of reference in a 'financing decision' calculation? I suggest that it is the current cost of borrowing from the organization's normal source, almost certainly its bank. That indeed is normally the discount rate chosen. Table 8.1 illustrates this use of the 'present value' method. Assume the following:

- A company is planning to acquire IT assets costing £100k on the last day of its financial year. At the end of four years it is estimated that the assets would be worthless and would be disposed of at nil cost.
- The company has received a quotation for a full payout finance lease that would require four amounts of £27.2k to be paid annually in advance, the first payment to be made on the same day.
- The company's bank would currently charge eight per cent per annum on incremental borrowing.

TABLE 8.1 *The 'financing decision' (lease versus purchase comparison)*

	Yr 0 £000	Yr 1 £000	Yr 2 £000	Yr 3 £000	Total £000
Lease payments, annual in advance	27.2	27.2	27.2	27.2	108.8
Discount factors @ 8%	1	0.9259	0.8573	0.7938	
Present values	27.2	25.2	23.3	21.6	97.3
Purchase price					100.0
Difference					2.7

The question is would the lease be cheaper in real terms than borrowing from the bank? The problem is solved by the now familiar process of discounting the lease cash flows, this time at eight per cent, then comparing the total of the present values so derived with the present value of the lump sum payment. The latter amount is of course undiscounted, because it would occur 'today' (Year 0). The same is true of the first lease payment. Table 8.1 shows that the present value of the lease is £97.3k, which, compared with the purchase price of £100k, shows a margin in favour of the lease of £2.7k.

This result might suggest the finance lease to be the best option in this case. However, while it would certainly be one of the decision criteria, it would be unwise to enter into any lease solely on the basis of calculations such as this. The decision should only be made after detailed examination of the full contractual terms and conditions, especially those governing matters such as early termination and extension. Unsatisfactory terms relating to these matters could make the above apparent margin of 2.7 per cent in favour of the lease pale into insignificance. It is even more important to examine carefully the terms and conditions in an operating lease, our next topic.

Checkpoint

Since the previous checkpoint we have:
- covered the main characteristics of finance leases and hire purchase;
- considered the effect of leasing on a financial case, distinguishing between the 'investment decision' and the 'financing decision'.

So far we have considered two particular kinds of lease: the finance lease and hire purchase. While their legal forms are different, both of them in practice cause the customer to assume the product risk (of obsolescence and decline in market value). Can leasing do anything for customers who wish to pass this product risk on to lessors? The answer is yes, and it is through the mechanism that has come to be known as the operating lease.

OPERATING LEASES

If asked to describe a lease, most people, if able to at all, tend to describe what is actually an operating lease or something like it. Operating leases are very important as ways of financing IT. One fundamental factor distinguishes an operating lease from a finance lease, and it is as follows:

> At the outset of an operating lease, the lessor deducts from the purchase price of the leased asset an amount, called the 'residual value' (RV), based on the asset's expected resale value at the end of the lease. During the primary period, often no longer than about three years, the customer will only have to pay the balance, plus interest. At the end of the primary period, the customer can usually return the leased asset to the lessor, with no further obligation.

RESIDUAL VALUE (RV)

Because the concept of residual value is fundamental to operating leases, it is worth spending time to become fully familiar with the idea. For example, assume that a machine costs £1000 today. Suppose that a lessor, prepared to lease the asset under an operating lease, estimates that the value at which it could be sold three years from today, its market value, will be £180. The first question is would the lessor be prepared to guarantee the full £180 by including it as the residual value in the operating lease? No, because the £180 can only be an estimate and the lessor will need a margin for error. The guaranteed residual value in the lease would be for a lesser amount, say £160.

Suppose that the lessor, who will have to pay £1000 for the asset, would indeed be prepared to guarantee a residual value of £160 in the lease. If the interest rate that the lessor will charge is, say, seven per cent, how much will the customer have to pay for the lease over the three-year period? If you wish to think about it for yourself and you need a hint, then remember that £160 receivable three years from today is not worth £160. The answer is shown in Table 8.2.

Table 8.2 shows that the present value of the RV, discounted at seven per cent, is in fact £130.61. This amount, deducted from the purchase price (£1000), leaves £869.39, which is the present value of the amounts that must be recovered from the customer. Suppose that the lease is to be payable over three years, annually in arrears, which means that the first payment is due at the end of Year 1. We need a way of working out what the payments would have to be. Table A1.3 in Appendix 1 allows us to do just that. It is called an 'annual equivalent annuity' table. 'Annual equivalent annuity' simply means the periodic payments that are equivalent in discounted terms, over a given number of periods, to a single amount today.

TABLE 8.2 *Example of residual value calculation*

	Yr 0 £000	Yr 1 £000	Yr 2 £000	Yr 3 £000	Ref	Total £000
Assumption – interest rate inherent in lease is 7%						
Purchase price	1000				*a*	1000.00
Estimated residual value (RV)				160	*b*	
Discount factor (7%)				0.8163	*c*	
Present value of RV (*b* × *c*)				130.61	*d*	130.61
NPV of lease (*a – d*), on which lease payments will be calculated					*e*	869.39
Annual equivalent annuity payable in arrears (3 years @ 7%) – see Note					*f*	0.3811
Amount of each payment, annual in arrears (*e* × *f*)						331.32

Note: Different annuity tables would be required for payments in advance or at different intervals.

What we want to know is the annual payment for three years in arrears if the discount rate is seven per cent. To use the table, start at the seven per cent row and move along until you come to the 3-year column. The factor that you find there is 0.3811. The payments for a three-year lease of £869.39 would be found by the simple calculation £869.39 × 0.3811, which comes to £331.32. This means that the lease would require from the customer three payments annually in arrears of £331.32. A proof of this calculation is shown in Table 8.3.

TABLE 8.3 *Proof of residual value calculation in Table 8.2*

	Yr 0 £	Yr 1 £	Yr 2 £	Yr 3 £	Total £
Lease payments, annual in arrears	0	331.32	331.32	331.32	993.96
Discount factors @ 7%	1	0.9346	0.8734	0.8163	
Present values (PV)	0	309.62	289.34	270.43	869.39

Obviously, different annuity factors are required if the lease is payable in advance rather than in arrears or if the payments are due quarterly or monthly rather than annually. In practice, however, as with the other financial calculations in this book, people nowadays use the functions built into computer spreadsheets or financial calculators rather than tables. However, the tables remain a useful aid to understanding the principles.

Options at the end of the primary period

The customer's options at the end of the primary period of an operating lease are dictated mainly by the need of the lessor to recover the residual value (the £160 in the above example). The customer usually, therefore, has one or both of the following options:

- return the asset to the lessor, who will then either sell or re-lease it;
- extend, but for payment sufficient to recover the expected further decline in residual value during the extension period.

Some lessors also offer the option to convert the operating lease to a full payout finance lease. This involves a single payment, by which the customer effectively buys the lessor's interest in the residual value and a one-year extension of the lease. Further extensions are then at peppercorn rates. Extension or conversion rates may be stated in the original contract or they may be left to be negotiated at the time when the option is exercised.

Who offers operating leases?

A feature of an operating lease is the option, indeed the obligation, eventually to return the leased equipment to the lessor. Therefore, any company offering IT operating leases is also going to be a trader in used equipment. We already know that banks have no interest in dealing in the assets that they finance, so banks themselves do not offer operating leases. The main providers of IT operating leases are:

- independent companies, some of which may be operationally independent subsidiaries of banks;
- manufacturers' leasing companies.

Early termination of an operating lease

On early termination of an operating lease, as of any lease, all outstanding amounts become payable. The equipment is returnable to the lessor, who will need to recover the residual value by selling or re-leasing it. Note, however, that the market value on early termination may be higher than the residual value originally written into the lease, which was estimated as at a later date. Whether the customer gets any benefit from this possibly higher value will depend upon the terms of the contract. If the contract is not specific, then the matter will be left to be negotiated at the time of termination. The outcome may be influenced, to some extent, by the relationship between lessor and customer, and by whether the lease to be terminated will be followed by another.

In a continuing relationship between lessor and customer the termination of one operating lease is likely to be caused by the wish to replace old equipment with new. Such exchanges are a common occurrence and are sometimes known as 'technology upgrades'. This is a confusing term because what is meant by it is replacement of old equipment with new, whereas 'upgrade' usually means new components replacing old within the same covers under the same serial number.

Rolled debt

When an operating lease is terminated and replaced by another, lessors do not necessarily require outstanding amounts to be paid in cash. They will sometimes 'roll' them into the next lease, simply quoting a rate that combines the new lease with debt from the old. This can be attractive, especially to customers with tightly controlled budgets. However, they should nevertheless understand that:

- Unless the amount of the debt has been disclosed, rolling debt obscures both the costs of terminating the old lease and entering into the new.

- After several 'rolled' terminations, quite large amounts of hidden debt may have built up without the lessee realizing it.

- Finance to pay off a debt is a loan. The accounting and tax treatment of loans is different from that of leases. To treat them as though they were the same is inaccurate, unless the amounts involved can reasonably be regarded as immaterial.

Operating lease upgrades

Broadly similar considerations apply to upgrades under operating leases as under finance leases, but with some important differences. Under finance leases, you will recall, it is the customer that receives almost all of any eventual proceeds of sale. The higher the proceeds, the more the customer gets. The lessor's interest in the proceeds is small, usually limited to one or two per cent of the original capital cost. With operating leases, however, eventual return of equipment to the lessor is a requirement. This, you will recall, is because the lessor will need to recoup its investment in the residual value. The proceeds of sale or re-lease of any particular leased asset will almost certainly make the difference between profit and loss for the lessor.

Therefore, operating lessors will try to ensure maximum market value for the equipment that they own. They will also seek to ensure the simplest state of affairs when the return takes place. This will normally be achieved if the leased asset is wholly owned by a single lessor. Operating lessors are therefore usually reluctant to allow upgrades to be financed other than with themselves, although it is sometimes done.

One of the things that can significantly affect the market value of IT equipment when it is returned is whether or not it consists wholly of manufacturers' standard components. The liberalization of the IT industry in the 1970s opened the market not just to suppliers of plug-compatible machines, but also to suppliers of components, such as memory. Some lessors require manufacturers' standard parts, if removed, to be refitted before a machine is returned.

As is the case with finance leases, an upgrade may be the subject of a new lease, or the original lease may be amended. In either case, the 'new' lease will usually reflect the fact that the effect of an upgrade is to extend the life of the base asset. If an upgraded asset is the subject of more than one lease, lessors will usually require all of them to expire at the same time. This is because of the obvious necessity of ensuring that the equipment is returned as a whole, complete with all its upgrades.

WHOSE BALANCE SHEET?

You may recall from the discussion about finance leases earlier in the chapter, that where a lease transfers 'substantially all the risks and rewards of ownership' to the customer, then the lease is called a finance lease, and the leased asset must appear on the customer's balance sheet, together with the debt owed to the leasing company. A full payout finance lease is self-evidently such a lease, because it transfers virtually 100 per cent of the risks and rewards of ownership to the customer. What about leases that do not transfer 'substantially all' of those risks? How did the rule-makers suggest that we identify them and how did they suggest we account for them?

The first question depends on what is meant by 'substantially all'. 'Virtually 100 per cent' obviously falls within the above definition of a finance lease. What about 95 per cent? Or 90 per cent or 80 per cent? The rule-makers no doubt intended that their definition was meant to be qualitative rather than primarily quantitative. However, the view that they took was that if a distinction is to be made, then a line must be drawn. The rule-makers chose to draw the line at 90 per cent. Once that was decided, the full version of their definitions of leases, which, expanded, became (in the UK) Statement of Standard Accounting Practice No. 21 (SSAP 21), is as follows.

The following extracts* from definitions in SSAP 21 are relevant in determining whether or not a leased asset has to be shown on the balance sheet of the lessee:

> A *finance lease* is a lease that transfers substantially all the risks and rewards of ownership of an asset to the lessee. It should be presumed that such a transfer of risks and rewards occurs if at the inception of a lease the present value of the minimum lease payments, including any initial payment, amounts to substantially all (normally 90% or more) of the fair value of the leased asset. The present value should be calculated by using the interest rate implicit in the lease. If the fair value of the asset is not determinable, an estimate thereof should be used.*

'Fair value' is usually but not necessarily taken to mean purchase price. After their rather long definition of a finance lease, the rule-makers then went to the other extreme in defining an operating lease. The SSAP 21 definition of an operating lease is:

> An *operating lease* is a lease other than a finance lease.*

In the Introduction to this chapter mention was made of International Accounting Statement No. 17 *Accounting for Leases*. It was also stated that SSAP 21 is very close to the international standard and contains the words '... compliance with SSAP 21 will ensure compliance with IAS 17 in all material respects'. Concerning finance leases, the respect in which the two standards differ significantly is that IAS 17 omits reference to the '90 per cent rule', thus requiring the decision (whether a particular lease is a finance lease or not) to be made on purely qualitative grounds. Appendix 2 contains, with permission, extracts from SSAP 21, IAS 17 and other relevant standards concerning leasing.

Residual value example revisited

In our example earlier in this chapter, under the heading 'Residual value', the cost of the asset was £1000. The 'present value of the minimum lease payments' was £869.39, which is 86.9 per cent of £1000. Therefore, under what came to be known as 'the 90 per cent rule' of SSAP 21, that particular lease would indeed, quantitatively at least, qualify as an operating lease.

How are operating leases accounted for?

How should customers account for operating leases? The answer is delightfully simple and is an important reason for the popularity of operating leases. The leased asset does not appear on the customer's balance sheet; neither do the outstanding amounts appear as a liability. Payments under operating leases are charged straight to the customer's profit and loss account as expenses and, like other expenses, they should normally be charged on a straight-line basis even if the payments are irregular. For example, suppose that on the first day of its accounting year, a company writes a three-year operating lease with an initial one-year holiday, and payments during Years 2 and 3, as in Table 8.4.

TABLE 8.4 *How operating leases are accounted for (1)*

	Year 1 £000	Year 2 £000	Year 3 £000
Payments	0	30	30

---

*The extracts from *Accounting Standards 2005/2006* are reproduced by kind permission of the Accounting Standards Board Limited. For further information please visit www.frc.org.uk/asb.

The lease would be charged to the profit and loss accounts of years one to three as in Table 8.5.

TABLE 8.5 *How operating leases are accounted for (2)*

	Year 1 £000	Year 2 £000	Year 3 £000
Operating lease charges	20	20	20

For the customer, this kind of 'off balance sheet financing' makes accounting much simpler and also ensures the least impact on some of the key financial ratios. In particular, with a finance lease or hire purchase, as with bank borrowing for outright purchase, both the asset and the debt are shown on the customer's balance sheet. This results in higher totals of both assets and debt. Because of this, both the return on capital employed (ROCE) and the debt/equity ratio are adversely affected. In the case of ROCE, this is because for much the same amount of profit there is a greater quantity of 'capital' (usually meaning, in this context, equity plus long-term debt). In the case of the debt/equity ratio it is because, for the same amount of equity, a greater quantity of debt is shown. See Chapter 13 for an explanation of these and other financial ratios. So, whose balance sheet does the asset appear on? The answer is the lessor's.

Operating leases and tax

As with most expenses, the tax treatment of operating leases generally follows the accounting treatment. The lease charges, adjusted if necessary as described above with respect to payment 'holidays', are treated as tax-deductible, just like most other business expenses.

Sale and lease-back

The principle of sale and lease-back is the same, whether the lease is a finance lease or an operating lease. However, if the lease is an operating lease, then by definition, the sale and lease-back removes the asset from the customer's balance sheet. However, the older an IT asset is when the sale and lease-back occurs, the less likely is it that the residual value will be high enough for the lease to qualify as an operating lease. It would usually be a non-full payout finance lease as described below.

RISK AND REWARD

By comparison with a finance lease, what advantages would customers expect to gain by (where possible) writing an operating lease for IT equipment? They are as follows:

- the guaranteed residual value written into the lease;
- lower lease payments during the primary period, the result of the residual value;
- off balance sheet finance;
- simpler accounting;
- avoiding the chore of disposal, by being able to return the equipment to the lessor at the end of the lease.

These are the fundamental benefits of an operating lease. What the operating lessee reaching the end of the primary period usually forgoes, by comparison with a finance lessee, are the following:

- The certainty of nominal (peppercorn) payments for continued use in a secondary period.
- Any 'profit' should the eventual market value of the leased asset exceed the residual value written into the lease, although this would usually not be a problem in respect of those operating leases that include an option to convert to full payout finance lease. Meanwhile, however, the lessee will have been protected from any 'loss' should the converse be the case.

For operating lessors, the risks and rewards associated with an operating lease are the converse of all the above. The major risk taken by an operating lessor is product risk: the risk of obsolescence and decline in market value. However, remember that operating lessors are dealers as well: they buy and sell equipment. They may also offer services of various kinds to their customers. An example is the provision of asset management services, described in the next paragraph.

Lessors have to keep accurate records of all their leased assets, from both an accounting and a tax viewpoint. Accounting for large numbers of assets can be a challenging task for many user organizations. The fact that the lessor, rather than the customer, has the task of maintaining these records is itself a major benefit of leasing for many companies. For a charge, some lessors will make their own asset management facilities available online to their customers. Customers can enquire into the status of their leased assets and can also use the facilities to record details of their own (non-leased) assets.

Points to look out for in an operating lease

The following is a summary of key points to consider:

- To what extent are the options available to the customer stated and priced in the contract?
- What does the contract say about upgrades? Could they be financed other than with the same lessor?
- What is the position regarding non-standard or second-hand parts?

- What does the contract say about extension? Is extension at a fixed rate or at fair market value? If the latter, how is fair market value determined? What period of notice to extend is required? Does the primary rate automatically continue if the required notice is not given?
- Under what terms can the lease be terminated early?
- Does the contract provide a conversion to full payout finance lease? What rights, if any, does the customer have to participate in any excess of market value over residual value and through what mechanism?
- Assuming follow-on business, will any termination debt be stated separately? What facilities does the lessor provide for financing termination debt?

When is an operating lease appropriate?

An operating lease would usually be appropriate for a company that does not require to take ownership and that:

- wants 'off balance sheet finance';
- wants the lessor to assume the product risk;
- wants the option of returning equipment to the lessor;
- is willing to accept usually higher (than full payout finance lease) secondary period payments;
- is willing to accept a nil or lower (than full payout finance lease) proportion of eventual sale proceeds.

> **Checkpoint**
>
> Since the previous checkpoint we have:
> - covered the main characteristics of operating leases;
> - discussed, with the aid of an example, what 'residual value' means and its fundamental importance in leasing.

NON-FULL PAYOUT FINANCE LEASES

We noted earlier that with most finance leases the customer pays 100 per cent of the asset cost plus interest and that such leases are usually called 'full payout finance leases'. Expressing that in terms of the SSAP 21 lease definitions quoted above: full payout finance leases are leases in which the 'present value of the minimum leases payments' comes to 100 per cent of the fair value (usually, cost) of the asset. It follows that non-full payout finances leases are those in which that percentage lies between 90 and 100 per cent. They have a residual value, but it is not big enough for the lease to qualify as an operating lease.

The most helpful way to think of a non-full payout finance lease is as a lease that would be an operating lease but for the fact that it fails to satisfy the '90 per cent rule'. Such a lease has to appear on the customer's balance sheet, which would make it unacceptable to a customer who required off balance sheet finance. In every other respect, its characteristics, benefits and possible pitfalls are usually as for operating leases.

Composite leases

In order to understand the principles of leasing it made sense to look at the two main kinds of lease (full payout finance leases and operating leases) separately and in their 'pure' forms. This we have done and the distinction between the two kinds of lease is still important. However, many IT investments today are complex and large, and financing arrangements tend to be correspondingly complex. As a result, the boundaries between particular kinds of lease are now sometimes less clear than they used to be.

Composite leases (not an 'official' term) are arrangements that, in a single contract, provide finance for the possibly many different elements in an IT development. These may include:

- IT and communications equipment from various manufacturers;
- software from various providers;
- services, which may be anything from project management, training and maintenance, through installation services to managed operations or full outsourcing.

In constructing such arrangements, the lessor must consider and price each element separately. Some items of hardware may qualify for operating lease rates, some only for finance lease rates. One-time charges for software licences with an expected life of two years or more would usually be leasable on finance lease terms. For a summary of the tax and accounting rules for software, see Appendix 4. The financing of services depends on the nature of the service. Services generally cannot be leased, although financing can be used to reschedule the timing and amounts of payments due to service providers. Financing for services is by means of loans.

On or off balance sheet?

From a cash flow point of view, all this may be a matter of indifference to the customer, who simply wants a 'bottom line price' in the form of a series of payments. However, what customers cannot be indifferent about is how such leases are accounted for. The accounting rules give no specific guidance on this question and, like much of lease accounting, it is an area where professional advice is likely to be sought with reference to particular situations. In general, the safest approach would usually be to apply the SSAP 21 (or IAS 17, if adopted) criteria to the elements being leased as though they were the subject of separate leases, and account for them accordingly.

EXCHANGE LEASES

This term is sometimes used to describe financial arrangements that have been packaged specifically around the idea of what were earlier described as 'technology upgrades', more accurately perhaps called asset replacements. They can be especially attractive to organizations that are constrained by rigid adherence to budgets. Under arrangements of this kind, a customer may install a tranche of various items of equipment for a specified period in return for agreed payments. At or after stated times, up to a given proportion of the assets, in terms of value, can be exchanged for new ones at no increase in periodic payments. To compensate the lessor for unpaid amounts on the replaced assets, the term of the lease is extended. Replacements above the stated proportions may be made, but if so then the periodic payments are increased.

Arrangements of this kind are based on operating lease principles. They consist of a series of leases, some of which are terminated early and replaced by others that have a later end date. The new leases will typically include termination charges from the leases terminated. Such arrangements may sometimes make an IT solution easier to sell and easier to buy. Both buyer and seller know that some items in a proposed solution are more advanced in their product life cycle than others and may soon be superseded by new technology. To the customer, here is a financial package that recognizes that fact and allows them to do something about it by exchanging old technology for new at the appropriate time. Furthermore, the initial term of the contract can be determined according to what the customer can afford, whether in cash or budget terms. The higher the periodic payments, the shorter the term; the lower the payments, the longer the term has to be. However, it is also the case that the longer the term, the less likely is it that the underlying leases would qualify as operating leases. As for the accounting treatment, here too professional advice is likely to be sought in respect of particular situations.

RENTAL

What is the difference, if any, between leasing and rental? There is no 'official' answer to this question. Both confer rights to use equipment or software in return for periodic payments. However, whereas leases other than hire purchase do not confer rights to purchase, arrangements described as 'rental' sometimes do. A description that appears to fit the facts, at least so far as goods are concerned, is that under a lease there is usually, discernible by the customer, a direct connection between the purchase price of the goods and the total of the periodic payments required. With rental of goods there is often no such discernible connection.

For example, a person renting a TV set may never know the purchase price and will probably not be interested. Over the period of the agreement they may actually be paying for the TV several times over. They do not mind, because they are not paying for a TV. What they are paying for is the right to use a TV, and what they want is a payment stream that matches their budget and their expected availability of cash. Repair and replacement services are usually included and they can if they wish cancel the agreement at short notice, and return the goods. It is this aspect that, you will recall, made true rental too risky for IT suppliers, and therefore too expensive for their customers, except for very short-term needs.

Pay-for-use arrangements

Financing arrangements are sometimes written under which a customer organization pays an IT supplier not for machines delivered but for processing power actually used. Using IT terminology, the customer is paying for 'mips' (millions of instructions per second) rather than for boxes. Typically, the customer will contract and pay for a minimum number of mips to be provided by the supplier over a defined period. If the customer requires more than the contracted number, then they pay at an agreed rate for the extra. How such arrangements are accounted for would, yet again, usually be a matter for professional advice. However, depending upon the particular circumstances, these arrangements may appear to be almost indistinguishable from rental.

INTERNATIONAL FINANCING

With the development by many organizations of international networks comes the need to finance them. This can be a complex process, especially if done piecemeal, using different financing organizations in different countries. Some lessors, themselves usually international companies with knowledge of the differing accounting and tax rules in various countries, offer international financing services to their customers. Typical features of such services are:

- A single set of contract terms and conditions, applicable in all the countries covered by the agreement, for supplying hardware, software and services from various suppliers.
- The option to add country-specific terms and conditions, where necessary to satisfy local laws.
- Invoicing to a single location and payment in the currency of choice.
- The ability to move equipment freely between countries, although doing so will usually have tax implications.

'SMALL TICKET' LEASING

This piece of leasing jargon refers to the leasing of small items of equipment such as personal computers (PCs). The principles of leasing are the same, whether for small items or large. However, there are some particular aspects of small ticket leasing that are worthy of note.

First, the costs of administering a lease are much the same whether the leased asset costs £1000 or £1 million. Therefore, while lessors may be willing to lease a single PC, they would be happier leasing large numbers of them under a single agreement. Second, small items such as PCs are typically delivered piecemeal over a period. A consequence of these two facts is that lessors are sometimes willing to write a single lease on all the small items to be acquired by the customer at any time during a particular period, typically one quarter. This saves administration costs for lessor and customer alike.

THE LEASING CONTRACT

Different lessors offer different terms and conditions. Perhaps the main difference between leasing contracts is the extent to which the customer's options are set out in the contract. At one end of the spectrum are contracts in which every option for the customer throughout the lease is stated and priced. These priced options may include:

- the primary period lease rate;
- secondary period rates for various renewal periods;
- conversion rates to full payout finance lease, if offered.

The mechanism for determining the extent to which the customer may, on early termination, participate in proceeds of sale may also be described in the contract. At the other end of the spectrum are contracts in which none of the above is specified except the primary period rate.

Swings and roundabouts

The more specific the contract, the more certainty does the customer have. However, such a contract leaves little scope for the lessor to make up on the swings what it may lose on the roundabouts if, for example, it starts to look as though it may have overestimated the residual value. The pricing of the primary period rate and the options will take this additional risk into account. On the other hand, the less specific the contract, the less risky it will usually be for the lessor. The lessor may, therefore, be able to build in a higher residual value, in the knowledge that it has some room for manoeuvre when the customer comes to upgrade, terminate early or extend. Neither kind of contract is 'good' or 'bad'. The important thing is to consider the deal on offer as a whole. The customer that opts for certainty should not necessarily expect to get it for nothing. The customer attracted by cheaper primary period payments should not necessarily expect to find its subsequent options so cheap when it comes to exercise them. In IT leasing, as in most aspects of life, there is no such thing as a free lunch.

THE FUTURE

Financing and especially leasing are continually evolving subjects, as are the rules and accounting standards under which they operate. They are matters of continual debate in the IT and accounting professions worldwide. Over recent decades they have played a significant role in helping IT users to afford what might otherwise have been unaffordable, and will no doubt continue to do so into the future.

Summary

The main points covered in this chapter, linked to its objectives, have been the following:

- *A lease is a contract under which the owner of an asset (the lessor) permits someone else (the lessee) to use it during a defined period in return for agreed payments. All components of an IT acquisition can be financed. Hardware and most lump sum charges for software licences can be leased. Payments due for services can be financed by means of a loan.*
- *The main providers of IT leasing are banks, independent leasing companies and IT manufacturers.*
- *A finance lease is a lease that transfers substantially all the risks and rewards of ownership of an asset to the lessee. Hire purchase is a lease with a purchase option. It is a method of providing extended payment terms for an asset that the hirer will eventually own. An operating lease can be described as a lease that includes a sufficiently large guaranteed residual value.*
- *In leasing terms, 'residual value' is an amount, based on an asset's expected value at the end of a lease, deducted by the lessor from the asset's cost in determining the payments due under the lease.*
- *During the currency of a lease the lessor owns the leased asset. Under an operating lease the leased asset is on the balance sheet of the lessor. Under finance leases and hire purchase the leased asset is on the balance sheet of the customer (the lessee).*
- *The currently relevant UK, EU, US and international rules and accounting standards that have an impact on IT leasing are summarised in Appendix 2.*

9 Outsourcing: Financial Aspects

WITH HUGH PIKE BSc MBA

Objectives

When you have studied this chapter you should be able to:

- *describe what outsourcing is, with particular reference to IT, and the main reasons for considering it;*
- *describe the particular financial characteristics of outsourcing and the financial implications of outsourcing decisions;*
- *describe the factors that typically have to be taken into account in building a financial case for outsourcing vis-à-vis in-house provision;*
- *construct a financial case for outsourcing vis-à-vis in-house provision from given data;*
- *explain how financial cases for outsourcing are typically evaluated.*

Outsourcing is a complex subject with strategic, operational, legal and financial implications. The main purpose of this chapter is to shed some light on one aspect of it: the mechanics of its cost-justification and accounting at the level likely to be encountered by an IT decision maker who may not happen to be financially expert. It may also be of use to financial people for whom decisions about outsourcing are not an everyday occurrence. Wider aspects of the subject are treated in the books listed in Further Reading.

WHAT IS OUTSOURCING?

Outsourcing means different things to different people. A working definition of IT outsourcing is as follows: a contractual relationship for the provision and management of IT services by an external supplier, under which:

- the services are customized to the customer's requirements, such that payment by the customer will be related to the achievement of agreed service levels and specified results;
- the services may be carried out at the customer's premises or at those of the supplier;
- the outsourcing may, and typically does, include the transfer of fixed assets and/or people from the customer to the supplier.

Whatever is being considered as a candidate for outsourcing, the fundamental questions are much the same:

- Do we have the expertise and resources to do this effectively ourselves?
- Even if we do, would having it done by an outside specialist organization result in better service or be more economical by, for example, liberating resources for more productive work?
- If so, should we outsource the whole function or just parts of it, and if so, which parts?

Early examples of outsourcing

Some examples of what could be called outsourcing, although it was not called that at the time, were to be found in the very early days of commercial computing, as far back as the 1960s. 'Service bureaux' offered either specific services, such as data entry, or specific applications, such as payroll, accounting and stock control. These bureau services were offered both by IT manufacturers and by large IT user organizations as a way of earning revenue from spare capacity on the (then) very expensive IT equipment in which they had invested and from the expertise that they had acquired.

Later, specialist companies were founded, often as subsidiaries of large commercial organizations, which offered specific services, IT maintenance chief among them. Today, once again, IT manufacturers are among those offering outsourcing services, together with IT consultancies and other specialist companies. The services on offer cover the full spectrum, from individual applications to the provision and management of a customer's total IT requirements.

OUTSOURCING IN PERSONAL LIFE

As with much of business life, an analogy with personal life will be useful, especially to those for whom outsourcing is an unfamiliar concept. We as individuals all use outsourcing. For example, while it is perfectly possible to do so, few people generate their own electricity. The means of doing so are not well understood by most people and to do so would in any case probably not be economical. Electricity generation comes outside our core 'business' of living, and we normally wish our limited time and resources to be spent on more productive things. So, most of us are content to let the power company do the job for us. They have the expertise and the money to invest in expensive equipment and keep it up to date, and they can achieve economies of scale that allow them to charge their customers affordable rates while still making a reasonable profit.

Some capital equipment (generating plant) is installed on supplier premises. Other equipment (a meter) is installed on customer premises.

Both pieces of equipment are owned by the supplier and are therefore shown as assets on their balance sheet. The depreciation of these assets is among the costs taken into account by the supplier when fixing its prices. These, and its other fixed costs are usually recouped by means of a fixed quarterly charge to the customer, while the variable costs of actually generating electricity are recouped on a usage basis. Alternatively, all costs may be recouped by making a higher usage charge, with no standing charge.

The relationship between supplier and customer is governed by a contract, which contains penalty clauses for non-provision of service by the supplier or non-payment by the customer. Subject to the adjustments below, payments made by the customer are regarded as revenue in the hands of the supplier and as 'revenue expense' by the customer. In the books of the supplier at its accounting date, amounts due but not yet paid for electricity supplied are treated as debtors; any standing charges received in advance are treated as deferred revenue. In the 'books' of the customer the reverse is the case. The cost of electricity used but not yet paid for is a creditor; any standing charges paid in advance are treated as prepayments.

Provided that we are prepared to accept certain reasonable constraints imposed by the supplier (for example, a particular voltage, standard interfaces for 'plugging in' and so on), then electricity can be regarded as a utility, which we use when we need it and for which we pay mainly for the amount used. Water and other utilities could provide similar analogies.

In summary, the reasons why we as individuals typically outsource our requirement for electricity and other utilities, are the following:

- They are necessary things, but they are peripheral to our core 'business' of living.

- We have better things to do with our limited time and resources.

- We may not have the expertise to provide them ourselves.

- Because it is the core business of the supplier, for which they have both the infrastructure and the expertise, they can almost certainly provide it more cost-effectively and efficiently than we could.

- We can benefit from improving technology without having to learn about, acquire and finance it ourselves.

- We can 'smooth' our cash outflow because we do not have to bear the heavy upfront cost of the necessary equipment ourselves. By outsourcing, we are converting capital cost into revenue expense. 'Smoothing' simply means spreading the payment for goods or services over time.

- We can reasonably expect higher availability.

- Outsourcing helps us manage risk. If the supply fails, then because of contractual obligations the supplier is motivated to restore it quickly.

If our own personal generator should fail, then what? Doing it ourselves is not a risk-free option.

OUTSOURCING IN BUSINESS

Businesses also outsource their electricity requirements, although they sometimes provide their own in-house back-up generators to cover critical situations, as do some individuals. The numbers are bigger, but the same principles apply. For most, outsourcing is the obvious thing to do for a function such as power supply, which is not part of their core business. However, for some years now many other business activities have also come under that heading: for example, office cleaning, payroll, accounting, secretarial services, transport, equipment maintenance... and IT.

The reasons, given above, why we as individuals outsource are the same reasons why businesses often do so, with one important addition. Most individuals do not draw up a personal balance sheet and profit and loss account, although we could and would find it a useful thing to do in pursuit of that most elusive of personal skills – keeping our financial affairs in order. Businesses, by contrast, are required to do so, both by commercial law and tax law.

However, as will be discussed in Chapter 13, many businesses like to show a lean and mean balance sheet with as few assets as possible. The fewer the assets, the less the 'capital employed' (money, to you and me) needed to finance them. The less the capital employed, the more impressive will be the return on capital employed: that key ratio that compares the profit earned with the money used to earn it. In Chapter 8 we saw how leasing can be one way of getting assets 'off balance sheet', by paying to use assets that belong to someone else. Outsourcing can have a similar effect.

FINANCIAL CHARACTERISTICS OF OUTSOURCING

Whether or not to outsource is a big decision for an organization and large amounts of money are usually involved. From a financial point of view, most of the big decisions that organizations make are usually regarded as 'investment decisions'. They involve the investment of often large amounts of money and the expectation of an eventual 'return', sufficient in percentage terms to justify the investment. Whether to keep the old car or buy a less old one (see Chapter 1) was an investment decision, albeit a rather small one. Whether to undertake the proposed new IT applications in Example 3.1 of Chapter 3 was another.

Service contracts are not like that, however, and outsourcing contracts are essentially service contracts. Think of one of the simpler kinds of IT service contract: maintenance. Suppose that under your current IT maintenance contract you would be spending £100k per year for the next five years. Now suppose that an alternative supplier has offered to do the same job for £80k per year for an equivalent level of service. Here, there is no upfront 'investment'; indeed, the first payment in this example would be less (by £20k) than it would otherwise have been, as would the remaining payments. Words such as 'investment' and 'return' have no applicability. The decision to be made here is not an 'investment decision' but a 'cost reduction' decision. The same is true of an outsourcing decision, regardless of which reasons were foremost for considering outsourcing in the first place and regardless of the fact that there may be substantial initial transition costs.

RISK AND SERVICE LEVELS

If outsourcing is indeed primarily a cost reduction decision, then it follows that the methods to be adopted for evaluating both the risk and the financial case will be those appropriate to cost reduction decisions. For a straight 'cost reduction' proposal like the one for cheaper maintenance outlined above, I suggest that the basis for decision would, in plain English, be:

> **Is the expected total saving over the duration of the contract big enough in proportion to the total 'status quo' expenditure to more than cover the risk of changing from the devil we know to one that we don't know?**

Continuing the maintenance contract example, provided only that the level of service from the new provider would indeed be at least equivalent to that provided by the old one, then would the expected total cost savings of £100k (£20k per year for five years) on current total costs of £500k, a reduction of 20 per cent, be regarded as worthwhile? The answer would almost certainly be yes. The risk would be managed by ensuring that agreed service levels were specified in the contract or in a separate service level agreement, together with penalties for failure to meet them. It may be considerably easier to manage risk when someone else is doing the work and is contractually liable for it than when you are doing it yourself.

Now suppose that the total cost savings over the five-year period were expected to be not £100k but £5k (£1k per year) on current total costs of £500k, a reduction of only one per cent in total costs rather than the 20 per cent just considered. Would it be worthwhile to change suppliers for such a saving? The answer would almost certainly be no. In either case the decision would be based on the commercial judgement of the decision maker.

FINANCIAL EVALUATION METHODS

Where there is no 'investment' and therefore no 'return' on investment it would be inappropriate to apply investment evaluation methods such as return on investment (ROI), internal rate of return (IRR) or payback, whose very names suggest their inapplicability. This applies to simple maintenance contracts; it applies equally to outsourcing proposals, however much bigger and more complex they may be.

Service suppliers such as maintenance contractors usually offer a discounted one-time payment as an alternative to monthly or other periodic payments. These offers are usually made attractive to customers because suppliers want both to get cash upfront and lessen the risk of customers walking away in mid-contract. So the discount is usually substantial and the option usually gives customers price protection for the duration of the contract. However, just because such offers involve a large upfront payment, that payment does not of itself convert a cost reduction decision into an investment decision. What it does is oblige the customer to make an additional financing decision, which would involve the use of net present value (NPV) to determine the real value of the discount being offered compared with making regular periodic payments.

Conversely, leasing is a way of smoothing the large initial investments necessary in many IT and other projects. However, leasing does not of itself convert an investment decision into a cost reduction decision just because it has the effect of removing the large upfront payment. What it also does is oblige the customer to make an additional financing decision to determine the real value of leasing compared with paying the lump sum.

I repeat that whatever may have been the main reasons for considering outsourcing in the first place, however big and complex the proposal may be, and regardless of whether the outsourcing charges are smoothed or unsmoothed, the financial decision to be made is essentially a cost reduction decision and not an investment decision. It follows that the method used to evaluate outsourcing proposals will nearly always be the rather simple one illustrated above in the context of the maintenance contract and that the methods developed for evaluating investment decisions (ROI, IRR, NPV, payback) will usually not be applied.

To the extent that a substantial upfront payment may be required by an outsourcing supplier, a financial case for outsourcing may well look like a case for an 'investment decision', and if being processed by spreadsheet or other computer model, then the arithmetic of all the above-named evaluation methods may well be done anyway, because such spreadsheets are usually designed with payback, NPV, IRR and ROI calculations built in. Needless to say, spreadsheets do not understand the significance or otherwise of the numbers that they produce. However, people evaluating outsourcing proposals will usually pay them scant regard or ignore them altogether, concentrating, as illustrated above, on the proportion of total estimated saving to total estimated status quo cost.

In the past, outsourcing suppliers have sometimes presented their proposals already smoothed. Although financing would almost always have been used to achieve this, the financing may not always have been obvious to the customer. However, it is now most likely that the 'natural' and the 'smoothed' cash flows would be shown separately. In the wake of several high-profile financial scandals in recent years, the financial regulatory environment is undergoing a process of radical change. Legislation designed to prevent fraudulent accounting and to make corporate executives more accountable for the accuracy of accounts and other information produced by their companies and corporations has been passed in some countries. Examples are the *Sarbanes-Oxley Act of 2002* in the USA and the *Companies (Audit, Investigations and Community Enterprise) Act of 2004* in the UK. The business world is still coming to terms with these new rules and with the enormity of the scandals that precipitated them.

SERVICE ENHANCEMENTS

Another way in which an outsourcing decision may differ financially from many other big IT decisions is that, inherent in the nature of outsourcing (the partial or complete taking over of IT operations and management by an outside specialist organization) is the likelihood that it might per se result in service enhancements. Examples might include higher availability or faster response times, and a resulting increase in productivity. Once a customer becomes convinced of the likelihood of such enhancements, the enhancements themselves might then become a further factor in favour of outsourcing. This might be thought to be a wholly benign cycle. However, an attendant difficulty is in deciding how to take the inherent enhancements into account in the financial case and the decision process.

A reasonable approach might be to recognize that two quite different things are happening when considering a typical outsourcing proposal – a like-for-like transfer of function and an enhancement of function – and treat them as the subjects of two different decisions. However, in practice it can be difficult to differentiate the two things for reasons that will become apparent shortly. In this respect, relevant considerations for the customer include the following:

- If the enhancements inherent in the outsourcing proposal will bring quantifiable benefits, then the amount of the benefits should be included in the financial case for outsourcing.
- If not, then they should be ignored. However, a supplier would no doubt resist strongly any suggestion by the customer that they (the

supplier) should somehow remove the enhancements and reduce the price correspondingly.

- If the enhancements are sufficiently desirable to be contemplated even if the status quo were to continue, and if it would be both technically and economically feasible to provide them in-house, then both the benefits and the additional costs of providing them should be estimated and built into the in-house financial case, so that like is being compared with like.

The second bullet point above illustrates the main difficulty that inherent enhancements can cause the decision maker in practice. The point is that the enhancements usually come with the deal, regardless of whether customers want them or not. That said, customers are usually happy to accept them.

As an analogy, imagine that you have bought and paid for a new washing machine. Subsequently, the salesperson discovers that the model that you have bought is no longer available from the manufacturer and offers you at no extra cost a new, enhanced model. You would almost certainly accept the offer, even if you didn't particularly want or need the enhancements. What would almost certainly be futile would be to ask for them to be removed and for a corresponding reduction in price. If the new model was only available at a higher price, then you would evaluate the benefits to determine whether the higher price was worth paying.

The course most often adopted is to attempt to identify and quantify the benefits, if any, expected to result from the enhancements. By summarizing them into a single line it becomes a simple matter to evaluate the financial case both with and without the enhancements. In the example that follows, I have included the assumed benefits of enhanced service in the financial case for outsourcing, and have assumed that it would not be economically feasible to provide them in-house.

INFLATION

In Chapter 1 it was pointed out that in producing financial cases people can and do use either inflated or uninflated values. For either approach, the starting point is to determine today's uninflated values; then, if required, to identify those items that will be subject to inflation, choose an appropriate rate and calculate future amounts accordingly.

The question is this: in a 'status quo versus outsourcing' financial case is it equally appropriate to use inflated or uninflated values? The answer is no. Inflated values should be used, for the following reason. For the customer, outsourcing involves the effective taking over by the supplier of a large number of individual in-house cost items and their replacement by a single item, which is the outsourcing charge, usually over a period of between seven and ten years. It is certain that the supplier, in setting its price, will take into account the expected inflation of its costs over the contract period. Not to do so would practically ensure a loss-making contract. If, therefore, the customer does not also take inflation into account in its financial case, then outsourcing charges, whether 'smoothed' or not, that have been arrived at after taking into account inflation will be being compared with uninflated in-house costs. Like will not be being compared with like.

Even at low rates of inflation the differences are not trivial. At the time of writing, 2005, inflation in the UK is approximately three per cent. For those future costs that do indeed increase at the rate of inflation, even such a low rate as three per cent will cause them to be 16 per cent higher after five years, and 34 per cent higher after ten. Imagine a higher rate of inflation, say seven per cent. After ten years, increasing at seven per cent per year, a cost will have almost doubled. During the early 1990s inflation rates in many countries were substantially higher than seven per cent.

Remember that a typical outsourcing contract may run for ten years, during which time there might be many changes in the economic environment. With that in mind, there are two ways in which suppliers typically take inflation into account in setting their charges. The first, and the most risky for the supplier but the most certain for the customer, is to make an estimate of average inflation over the whole contract period and inflate their expected costs accordingly in the process of calculating their charges. The second is to state, in the contract, charges for an initial period, together with a formula for applying some level of indexation thereafter that will compensate for inflation in accordance with a recognized index, such as an index of wages and salaries. Whatever the method employed it is of course ultimately a matter for agreement between supplier and customer. In the example that follows later in this chapter I shall, for simplicity, be assuming the first of these two methods.

HOW TO BUILD AN OUTSOURCING FINANCIAL CASE

The main headings to which consideration would nearly always have to be given in an outsourcing decision are the following, although in practice there may of course be others. Under each heading is a brief checklist of the main points that will usually have to be considered in that context. All of these main points feature in the worked example that follows shortly and are explained in detail in the narrative commentary thereon.

- **Hardware** Trade-in or transfer values of existing hardware; purchase prices or lease payments for new; lease termination, extension or assignment charges; maintenance, power and insurance; (in profit and loss financial cases only) depreciation; and losses or profits on disposal.

- **Software** Licence fees: lump sums or financing payments; annual maintenance charges; licence transfer fees; (in profit and loss cases only) amortization; and losses on transfer or cessation of use.

- **Premises** Sale price or rent of existing; purchase price or rent of new; any sub-rent receivable; and running costs.

- **People** Salaries and overheads; redundancy payments; cost of people retained or hired for liaison with an outsourcing supplier; and outsourcing consultancy fees.

- **Administrative overheads** If these will change as a result of out-sourcing, then they should be included.

- **Service enhancements** See the similarly titled section earlier in this chapter.

- **Outsourcing charges** See the above explanations of 'smoothing' and the section entitled 'Inflation'.

To remind you, the golden rule for financial cases designed to assist decision-making is restated as follows:

- In cash flow financial cases, include future cash outflows and inflows that differ among the alternatives. Include cash paid and received in respect of purchase and sale of capital assets, but never their associated depreciation or losses or profits on disposal.

- In profit and loss financial cases, include future expenses and revenues that differ among the alternatives. Include depreciation and losses or profits on disposal of capital assets, but never their associated cash flows.

- Exclude sunk costs: costs already incurred that cannot be recouped.

> **Checkpoint**
>
> So far in this chapter we have covered the first three of its five objectives. In particular:
>
> - we have discussed what outsourcing is, with particular reference to IT, and the main reasons for considering it;
>
> - we have discussed the particular financial characteristics of out-sourcing and the financial implications of outsourcing decisions;
>
> - we have listed the factors that typically have to be taken into account in building a financial case for outsourcing vis-à-vis in-house provision.

A WORKED EXAMPLE

As with most of the topics in the book, this one will be further discussed in the context of a worked example. Especially if outsourcing is your particular interest, then this example is one from which you have much to gain by attempting to work through it yourself. Alternatively, you can simply read it as part of the narrative. The example is designed to illustrate in a simple and logical way as many as possible of the factors that frequently feature in decisions about whether the IT function should be outsourced or remain (or return) in-house. You are once again invited to accept any artificiality in the example as a price to pay for its being as comprehensive as possible and therefore a basis for building your own real and no doubt more complex cases.

The approach adopted will be to illustrate, with numbers, the financial factors (listed above) that need to be considered in a typical outsourcing decision, and in building an appropriate financial case in both cash flow and profit and loss form. In the narrative commentary that follows you will be taken step by step through every line of the solution. Except for anything blindingly obvious, each line will be described in the text and different options discussed where appropriate. I repeat that, even if you prefer to ignore the numbers, just reading the text will contribute significantly towards achieving the learning objectives of the chapter.

EXAMPLE 9.1: DESCRIPTION

Assume that Customer Ltd is considering whether to outsource its IT function. Management has considered the various arguments in favour of outsourcing and most of them seem to apply to the company. Discussions are in progress with Supplier Ltd, an IT outsourcing company, and some work has been done to collect data on the likely costs and benefits. Some organizations use the services offered by outsourcing consultants (see the section on Managing the Process at the end of this chapter), in which case it would be the consultants with whom the organization would be dealing in these early stages. Customer Ltd's management recognizes that seven to ten years is a reasonable and typical period over which to contract for such a major change to their business. However, to avoid filling pages unnecessarily with numbers, I have chosen a shorter five-year evaluation period. In this example, for the sake of simplicity, just one outsourcing proposal is being compared with the in-house status quo. In practice, several competing proposals might be under consideration.

The input data

You will find the input data in Table 9.1. In that table, items typically likely to be subject to inflation are marked with the letter 'I' in the 'Ref' column to the right of the numbers. I suggest that you glance at Table 9.1 now. However, should you wish to treat the example as an exercise and attempt it yourself, then before doing so:

1. Read the following sections first, up to the heading 'Commentary on the tables'.

2. Look ahead at Tables 9.2–9.8 and either draw up rough versions of them or use simple spreadsheets on a computer for your workings.

TABLE 9.1 *Example 9.1 – Input data*

	£000	Ref

Note: Items subject to inflation are marked 'I' and items to be transferred to supplier are marked 'T' in the 'Ref' column.

	£000	Ref
Mainframes, midrange and peripherals (owned)		T
Book value on Day 1 of Yr 1	1500	
Depreciation (straight line), per year	500	
Market value on Day 1 of Yr 1 and Yr 2 respectively	400 200	
Maintenance, power and insurance, Yr 1	100	
Current intention if continue in-house:		
Trade-in at market value at beginning of Yr 2	200	
Purchase new equipment at beginning of Yr 2	1600	
Depreciation of new equipment (straight line) Yr 2 to Yr 5, per year	400	
Maintenance, power and insurance, from Yr 2, per year	60	I
External net revenue from spare capacity during Yr 1 to Yr 5 (ceases if outsource)	90	I
Software licences on the above existing and new equipment		T
Book value on Day 1 of Yr 1	250	
Amortization (straight line), Yr 1 to Yr 5	50	
Annual maintenance charges	40	I
Transfer fees to be borne by customer if licences assigned	150	
Mainframes, midrange and peripherals (operating leases – assignable at no charge)		T
One remaining annual payment (Yr 1)	300	
Maintenance, power and insurance (Yr 1)	80	I
Current intention if continue in-house:		
Return leased equipment to lessor at end of Yr 1		
Lease new equip – primary term 3 years from Yr 2, per yr (fixed)	350	
Secondary term of above – 1 year (Yr 5, fixed)	200	
Maintenance, power and insurance, Yr 2 to Yr 5, per year	50	I

Table continues...

TABLE 9.1 *Continued*

		£000	Ref
Software licences on the above existing and new equipment			T
Book value on Day 1 of Yr 1		140	
Amortization (straight line), Yr 1		70	
Annual maintenance charges		40	I
Current intention if continue in-house:			
Acquire new licences, and cease using old ones, at beginning of Yr 2		400	
Amortization (straight line), Yr 2 to Yr 5, per year		100	
Annual maintenance charges		50	I
Transfer fees to be borne by customer if licences assigned		NIL	
PCs – desktops and laptops (owned)			
Book value on Day 1 of Yr 1, Yr 2 and Yr 3 respectively	500 250	0	
Depreciation (straight line), Yr 1 and Yr 2, per year		250	
Market value on Day 1 of Yr 1, Yr 2 and Yr 3 respectively	100 50	0	
Maintenance, power and insurance, Yr 1 and Yr 2, per year		50	I
Current intention if continue in-house:			
Scrap and replace at beginning of Yr 3			
Annual operating lease payments, Yr 3, Yr 4 and Yr 5, per year		300	
Maintenance, power and insurance, Yr 3, Yr 4 and Yr 5, per year		30	I
Software (ignored for this example)			
Premises (owned, and would be sold if outsourcing undertaken)			
Book value on Day 1 of Yr 1		1200	
Depreciation (straight line), per year		40	
Market value on Day 1 of Yr 1		1600	
Running costs, Yr 1 to Yr 5, per year		100	I
Premises (rented, and to be sublet to supplier if outsourcing undertaken)			
Rent payable, Yr 1 to Yr 5, per year (fixed)		200	
Sub-rent receivable if outsourcing undertaken, Yr 1 to Yr 5, per year (fixed)		260	
Running costs (payable by supplier if outsourcing undertaken), Yr 1 to Yr 5, per year		80	I

Table continues...

TABLE 9.1 *Continued*

	£000	Ref
People (pay £25k per year and overheads £15k)		
20 people on Day 1 of Yr 1	800	I
Of whom if outsourcing undertaken:		
transferable to supplier (15 × £40k) on Day 1 of Yr 1	600	
kept for liaison between customer and supplier	80	I
(2 × £40k), per year		
made redundant – redundancy payments (3 × £25k) on Day 1 of Yr 1	75	
Administrative overheads		
Per year if IT remains in-house	500	I
Per year if outsourcing undertaken	400	I
Outsourcing charges		
Smoothed, Yr 1 to Yr 5, per year	1600	
Net benefit from enhancements if outsourcing undertaken, Yr 1 to Yr 5, per year	300	I

Assume not technically or economically feasible to provide these enhancements in-house.

How to approach the task

There is no textbook way of approaching this task. No doubt for this very reason, each organization has its own way of doing things. What follows should help you to understand the principles involved sufficiently to be able to relate them to your particular organization's way of doing things. To guide you through the almost certain differences, and hopefully to minimize any annoyance at not finding your particular approach faithfully reproduced, here are a few general comments:

- I have adopted the same style as for the other major worked example, in Chapter 3. In particular, I have tried to ensure that even if you wish to ignore the numbers you can still read the example as narrative.

- You will recognize the following tables, although they cover five years rather than the four that you have become used to.

- I have maintained the convention of showing both cash outflows and expenses as negative numbers, while showing cash inflows and revenues as positive unsigned numbers. I have done this for clarity and the avoidance of confusion, although in practice many organizations omit the minus signs in printed output.

Throughout the book I have made the point that, in theory, cash flow is by far the most important way of mathematically evaluating investment opportunities, and have given reasons why this is so. However, we have also discussed the fact that decisions about outsourcing are not investment decisions but cost reduction decisions, and in practice these are often based primarily on their effect on profit or loss, rather than cash flow.

Even where investment decisions are being made, especially in large departmentalized organizations, it is important to know what the profit and loss effect of an investment will be, both for the organization as a whole and for affected individual departments. This is not least because departmental performance is usually measured in profit and loss terms and because that performance is often the basis for awarding bonus and incentive payments. These practical realities sometimes result in decisions being made primarily with reference to the profit and loss effect and only secondarily or not at all on the basis of cash flow.

Therefore, here also I shall follow the practice in the earlier example of looking at the financial case in both cash flow and profit and loss terms, leaving you, the reader, to take from it whatever is relevant for your particular purpose. One practical reason for analysing both cash flow and profit and loss effects, especially with respect to capital expenditure, is that until you have estimated the cash flows you cannot work out what the impact on profit or loss will be.

The 'whole project' approach

For this example, and for large financial cases in general, it will be found that the 'whole project' method of setting out financial cases is the most convenient to adopt. This was explained in Chapter 1, but briefly to recap, it involves:

- listing all the costs and income associated with the status quo;
- listing all the costs and income associated with the proposal for change;
- comparing the respective totals to determine the savings.

STEP BY STEP TO THE SOLUTION

Based on the above, the step-by-step approach followed in this example is as follows, each step following logically from the preceding one:

1. Estimate what the relevant cash outflows and inflows would be in today's values over the chosen evaluation period if the status quo, in this case in-house operation, were to be maintained throughout the period. This includes estimating the likely timing, costs and financing methods of expected changes to equipment, software, people, premises and overheads likely to be necessary, and any proceeds of disposal.

2. Identify those cash flows likely to rise, at least approximately, in line with expected inflation.

3. Recalculate the numbers listed in (1), incorporating inflated values where appropriate.

4. Estimate the relevant cash flows for the outsourcing proposal, using inflated values where appropriate.

5. Compare the respective totals in (3) and (4) to determine the estimated net cash flow savings.

6. Repeat steps (3) to (5) above, substituting expenses and revenues for cash outflows and inflows, in order to determine the estimated net expense savings.

THE TABLES

Following, in the sequence in which they are first referred to, are seven tables, to which reference will be made in the narrative. The case for using inflated values has been made above. However, the point is also illustrated in the tables listed below. Table 9.2 includes only uninflated cash flows; in Table 9.3 those cash flows likely to increase with inflation (marked with an "I") have been inflated at a rate of three per cent per annum from the year following that in which they first occur. All subsequent tables in the example, whether cash flow or expense, are derived from the inflated numbers in Table 9.3.

Tables showing cash outflows and inflows

- **Table 9.2** The in-house status quo, in detail and including the currently intended likely developments over the next five years, looked at from a cash flow viewpoint, all at today's (uninflated) values.

- **Table 9.3** As Table 9.2, but reworked to include inflation as appropriate.

- **Table 9.4** The outsourcing proposal, in detail, also from a cash flow viewpoint.

- **Table 9.5** A comparison of the 'outsourcing' total net cash flows (from Table 9.4) with the 'status quo' total net cash flows (from Table 9.3).

Tables showing expenses and revenues

- **Tables 9.6–9.8** These contain information similar to that in Tables 9.3–9.5, but looked at from a profit and loss viewpoint, that is showing expenses and revenues rather than cash outflows and inflows.

Supplementary tables

The following two additional tables list the differences between the 'cash flow' and 'expense' tables of the status quo and outsourcing situations respectively. They are included here only as aids to understanding and do not form part of the financial case.

- **Table 9.9** Lists the differences between the net cash flows (Table 9.3) and net expenses (Table 9.6) of the 'status quo' situation.

- **Table 9.10** Lists the differences between the net cash flows (Table 9.4) and net expenses (Table 9.7) of the outsourcing proposal.

A quick tour of the tables

I suggest that you now take a quick first look at the tables. They may look a bit daunting because there are so many numbers, but do not be put off by this. We shall be going through the logic of each one a line at a time, step by step. And remember if you prefer to ignore the numbers, then do so and just continue reading the narrative.

Note that even those tables that concern cash flows do not contain a 'Year 0' column. The reason why this is so concerns financial evaluation methods (see above), and the fact that outsourcing, whatever the main reasons for considering it, is regarded from a financial viewpoint as a cost reduction decision, not an investment decision. Because of this, methods that are designed to evaluate investment decisions are not appropriate and are therefore generally not used. In fact, net present value (NPV) could be used, because it can be applied to any set of cash flows. However, the practice is usually not to do so. We shall shortly be looking at all the tables in detail. However, for now just look at three of them:

- **Table 9.3** Status quo – cash flows as currently intended, inflated at three per cent where relevant;

- **Table 9.6** Status quo – expenses as currently intended, inflated at three per cent where relevant;

- **Table 9.9** Status quo – reconciliation between Table 9.3 (cash flows) and Table 9.6 (expenses).

Note the differences between them. To help you, items that differ between Tables 9.3 and 9.6 are shown in italics. You will note that the total net expense in Table 9.6 (£16,514k) is substantially different from the total net cash outflow in Table 9.3 (£13,924k). This is due entirely to the following:

- Table 9.3 (cash flows) includes the purchase price of capital equipment, software and premises, and any proceeds of sale, trade-in or transfer, while depreciation and losses or profits on disposal are ignored because they are not cash items.

- In Table 9.6 (expenses) the reverse is true; cash costs and cash proceeds of disposal of fixed assets are ignored, because they do not directly affect the profit and loss account. However, all depreciation, amortization and losses on disposal are included. Table 9.9 lists all these differences and reconciles the totals of the two tables.

In a real situation there may be other differences between Tables 9.3 and 9.6. These would mostly be timing differences arising from revenues being earned before cash is received and expenses being incurred on credit before cash is paid. However, in financial cases such differences are often trivial and even if not they tend to be ignored. For all revenue and expense items in this example it will be assumed that there are no timing differences, by which I mean that cash is received at the same time as revenue is earned and that cash is paid at the same time as costs are incurred.

TABLE 9.2 *Example 9.1 – Status quo – cash flows as currently intended, uninflated*

	Yr 1 £000	Yr 2 £000	Yr 3 £000	Yr 4 £000	Yr 5 £000	Total £000
Mainframes, midrange and peripherals (owned)						
Existing equipment – trade-in		200				200
New equipment – purchase price		−1600				−1600
Maintenance, power, insurance	−100	−60	−60	−60	−60	−340
Software licences (already paid)						
Software annual maintenance	−40	−40	−40	−40	−40	−200
External net revenue	90	90	90	90	90	450
Mainframes, midrange and peripherals (operating leased)						
Existing lease payments (fixed)	−300					−300
New lease payments (fixed)		−350	−350	−350	−200	−1250
Maintenance, power, insurance	−80	−50	−50	−50	−50	−280
Software licences (paid outright)		−400				−400
Software annual maintenance	−40	−50	−50	−50	−50	−240
PCs – desktops and laptops						
Existing equipment – scrapped		0				0
New equipment – lease (fixed)			−300	−300	−300	−900
Maintenance, power, insurance	−50	−50	−30	−30	−30	−190
Software (ignored for this example)						
Premises (owned)						
Running costs	−100	−100	−100	−100	−100	−500
Premises (rented)						
Rent payable (fixed)	−200	−200	−200	−200	−200	−1000
Running costs	−80	−80	−80	−80	−80	−400
People						
Pay and overheads	−800	−800	−800	−800	−800	−4000
Administrative overheads	−500	−500	−500	−500	−500	−2500
Status quo – total net cash flows	−2200	−3990	−2470	−2470	−2320	−13 450

TABLE 9.3 *Example 9.1 – Status quo – cash flows as currently intended, inflated at 3% where relevant*

	Ref	Yr 1 £000	Yr 2 £000	Yr 3 £000	Yr 4 £000	Yr 5 £000	Total £000

Note: Items subject to inflation are marked 'I' in the 'Ref' column.

Mainframes, midrange and peripherals (owned)

	Ref	Yr 1	Yr 2	Yr 3	Yr 4	Yr 5	Total
Existing equipment – trade-in			200				200
New equipment – purchase price			−1600				−1600
Maintenance, power, insurance	I	−100	−60	−62	−64	−66	−352
Software licences (already paid)							
Software annual maintenance	I	−40	−41	−42	−43	−44	−210
External net revenue	I	90	93	96	99	102	480

Mainframes, midrange and peripherals (operating leased)

	Ref	Yr 1	Yr 2	Yr 3	Yr 4	Yr 5	Total
Existing lease payments (fixed)		−300					−300
New lease payments (fixed)			−350	−350	−350	−200	−1250
Maintenance, power, insurance	I	−80	−50	−52	−54	−56	−292
Software licences (paid outright)			−400				−400
Software annual maintenance	I	−40	−50	−52	−54	−56	−252

PCs – desktops and laptops

	Ref	Yr 1	Yr 2	Yr 3	Yr 4	Yr 5	Total
Existing equipment – scrapped				0			0
New equipment – lease (fixed)				−300	−300	−300	−900
Maintenance, power, insurance	I	−50	−52	−30	−31	−32	−195
Software (ignored for this example)							

Premises (owned)

	Ref	Yr 1	Yr 2	Yr 3	Yr 4	Yr 5	Total
Running costs	I	−100	−103	−106	−109	−112	−530

Premises (rented)

	Ref	Yr 1	Yr 2	Yr 3	Yr 4	Yr 5	Total
Rent payable (fixed)		−200	−200	−200	−200	−200	−1000
Running costs	I	−80	−82	−84	−87	−90	−423

People

	Ref	Yr 1	Yr 2	Yr 3	Yr 4	Yr 5	Total
Pay and overheads	I	−800	−824	−849	−874	−900	−4247

	Ref	Yr 1	Yr 2	Yr 3	Yr 4	Yr 5	Total
Administrative overheads	I	−500	−515	−530	−546	−562	−2653
Status quo – total net cash flows		−2200	−4034	−2561	−2613	−2516	−13924

Note: Items in italics are those that differ between Tables 9.3 and 9.6.

TABLE 9.4 *Example 9.1 – Outsourcing – cash flows, inflated at 3% where relevant*

	Ref	Yr 1 £000	Yr 2 £000	Yr 3 £000	Yr 4 £000	Yr 5 £000	Total £000
Note: Items subject to inflation are marked 'I' in the 'Ref' column.							
Outsourcing charges		−1600	−1600	−1600	−1600	−1600	−8000
Mainframes, midrange and peripherals (owned)							
Existing equipmt. transferred at MV		400					400
Maintenance, power, insurance							
Software licences transfer fees		−150					−150
Software annual maintenance							
External net revenue							
Mainframes, midrange and peripherals (operating leased)							
Existing lease payments							
New lease payments							
Maintenance, power, insurance							
Software licences							
Software annual maintenance							
PCs – desktops and laptops							
Existing equipment scrapped				0			0
New equipment – lease (fixed)				−300	−300	−300	−900
Maintenance, power, insurance	I	−50	−52	−30	−31	−32	−195
Software (ignored for this example)							
Premises (owned)							
Proceeds of sale		1600					1600
Running costs							
Premises (rented)							
Rent payable (fixed)		−200	−200	−200	−200	−200	−1000
Sub-rent receivable (fixed)		260	260	260	260	260	1300
Running costs borne by subtenant							
People							
Pay and overheads	I	−80	−82	−84	−87	−90	−423

Table continues ...

TABLE 9.4 *Continued*

	Ref	Yr 1 £000	Yr 2 £000	Yr 3 £000	Yr 4 £000	Yr 5 £000	Total £000
Redundancy			−75				−75
Administrative overheads	I	−400	−412	−424	−437	−450	−2123
Benefits from enhancements	I	300	309	318	328	338	1593
Outsourcing – total net cash flows		5	−1777	−2060	−2067	−2074	−7973

Note: Items in italics are those that differ between Tables 9.4 and 9.7.

TABLE 9.5 *Example 9.1 – Comparison of inflated 'status quo' and 'outsourcing' cash flows*

	Yr 1 £000	Yr 2 £000	Yr 3 £000	Yr 4 £000	Yr 5 £000	Total £000

Note: Relevant cash flows within these totals have been inflated at 3% per annum.

Total net cash flows

		Yr 1	Yr 2	Yr 3	Yr 4	Yr 5	Total
Status quo (Table 9.3)		−2200	−4034	−2561	−2613	−2516	−13924
Outsource (Table 9.4)		5	−1777	−2060	−2067	−2074	−7973
Reduction in net cash outflows	£k	2205	2257	501	546	442	5951
Ditto	%	100	56	20	21	18	43

TABLE 9.6 *Example 9.1 – Status quo – expenses as currently intended, inflated at 3% where relevant*

	Ref	Yr 1 £000	Yr 2 £000	Yr 3 £000	Yr 4 £000	Yr 5 £000	Total £000

Note: Items subject to inflation are marked 'I' in the 'Ref' column.

Mainframes, midrange and peripherals (owned)

	Ref	Yr 1	Yr 2	Yr 3	Yr 4	Yr 5	Total
Existing equipment – depreciation		−500					−500
Existing equipment – loss on disposal			−800				−800
New equipment – depreciation			−400	−400	−400	−400	−1600
Maintenance, power, insurance	I	−100	−60	−62	−64	−66	−352
Software licences – amortization		−50	−50	−50	−50	−50	−250
Software annual maintenance	I	−40	−41	−42	−43	−44	−210
External net revenue	I	90	93	96	99	102	480

Table continues ...

TABLE 9.6 *Continued*

	Ref	Yr 1 £000	Yr 2 £000	Yr 3 £000	Yr 4 £000	Yr 5 £000	Total £000
Mainframes, midrange and peripherals (operating leased)							
Existing lease payments (fixed)		−300					−300
New lease payments (fixed)			−350	−350	−350	−200	−1250
Maintenance, power, insurance	I	−80	−50	−52	−54	−56	−292
Existing S/W licences – amortization		*−70*					*−70*
Ditto – loss on cessation of use			*−70*				*−70*
New S/W licences – amortization			*−100*	*−100*	*−100*	*−100*	*−400*
Software annual maintenance	I	−40	−50	−52	−54	−56	−252
PCs – desktops and laptops							
Existing equipment – depreciation		*−250*	*−250*				*−500*
New equipment – lease (fixed)				−300	−300	−300	−900
Maintenance, power, insurance	I	−50	−52	−30	−31	−32	−195
Software (ignored for this example)							
Premises (owned)							
Depreciation		*−40*	*−40*	*−40*	*−40*	*−40*	*−200*
Running costs	I	−100	−103	−106	−109	−112	−530
Premises (rented)							
Rent payable (fixed)		−200	−200	−200	−200	−200	−1000
Running costs	I	−80	−82	−84	−87	−90	−423
People							
Pay and overheads		−800	−824	−849	−874	−900	−4247
Administrative overheads		−500	−515	−530	−546	−562	−2653
Status quo – total net expenses		−3110	−3944	−3151	−3203	−3106	−16514

Note: Items in italics are those that differ between Tables 9.3 and 9.6.

TABLE 9.7 *Example 9.1 – Outsourcing – expenses, inflated at 3% where relevant*

	Ref	Yr 1 £000	Yr 2 £000	Yr 3 £000	Yr 4 £000	Yr 5 £000	Total £000

Note: Items subject to inflation are marked 'I' in the 'Ref' column.

	Ref	Yr 1	Yr 2	Yr 3	Yr 4	Yr 5	Total
Outsourcing charges		−1600	−1600	−1600	−1600	−1600	−8000
Mainframes, midrange and peripherals (owned)							
Existing equipment – depreciation							*0*
Existing equipt. – loss on transfer		−1100					−1100
Maintenance, power, insurance							0
Software licences – amortization							*0*
Software licences – transfer fee		−150					−150
Software licences – loss on transfer		−250					−250
Software annual maintenance							0
External net revenue							0
Mainframes, midrange and peripherals (operating leased)							
Existing lease – assign to supplier							0
New lease payments							0
Maintenance, power, insurance							0
Software licences – amortization							*0*
Software licences – loss on transfer		−140					−140
Software annual maintenance							0
PCs – desktops and laptops							
Existing equipment – depreciation		−250	−250				−500
New equipment – lease (fixed)				−300	−300	−300	−900
Maintenance, power, insurance	I	−50	−52	−30	−31	−32	−195
Software (ignored for this example)							
Premises (owned)							
Depreciation							
Profit on disposal		*400*					*400*
Running costs							0
Premises (rented)							
Rent payable (fixed)		−200	−200	−200	−200	−200	−1000
Sub-rent receivable (fixed)		260	260	260	260	260	1300
Running costs payable by subtenant							0
People							
Pay and overheads	I	−80	−82	−84	−87	−90	−423

Table continues …

TABLE 9.7 *Continued*

	Ref	Yr 1 £000	Yr 2 £000	Yr 3 £000	Yr 4 £000	Yr 5 £000	Total £000
Redundancy		−75					−75
Administrative overheads	I	−400	−412	−424	−437	−450	−2123
Benefits from enhancements	I	300	309	318	328	338	1593
Outsourcing – total net expenses		−3335	−2027	−2060	−2067	−2074	−11563

Note: Items in italics are those that differ between Tables 9.4 and 9.7.

TABLE 9.8 *Example 9.1 – Comparison of inflated 'status quo' and 'outsourcing' expenses*

		Yr 1 £000	Yr 2 £000	Yr 3 £000	Yr 4 £000	Yr 5 £000	Total £000
Note: Relevant items within these totals have been inflated at 3% per annum.							
Total net expenses							
Status quo (Table 9.6)		−3110	−3944	−3151	−3203	−3106	−16514
Outsource (Table 9.7)		−3335	−2027	−2060	−2067	−2074	−11563
Reduction in net expenses	**£k**	−225	1917	1091	1136	1032	4951
Ditto	**%**	−7	49	35	35	33	30

TABLE 9.9 *Example 9.1 – Reconciliation between 'status quo' Tables 9.3 (cash flow) and 9.6 (expenses)*

	Yr 1 £000	Yr 2 £000	Yr 3 £000	Yr 4 £000	Yr 5 £000	Total £000
Total net cash flows from Table 9.3	−2200	−4034	−2561	−2613	−2516	−13924
Add cash flows in Table 9.3, but not in Table 9.6						
Existing equipment – trade in		−200				−200
New equipment – purchase price		1600				1600
Software licences – purchase		400				400
Less depreciation and losses in Table 9.6, but not in Table 9.3						
Existing equipment – depreciation	−500					−500
Existing equipment – loss on disposal		−800				−800
New equipment – depreciation		−400	−400	−400	−400	−1600
Software licences – amortization	−50	−50	−50	−50	−50	−250
Ditto – amortization	−70					−70
Ditto – loss on cessation of use		−70				−70
New S/ware licences – amortization		−100	−100	−100	−100	−400
Existing PCs – depreciation	−250	−250				−500
Premises – depreciation	−40	−40	−40	−40	−40	−200
Total net expenses from Table 9.6	−3110	−3944	−3151	−3203	−3106	−16514

TABLE 9.10 *Example 9.1 – Reconciliation between 'outsourcing' Tables 9.4 (cash flow) and 9.7 (expenses)*

	Yr 1 £000	Yr 2 £000	Yr 3 £000	Yr 4 £000	Yr 5 £000	Total £000
Total net cash flows from Table 9.4	5	−1777	−2060	−2067	−2074	−7973
Add cash flows in Table 9.4, but not in Table 9.7						
Existing equipment transferred	*− 400*					*− 400*
Premises – proceeds of sale	*− 1600*					*− 1600*
Less depreciation and losses in Table 9.7, but not in Table 9.4						
Existing equipment – loss on transfer	*− 1100*					*− 1100*
Software licences – loss on transfer	*− 250*					*− 250*
Ditto – loss on transfer	*− 140*					*− 140*
Existing PCs – depreciation	*− 250*	*− 250*				*− 500*
Premises – profit on disposal	*400*					*400*
Total net expenses from Table 9.7	−3335	−2027	−2060	−2067	−2074	−11563

EXAMPLE 9.1: EXPLANATIONS

The following commentary explains individual lines in Tables 9.2–9.5. Not all items call for comment. Where a similar item has already been the subject of comment earlier, either in this or in earlier examples, there may be a brief comment together with a reference back to the original one. However, you will be guided every step of the way.

Status quo – cash flows as currently intended, uninflated (Table 9.2)

All the numbers in this table are at today's values, that is uninflated, as this would usually be the starting point for any financial case. As already discussed, however, to use uninflated values in an outsourcing financial case would not be comparing like with like, as the outsourcing supplier's charges would have been calculated taking expected inflation into account. Table 9.3 is a repeat of Table 9.2, but showing inflated values for all items to which inflation is likely to apply. For clarity, these items have been marked with the letter 'I'. All subsequent tables are derived from the numbers in Table 9.3. The commentary on Table 9.3 is equally applicable to Table 9.2.

Status quo – cash flows as currently intended, inflated at three per cent where relevant (Table 9.3)

In this table, items shown in italics are those that differ between Tables 9.3 and 9.6.

Mainframes, midrange and peripherals (owned)

In this table we are making estimates of the expected future cash flows of the status quo (stay-as-we-are) situation. The pieces of information relevant for this purpose are:

- the cash inflow in Year 2 of £200k representing the expected proceeds of sale of the existing equipment;
- the cash outflow of £1,600k, also in Year 2, representing the expected purchase price of its replacement;
- the estimated cash outflows on maintenance, power and insurance on both the existing and new equipment.

Book value, depreciation and any loss or profit on disposal do not represent cash flows and therefore have no place here. They will be important when, in Table 9.6, we come to consider the status quo in profit and loss terms of expenses and revenues. Trade-in is usually done at market value, although there can sometimes be exceptions (see comments on pages 176–177 in the context of Table 9.7).

Maintenance, power, insurance

These are relevant cash flows. They are also expenses and will therefore also appear in Table 9.6. This is the first example of cash flows likely to be subject to inflation-related increases.

Software licences

Although intangible, software licences with an expected life of more than two years are treated for accounting purposes just like any other long-term asset. They are initially shown on the licensee's balance sheet at cost. See Appendix 4 for how shorter term licences are treated. Whether the licences are for finite periods or are of indeterminate length for as long as maintenance charges are paid, they are depreciated over their expected useful lives, except that the word 'amortization' is usually applied to the depreciation of intangible assets. These licences had obviously been purchased before the start of our evaluation period. Therefore, neither the purchase price, which is a 'sunk cost', nor the amortization, which is not a cash flow, are relevant for this table of cash flows. The transfer fee is of course ignored in this 'status quo' table, but will be included in both Tables 9.4 and 9.7, which concern the outsourcing cash flows and expenses respectively.

Software annual maintenance

These are payments to cover fixes, new releases and often new versions also, although sometimes an additional charge will be made for a new version. Annual maintenance charges are relevant cash flows and are therefore included. Like hardware maintenance, they are also expenses and will therefore appear in Table 9.6 as well. As with equipment maintenance, above, it has been assumed that these payments and all similar ones in this example are not fixed and are therefore subject to inflation-related increases.

External net revenue

A plausible source of attributable revenue, expected to continue throughout the evaluation period if the status quo is maintained, has been deliberately included as an illustration of 'opportunity cost', although it is recognized that it may not feature in many outsourcing decisions. The opportunity cost in this case would be the revenue forgone if the decision is taken to outsource.

Mainframes, midrange and peripherals (operating leased)

Operating leases can be thought of as being like rental (i.e. paying for the use of assets that belong to someone else). The lease payments, assumed to be fixed, are treated both as cash outflows (Table 9.3) and as expenses (Table 9.6). Operating leases usually, as assumed here, include the option to return leased assets to the lessor at the end of the primary term of the lease (see Chapter 8).

Maintenance, power and insurance

Leases of all kinds usually require the lessee to maintain and insure the leased assets.

Software licences

In this example a single lump sum licence payment is assumed. However, especially when a software licence is part of a bigger acquisition including hardware or services, it could be financed, together with the other elements acquired, so that payment for everything could be spread over time. The instrument for financing a software licence would usually be a finance lease, although if it is wrapped up in a larger deal this fact may be transparent to the customer. As with the other software licences, referred to above, book value, amortization and the loss on cessation of use are irrelevant for this table of cash flows.

PCs – desktops and laptops

These PCs were obviously purchased before Year 1. Therefore, the cash outflow representing their purchase price is a 'sunk cost' and ignored in the cash flow financial case; their depreciation is ignored because it is not a cash item. The only relevant capital cash flow would be any expected future proceeds of sale or trade in. In this case, that figure is assumed to be nil. The relevant 'revenue expense' cash flows for the new PCs are the lease payments and the payments for maintenance etc. Like all the revenue and 'revenue cost' cash flows, they will also appear in the profit and loss financial case (Table 9.6).

Premises (owned)

Once again, no capital cash flows are shown because:

- the purchase price was a pre-evaluation sunk cost; and
- depreciation is not a cash item.

The cash flows representing the running costs are included in both the cash flow and profit and loss financial cases.

Premises (rented)

The future rent and running costs are shown both here as cash outflows and, in Table 9.6, as expenses. The rent is stated to be fixed; the running costs are assumed to be subject to inflation.

People

People costs are both cash outflows and, ignoring timing differences, expenses.

Regarding people, brief mention should be made of the *Transfer of Undertakings (Protection of Employment) Regulations 1981* (TUPE), which apply to situations, including outsourcing, in which employees of one company (in this case the customer) are transferred to the employment of another (the outsourcing supplier), or vice versa if a previously outsourced function is being moved back in-house. TUPE imposes obligations to consult with affected staff and protects their terms and conditions of employment. See the books listed in Further Reading for more detailed information on such matters.

Administrative overheads

These are all assumed to be cash outflows subject to inflation and, in Table 9.6, as expenses. In a real situation, these totals might include the depreciation of assets, for example buildings and IT systems used for administrative purposes. If that were so, then the amounts of such depreciation would be excluded from this cash flow table, but would be included in the profit and loss version (Table 9.6).

Status quo – total net cash flows

This line shows the total estimated net cash outflows (£13,924k) expected to result from a decision to continue with the in-house situation, and the years in which they would occur. Table 9.4, which we shall consider shortly, contains the equivalent for the outsourcing situation. Table 9.5 will compare the two sets of totals, this comparison being an important part of the eventual decision process.

Outsourcing – cash flows, inflated at three per cent where relevant (Table 9.4)

This table is similar to Table 9.3, but instead of reflecting the status quo cash flows it shows the expected relevant cash inflows and outflows that would occur if the outsourcing proposal were to be accepted and if cutover were to take place at the beginning of Year 1. For ease of eventual comparison, this table has much the same format as Table 9.3. However, many of the lines contain no numbers, because they represent items of cost that would be taken over by the supplier and are consequently now included in the supplier's outsourcing charges. Empty lines are not referred to in the following commentary.

Outsourcing charges

Outsourcing contracts always involve substantial initial costs, often called transition costs. This means that, as with many kinds of long-term contract, the supplier's costs are 'front-loaded', and would ideally be recouped from the customer as and when they are incurred. However, from the customer's point of view, the value of the service received would normally be much the same in the first year of the contract as in the last, so customers would like the payment pattern to reflect that fact.

The usual solution to these conflicting requirements will be familiar to those who have read Chapter 8 on leasing or who already understand its principles. One of the many reasons why organizations use leasing is to spread, or smooth, the initial payment for long-term IT or other assets over the period that will benefit from their use. Outsourcing is a long-term service, and you cannot lease a service. What you can do, however, is to use financing to smooth the payments to be made by the customer, while at the same time ensuring that the supplier gets paid the full amounts on the due dates.

Some outsourcing suppliers have their own subsidiary finance companies and will offer smoothing as a service to their customers. Those that do not will usually suggest a selection of third party finance companies from which the customer can choose a financing partner. In either case, the finance company will offer a payment stream tailored to meet the needs of the customer. This may be a smoothed stream of regular payments or, as with leasing, it may be a series of irregular payments including, for example, holidays or step payments to accommodate the cyclical nature of a particular customer's business or some other circumstance such as a temporary shortage of cash.

Reverting to the present example, there are in theory two different decisions to be made here. The first is what, in the context of outsourcing, I have called the 'cost reduction decision'; the second is the financing decision. You may recall from Chapter 8 that a financing decision is usually based on a net present value (NPV) calculation, using as a discount rate the customer's current cost of incremental borrowing from their normal source, typically a bank. You may also recall from earlier in this chapter that, nowadays, suppliers would typically quote both smoothed and unsmoothed payment streams. Here, for the sake of simplicity, I have taken a short cut, ignored both the 'natural' payment stream and the financing decision, and used the smoothed payment stream proposed by the supplier.

Mainframes, midrange and peripherals (owned)

Note that the relevant cash flow of £400k represents the price to be paid by the supplier to acquire the equipment from the customer. In theory, this need not be paid in cash but could be taken into account in working out the outsourcing charges. However, in practice it is nearly always done as a cash transaction, because a large injection of cash at the start of the contract is often a major incentive for customers to undertake outsourcing. The transaction would usually be done at a price equal or close to market value. Reasons why it might possibly be done at a higher price will be mentioned on pages 176–177 in the context of Table 9.7.

Maintenance, power and insurance

These are not shown, because from the beginning of Year 1 they will be the responsibility of the supplier and their costs, including assumptions about inflation, will have been taken into account by the supplier in calculating its outsourcing charges.

Software licence transfer fees

Transfer fees are not always imposed by a software licensor, but where they are, then they may be substantial. It is a matter for negotiation whether they are paid by the customer or by the outsourcing supplier. If paid by the customer, then it may mean a substantial cash outflow at the beginning of the contract; if paid by the supplier, then the amount, together with all the other costs estimated to be incurred on the contract, will be uplifted by whatever profit percentage is applied in calculating the outsourcing charges. It is difficult to make this a win–win situation.

Software annual maintenance

Not shown, because from the beginning of Year 1 these payments will be the responsibility of the supplier.

External net revenue

As discussed under Table 9.3, the cessation of this source of revenue is an example of an opportunity cost attributable to the outsourcing proposal.

Mainframes, midrange and peripherals (operating leased)

It is assumed that the existing leases will be assigned to the supplier.

PCs – desktops and laptops

These cash flows are the same as in Table 9.3, because the customer will retain this equipment. The cash flows could, therefore, have been omitted from both the status quo and outsourcing tables, but have been included for clarity.

Premises (owned)

The sale would only take place if the outsourcing is undertaken. Therefore, the sale proceeds of £1,600k are a relevant cash inflow.

Premises (rented)

The company will continue the rental contract, and the sub-rent will only be receivable if the outsourcing is undertaken, so both are relevant cash flows here. The running costs will be borne by the subtenant.

People

The only relevant IT people costs in the outsourcing scenario will be those relating to the two people retained for liaison with the supplier (2 × £40k), and the redundancy payments (3 × £25k). The remaining people will be transferred. Mention has been already been made of the TUPE regulations that apply to people transferred to the employment of another under-taking, for example an outsourcing supplier.

Administrative overheads

As stated in the input data, these are assumed to be £100k lower in Year 1 than in the in-house situation. Remember that any depreciation within the total figure of overheads should be excluded from this list of cash flows, although it would be included in the corresponding profit and loss analysis (Table 9.7), because depreciation is an expense but not a cash flow.

Benefits from enhancements

See the section headed 'Service enhancements' earlier in this chapter, and also the discussion of benefit quantification in Chapter 2. As I have included these benefits, they will of course contribute to the financial case for outsourcing in Table 9.5. However, because I have included their totals as a single line, it would be a simple matter to produce another version of the financial case that excluded them. To remind you, it has been assumed that it would not be technically or economically feasible to provide these benefits in-house. If it had been, then both the benefits and the costs of providing them in-house would have to be included in Table 9.3.

Outsourcing – total net cash flows

This line shows the total estimated net cash outflows (£7,973k) expected to result from a decision to outsource, and the years in which they would occur. In Table 9.5 these will be compared with the totals of the 'status quo' net cash outflows from Table 9.3. This comparison will be important in the decision process.

Comparison of inflated 'status quo' and 'outsource' cash flows (Table 9.5)

This table represents the summary cash flow financial case. It is a comparison of the estimated net cash flows of both scenarios: outsourcing and the status quo in cash flow terms. Subtracting the outsourcing cash flows from those of the 'status quo' situation gives the net reduction in cash outflows that would result from a decision to implement outsourcing from the beginning of Year 1. The total net reduction in cash outflow of £5,951k represents approximately 43 per cent of the status quo cash flows of £13,924k. This might typically be thought, at first glance, to be a good margin in favour of outsourcing. However, note that three-quarters of that reduction actually comes from Years 1 and 2, with their various distortions due to the disposal and acquisition of assets. When, from Year 3 onwards a more or less steady state is reached in the comparison between the two scenarios, the net reduction in cash outflow drops to an average of approximately 20 per cent of the status quo cash flows. This would still be regarded as attractive by many organizations. It is always desirable to look at the year by year numbers, as we have just done, as well as at the totals, because there will always be similar distortions in the early years, although they may be less pronounced than they are in this contrived example.

That concludes the commentary on the 'cash flow' tables (Tables 9.2–9.5). The following commentary explains individual lines in the 'profit and loss' tables (Tables 9.6–9.8). As hitherto, not all items call for comment. Where a similar item has already been the subject of remark, either in this or in earlier examples, there may be a brief comment together with a reference back to the original one.

Status quo – expenses as currently intended, inflated at three per cent where relevant (Table 9.6)

In this table, items shown in italics are those that differ between Tables 9.3 and 9.6.

This is the 'profit and loss' equivalent of Table 9.3. Many of the items in it have already been referred to in the commentary on that table, and all the revenue (non-italicized) items are the same. For all the capital items (italicized), what is included here is their depreciation or amortization, and any losses or profits on disposal, never their cash flows. As already stressed, 'revenue' and 'revenue cost' items will nearly always appear unchanged in both sets of data, timing differences being ignored.

Mainframes, midrange and peripherals (owned)

In Year 1, the depreciation of the equipment, £500k, is charged as an expense. This will reduce the book value from £1,500k to £1,000k. Also by the beginning of Year 2, however, the expected market value will have fallen to £200k, so the loss on disposal of the equipment in Year 2 will be £800k, the difference between the book value and the market value.

New equipment – depreciation

The depreciation is at its stated rate of £400k per annum from Year 2. Note that its purchase price of £1,600k, shown as a cash outflow in Table 9.3, does not appear here, because the purchase price of a capital asset does not affect the profit and loss account directly (only through the mechanism of depreciation).

Software licences – amortization

The capital cost of these licences did not appear in Table 9.3 because they were a sunk cost. However, their amortization (£50k per annum) continues as an expense until they cease to be used or until they are fully written off. Remember that 'amortization' simply means the depreciation of intangible assets.

Software annual maintenance

As already noted, these and other 'revenue costs' appear both here, as expenses, and as cash outflows (Table 9.3).

External net revenue

This appears both here, as revenue, and as a cash inflow in Table 9.3.

Mainframes, midrange and peripherals (operating leased)

Payments under operating leases are both expenses and cash outflows.

Existing software licences – amortization

Software licences for a period longer than two years are treated like other fixed assets and amortized over their expected useful lives, as shown in Year 1 (£70k).

Ditto – loss on cessation of use

At the cessation of use at the beginning of Year 2, any remaining book value must be written of as a loss, in this case of £70k.

New software licences – amortization

The new licences will be amortized over their expected useful lives.

Software annual maintenance

Comments as above.

PCs – desktops and laptops

Depreciation is applied until the equipment is to be disposed of, at which point the book value happens to be nil. As the equipment is expected to be scrapped, market value (nil) will equal book value (nil), so there will be no loss or profit on disposal. It has been decided to lease replacement equipment from Year 3. The lease payments appear both as expenses, as here, and as cash outflows in Table 9.3. Were the new equipment to be purchased instead of leased, then the purchase price would be a cash outflow in Table 9.3, while its depreciation would be shown here as an expense.

Premises (owned)

It may not need to be said, but the reason why inflation is not applied to depreciation is that depreciation is simply an arithmetic operation: the division by n of the purchase price of an asset, where, with straight-line depreciation, n is the number of years of expected useful life.

Premises (rented), people and administrative overheads

Comments as for Table 9.3.

Status quo – total net expenses

This line shows the total estimated net expenses (£16,514k) expected to result from a decision to continue with the in-house situation, and the years in which they would occur. Table 9.7 will contain the equivalent for the outsourcing situation. The profit and loss financial case (Table 9.8) will compare the two sets of totals, this comparison being an important part of the eventual decision process.

Outsourcing – expenses, inflated at three per cent where relevant (Table 9.7)

This table is similar to Table 9.6, but instead of the status quo it shows the relevant expenses, losses and profits expected to occur if the outsourcing proposal were to be accepted, and if cutover were to take place at the beginning of Year 1.

Outsourcing charges

Comments as for Table 9.4.

Mainframes, midrange and peripherals (owned)

Existing equipment – loss on transfer

The loss on transfer of the equipment to the supplier in Year 1 of £1,100k is the difference between the book value (£1,500k) and the market value (£400k). As described in Chapter 7, loss on disposal (or transfer) of assets is a perennial problem for organizations that buy IT and other high technology assets rather than, for example, leasing them through operating leases. Human nature is understandably reluctant to admit that a very expensive asset just purchased, which is unlikely to wear out for many years, will nevertheless have a useful life of only, say, three years, even though that life may be prolonged by upgrades. As a result, estimates of useful life are often exaggerated. Consequently, on disposal by whatever means, book values of such assets often exceed their market values by substantial amounts. The resulting loss is a charge against profit, which, if sufficiently large, can cause company or departmental management to cancel or postpone an otherwise cost effective proposal.

A possible way of eliminating the loss in this example might be for the customer to retain ownership of the equipment, at the same time granting a licence to the supplier to operate and maintain it. However, among the implications of doing so would be the following:

- The book value of £1,500k would still eventually be a charge against profit, but via the mechanism of depreciation and spread over three years.
- The customer would forego the cash inflow of £400k, which would otherwise have been paid by the supplier. This might be much needed and may have been a significant reason for contemplating outsourcing in the first place.
- The situation regarding software licences and transfer charges would have to be examined very carefully. See relevant books listed in Further Reading.

A theoretical alternative might be for the supplier to agree to transfer the equipment at its book value, either directly or through a leasing company, thus eliminating the loss at the time of transfer, or at a lower figure that would at least reduce the loss. However, as already mentioned in Chapter 3, among the implications of doing this would be the following:

- To the extent of any significant uplift in transfer price above market value, the transaction becomes an artificial transaction, with accounting, corporation tax, value added tax and legal implications for the customer, the supplier and any finance company involved. The safest course is not to do it, but if it is contemplated, then professional advice should be sought.
- Even if it were to be done, then the supplier would need to recoup the excess of the transfer price over the market value in its outsourcing charge to the customer. In doing so, the supplier would apply its normal profit uplift, so that the customer would ultimately pay substantially more than the amount of the loss avoided.

Decline in the value of most assets is a fact of life and cannot be wished away. If inadequate depreciation is written off during an asset's life, then the inevitable effect will be a corresponding so-called 'loss on disposal':

the difference between book value and market value. This difference is the resultant of three things:

- the rapid decline in market value of high technology assets generally;
- the period chosen as representing expected useful life;
- the method of depreciation chosen.

The economic characteristics of high technology assets are not going to change. Therefore, if it is wished to avoid, or lessen, loss on disposal problems in future, the choice is to adopt either more realistic estimates of useful life or a different method of accounting for depreciation. As discussed in Chapter 7, the two main accounting methods used to reflect the depreciation of any fixed assets are (a) the 'straight line' method, and (b) the 'reducing balance' method, a theme that has several variations. In some countries, including the UK, the straight line method is the most widely used; in some other countries, the reducing balance methods are favoured, sometimes because they are similar to the tax rules for depreciation in those countries.

To remind you, the most common 'reducing balance' method is to calculate the depreciation for each year as a percentage (for example, 50 per cent) of the asset's book value at the beginning of that year. The effect of this is that the book value declines more rapidly in the first couple of years, thus reflecting more closely the typical decline in market value. The obvious advantage of this method, provided a sufficiently high percentage is applied, is the likelihood of a lower eventual loss on disposal, thus lessening the problem that gave rise to this discussion. Its main disadvantage, however, is precisely the resulting high charge for depreciation in Year 1, which may cause what could be an unacceptable reduction in both company and departmental profit in that year.

Software licences – transfer fee
Comments as for Table 9.4.

Software licences – loss on transfer
As already discussed, and as detailed in Appendix 4, software licences having an expected useful life of more than two years are accounted for in the same way as hardware. They, or more accurately the rights that they confer, are shown as assets on the customer's balance sheet and are then amortized over their expected useful lives. If a licence has been taken out for a finite period, then that may, but not necessarily, suggest its expected useful life. If the licence is not for a finite period, but is to run for as long as annual maintenance payments are made, then the useful life must be estimated and amortization applied accordingly. On transfer, or otherwise on cessation of use, any remaining book value (£250k in this case) represents a loss, an expense to be charged against both the company and,

if appropriate, departmental profit, just like a loss on disposal or transfer of hardware assets.

It is assumed here that the supplier pays nothing to the customer in respect of the licences transferred. If there were any payment from the supplier, then, as with the transfer of hardware assets, the loss would be reduced by the amount of any such payment.

PCs – desktops and laptops

These expenses are the same as in Table 9.6, because the customer will retain this equipment if the outsourcing proposal is accepted. The expenses could, therefore, have been omitted from both the status quo and outsourcing financial cases, but they have been included for clarity.

Premises (owned)

Whereas IT equipment and other high technology assets will usually incur a loss on disposal, land and buildings will often have appreciated, as in this case, so that market value exceeds book value. The profit on disposal of £400k is the difference between the book value (£1,200k) and the market value (£1,600k).

Premises (rented)

The rent payable will be as in Table 9.6, because the premises will be retained. However, there will now also be rent receivable from the subtenant.

People, administrative overheads and benefits from enhancement

Comment as for Table 9.4.

Outsourcing – total net expenses

This line shows the total estimated net expenses (£11,563k) expected to result from a decision to outsource, and the years in which they would occur. In Table 9.8 these will be compared with those of the expected status quo expenses from Table 9.6, this comparison being an important part of the eventual decision process.

Comparison of inflated 'status quo' and 'outsource' expenses and revenues (Table 9.8)

This table represents the summary profit and loss financial case. It is a comparison of the estimated net expenses of both scenarios: outsourcing and the status quo. Subtracting the outsourcing net expenses from those representing the status quo gives the reduction in net expenses that would result from a decision to implement outsourcing from the beginning of Year 1. The total reduction in net expenses of £4,951k represents 30 per cent of the status quo net expenses of £16,514k. As with the cash flow financial case considered earlier, this would typically be thought a reasonable margin in favour of outsourcing. Unlike the cash flow case, however, the upfront distortions due to losses and profits on disposal and transfer of assets cause an increase in net expenses in Year 1, of £225k. The average decrease in net expense of 34 per cent in Years 3 to 5, once a steady state has been reached, would be regarded as attractive by many organizations. To repeat, it is always necessary to look at the year by year numbers, especially those in the later years when a steady state is likely to have been reached, because there will always be distortions in the early years.

The following commentary explains Tables 9.9 and 9.10. Neither table forms part of the financial case. They are included here only as aids to understanding the differences between the earlier cash flow and expense tables.

Reconciliation between 'status quo' Tables 9.3 (cash flow) and 9.6 (expenses) (Table 9.9)

This table lists the differences between the italicized cash flows (in Table 9.3) and expenses (in Table 9.6) of the 'status quo' situation, and shows how collectively they explain the difference between the two tables.

Reconciliation between 'outsourcing' Tables 9.4 (cash flow) and 9.7 (expenses) (Table 9.10)

This table lists the differences between the italicized cash flows (in Table 9.4) and expenses (in Table 9.7) of the outsourcing proposal.

EXAMPLE 9.1: SUMMARY

Remember that this has been a contrived and artificial example. Nevertheless, it includes most of those financial and accounting factors that generally feature in outsourcing decisions. It has already been said that, subject to the need to look carefully at the year by year 'steady state' numbers and not just the totals, this particular outsourcing proposal as a whole might be regarded as reasonably attractive from a purely financial viewpoint. However, there are some aspects of it that could be show stoppers in particular situations, especially bearing in mind that enhancement benefits of £300k per annum have been attributed to the outsourcing case. It will be worth considering these potential show stoppers and what, if anything, might be done to mitigate them. For the following discussion it will only be necessary to look at Tables 9.5 and 9.8.

Starting, literally, with a positive in Table 9.5, the total of the reduction in net cash outflow of £4,462k in Years 1 and 2 of course looks extremely attractive. However, for some organizations the steady state cash position, showing an average reduction in net cash outflows over Years 3, 4 and 5 of about 20 per cent, might be barely acceptable. In those circumstances, the organization might look carefully at the enhancement benefits and rework the case excluding them. If this is done (table not shown), then the total percentage cost reduction in net cash outflow falls to 31 per cent, and in the steady state years (3, 4 and 5) it falls on average to six per cent. In these circumstances there would probably be pressure to be more cautious about the attributed value of the enhancements.

Turning to the profit and loss effect (Table 9.8) the situation is reversed. The steady state of Years 3, 4 and 5 shows an average reduction in net expenses of about 34 per cent, which would usually be regarded as satisfactory. However, the Year 1 increase of £225k in net expense, and consequent reduction in profit, may be unacceptable, both from a company and departmental viewpoint. The major contributor to this increase is the loss on transfer, £1,100k, relating to the existing mainframe and midrange equipment. In these circumstances the temptation to eliminate that increase by, for example, trying to negotiate a transfer price that is at least £225k above market value might be considerable. I repeat my earlier comment that if this is contemplated, then professional advice should be sought.

It might be thought that another way round the problem of an increase in net expense in Year 1 might be to negotiate an outsourcing payment that is £225k lower in Year 1, compensated for by higher payments in Years 2 to 5. Unfortunately, the accounting rules state that in those circumstances, regardless of the payment pattern, if the annual value from the contract is to be more or less equal year by year, then the total outsourcing payments would in effect have to be 're-smoothed' for the purpose of charging them as expenses to the profit and loss account. The effect of this would of course be to nullify what it had been intended to achieve.

That concludes the example. Its purpose has been to illustrate as many as possible of the factors that usually need to be considered in financial cases for outsourcing versus in-house IT operations, and to provide a basis for building such financial cases in real life.

OUTSOURCING DECISION CRITERIA

This chapter has concentrated on one particular aspect of outsourcing: the mechanics of its cost-justification and accounting at the level likely to be encountered by an IT decision maker who may not happen to be financially expert. It may also have been of use to financial people for whom decisions about outsourcing are not an everyday occurrence.

In the early days of IT outsourcing, a challenge for suppliers was to convince prospective customers that the benefits of a contractual outsourcing relationship would outweigh the risks perceived to be inherent in losing direct control over the people providing IT services. Today, IT outsourcing is well-established and is adopted by organizations large and less large across all sectors of industry and commerce, and the public sector, and including organizations for which IT is, as the jargon has it, 'mission-critical'. However, it is not compulsory, and indeed sometimes organizations decide to revert from outsourced to in-house provision. So let us conclude by revisiting the decision criteria. We first looked at them in the context of the analogy with outsourcing in personal life. Translated to the business world, and IT specifically, factors to consider when contemplating IT outsourcing include the following:

- For most organizations, IT, although vital, is peripheral to their core business.
- Do we have better things to do with our limited time and resources?
- Do we have the expertise to do for ourselves all the IT things that we need to do?
- Could a specialist supplier, which can be presumed to have the necessary infrastructure, expertise and experience, provide our IT more cost-effectively than we could?
- Would we benefit from having access to continually improving technology without having to learn about, acquire and finance it ourselves?
- Both outsourcing and operating leasing are ways of converting capital cost into revenue expense, of smoothing cash flows and taking assets off balance sheet. If these are among our requirements, then what are the pros and cons of each approach for us?
- Availability is critical to us. Doing it ourselves is not a risk-free option. Equally, to what extent is an outside supplier able to ensure the service levels that we require?

MANAGING THE PROCESS

Although the following points are not primarily financial, for the sake of completeness it may be helpful to summarize the things that have to be done during the process of evaluating and implementing outsourcing. They include the following:

- assessing the current IT situation and business environment;
- determining what is to be outsourced;
- setting objectives for the required outcomes, including service levels, availability and cost reduction criteria;
- issuing an Invitation To Tender to a number of chosen suppliers;
- managing the bid process;
- building and evaluating the financial cases;
- selecting a supplier;

- negotiating the outsourcing contract and, if separate, the service level contract;
- making a final decision on whether to proceed;
- managing the transition;
- monitoring implementation of the outsourced service;
- managing the ongoing contractual relationship.

Such a list of tasks can be a daunting prospect even for a large organization. Although many organizations will typically have significant experience of procurement, some of it on a large scale, outsourcing can be much more complex and multifaceted than some other procurements. The long-term relationships involved in outsourcing contracts make it critical to get it right.

In this context, mention should be made of IT outsourcing consultants, or IT sourcing consultants as they are sometimes known. These are specialist organizations that advise customers on outsourcing matters, put them in touch with potential suppliers and, typically, manage the process of supplier selection. They generally provide an objective comparison between suppliers on a like-for-like basis in order to assist the customer in the selection process and bring the benefits of experience gained in similar situations. They may also act in a liaison role between customer and supplier during the currency of the contract.

Summary

The main points covered in this chapter, linked to its objectives, have been the following:

- *IT outsourcing is a contractual relationship for the provision and management of IT services by an external supplier, under which the services are customized to the customer's requirements, such that payment by the customer will be related to the achievement of agreed service levels and specified results.*
- *Among the characteristics of outsourcing that raise particular financial issues are (a) the fact that it involves cost reduction rather than investment, (b) the transfer of assets and people, and (c) service enhancements.*
- *In the context of a structured example, we have encountered the factors that typically have to be taken into account in building a financial case for outsourcing vis-à-vis in-house provision.*
- *We have constructed a financial case for outsourcing vis-à-vis in-house provision from given data.*
- *We have discussed how financial cases for outsourcing are typically evaluated, and why investment evaluation methods such as internal rate of return (IRR) and return on investment (ROI) are usually inappropriate.*

10 Tasters: Budgeting, Costing and Pricing

Objectives

When you have studied this chapter you should be able to:

- *describe what is meant by budgeting and explain why it is such an important business activity, especially in departmentalized organizations;*
- *explain how budgeting, sometimes called 'responsibility accounting', is used as a motivation and measurement tool;*
- *distinguish between 'capital expenditure' and 'revenue expenditure', and give IT examples of each;*
- *describe what is meant by costing and explain why it is such an important business activity;*
- *describe what is meant by pricing and explain how costing information can be used as an aid to making pricing decisions.*

The purpose of this chapter is to provide an introduction to three other aspects of finance that are relevant to IT decision makers and that collectively could be said to form the backbone of the very large subject called management accounting: budgeting, costing and pricing. Each of these could be the subject of whole books and indeed many books have already been written about them.

BUDGETING

No laws govern budgeting or oblige companies to budget. However, most companies and other organizations operate budgeting procedures and most IT departments have to operate within budget constraints.

Part 2 of this book covers the fundamental principles of finance and accounting for those who start from zero knowledge or wish to brush up on knowledge that they already have. It notes how all business transactions can be recorded in that primary accounting document called the balance sheet. It looks at the role of the profit and loss account as an explanation of how the profit or loss made since the start of the business, or since the previous balance sheet, was arrived at; and the similar role played by the cash flow statement, but with respect to cash. It goes on to mention financial analysis, and to show how various comparisons – of numbers within the accounts, and with past years, industry averages, competitors and so on – can provide information about how a business has been performing.

However, characteristic of all that information is that it concerns the past. We as individuals may find it useful, even if possibly depressing, to find out from our personal 'accounts' that our expenditure exceeded our income last year, and what caused the excess. However, would it not have been even more useful if we had had some idea in advance that that was likely to be the case? If so, then we might have had a chance to do something about it. The same is true of businesses. Sometimes individuals do try to work out their personal finances in advance, however approximately. The process of doing so is called budgeting and the same word is used to describe the very similar activity carried out by almost all businesses. A budget is a financial plan setting targets for the revenues and expenditures of an organization for a specified period.

For a small business, the budgeting process may be as simple as it would be for most individuals, consisting of estimates of income and expenses, and the resulting profit or loss, and of cash availability month by month, highlighting periods during which overdraft facilities might be needed. The business would also need to budget for any planned capital expenditure, such as new premises or equipment, just as an individual would if buying a house or a car. This is for two reasons. The first is to determine whether the necessary financial resources are already available or can be borrowed. The second is that capital expenditure always has an effect on subsequent year-by-year revenue expenditure. If existing resources such as cash deposits or investments are to be used, then there will in future be less income from interest or dividends; if a loan is to be taken out, then there will be higher expense in the form of interest, and increased cash outflow on both the interest and the repayments. Either way, if the asset to be acquired is one that will depreciate in value, then this will be an expense that will further reduce profit. Profit will also be reduced, and cash outflow increased, by the running costs of the asset.

DEPARTMENTALIZED BUSINESSES

As a business gets bigger, there comes a point at which the owner or owners, or, in the case of a company, the board of directors, can no longer take all the decisions themselves. They have no choice but to divide the business up into manageable parts and to appoint a director or manager to be in charge of each part. The three most common ways of carving a business up are by function, by product or by region, or possibly all three. Division by function distinguishes between the major functions of a business. What these are will depend upon the kind of business it is, but they might typically include research and development, manufacturing, sales, distribution and finance. They might also include IT, although in some businesses the person in charge of IT reports to another functional head, typically but not necessarily the head of finance. Division by product distinguishes between the major products of a business. For example, a large IT manufacturer might have separate divisions for its main hardware and software products and its services. Division by geography may be by continent, country or region within a country.

As you can imagine, a worldwide multi-product company that carries out most of its functions in most or all of the countries in which it operates, will have a quite complex divisional or departmental structure. At the other end of the scale, the successful owner of a shop, who buys another shop and appoints a manager to run it, would have a quite simple structure: the two shops.

Mention of a manager highlights an important point, which is that however complex or simple the way of dividing up the business, if you are going to give someone responsibility for managing a part of it then you had better also provide them with the resources with which to do so, including financial resources. To do this we can expand slightly the original idea of a budget as simply an estimate of future income, expense and cash flow, to become a way of allocating financial resources to the managers of various parts of the business and delegating authority for managing those resources. Eventually the sum of the income, expense and cash flow budgets of all the divisions and departments will give the totals of those budgets for the business as a whole, although as a bargaining position, revenue budgets may be initially overstated, while expense budgets may be understated.

COST CENTRES AND PROFIT CENTRES

Exactly what financial resources are delegated depends upon the nature of the division or department. For this purpose, let us dispense with the rather cumbersome 'division or department' and coin the term 'centre' to mean either. Many centres do not earn revenue for the business but simply incur costs, and so are called 'cost centres'. An example would be an accounting department, which is necessary for the running of the business but which would be most unlikely to earn revenue. The obvious requirement for such a centre therefore is that its costs should be minimized and its budget would reflect that fact.

If there were such a thing as a centre that earned revenue without incurring any cost, then it would no doubt be called a 'revenue centre'. The obvious example of a centre whose purpose is to produce revenue is a sales division or department. Since, however, such a centre does indeed incur costs (salespeople's salaries, commissions and travel, for example) then it is clearly important to budget not just for the revenue required to be earned by that particular centre but for its costs also. Since those costs eventually become expenses, and since profit is the difference between revenue and expenses, it is perhaps not surprising that such a centre would usually be called a 'profit centre'.

CHARGE-OUT

Some functions in a business, for example the IT function, may be either cost centres or profit centres. If, as well as serving the company, IT services are provided to other businesses for a charge, then the IT function or part of it would be regarded as a profit centre; if not, then it would be regarded as a cost centre. Sometimes, even where no external services are provided, notional amounts are 'charged out' to user departments within the business. Charge-out may be at cost or at a marked up amount yielding a notional profit to the IT department. The purpose of such an approach is to encourage functional management to operate their function as though it were indeed an independent business. Especially is this so if the amounts charged to user department are reasonably accurate, which is more easily said than done, and if user departments are free to use external IT services if they can be obtained more cost-effectively. Such calculations may eventually be the basis for deciding whether to outsource part or all of the IT function.

RESPONSIBILITY ACCOUNTING

There would be little point in doing the considerable amount of work involved in budgeting if account were not kept of how individual centre managers actually perform when measured against their budgets. Budget-holding managers are indeed judged on, among other things, their performance against budget, and it is but a small further step to reward or penalize them on the basis of such performance. Many managers are paid bonuses based on their performance against budget. In this way managers responsible for divisions or departments are held accountable for the performance of those centres. Not surprisingly, the term 'responsibility accounting' is sometimes used to describe this whole process.

As in the example above of the sales division, it is usually obvious which centres in a business are responsible for generating revenues. However, if managers are to be held responsible for costs, then it is important that managers are only measured against those costs over which they can have some control. Many costs are obviously directly attributable to a particular centre. For example, the rent and insurance of a factory building are obviously direct costs of the manufacturing division as a whole, which will be the responsibility of the manufacturing director. It is therefore reasonable to include those costs in the total by which that person is measured. By contrast, the manufacturing director is likely to have no control whatever over whether extra money required by the company is raised by borrowing or by issuing further shares. This kind of decision is the responsibility of the financial director or chief financial officer, who would therefore be held accountable, for example, for any extra interest payable.

THE IMPORTANCE OF OPERATING PROFIT

One reason why operating profit is such an important number in the profit and loss account is precisely that it represents the revenues earned less all the operating, or non-financial, expenses of the business. These expenses are the ones that are usually capable of being charged to the responsibility of the operating, as distinct from financial, managers within the business, even if the process of assigning responsibility is not necessarily easy. Interest, tax and dividends belong in deep finance territory. There is one respect, however, in which an operating manager, such as an IT manager, may be given discretion to encroach into deep finance territory, and that is in the matter of leasing. Managers may be given authority to incur capital expenditure up to a given amount. While in some companies the decision as to how equipment (IT equipment, for example) is to be financed is always left to the finance function to decide, in others managers are given discretion whether to purchase or lease.

It should by now be apparent that much of the information needed to determine the actual revenues and costs of individual divisions or departments is the same as that needed to determine the financial results of the business as a whole, but analysed in different ways. For example, the sales achieved by Supermarkets A and B in a supermarket chain will no doubt be used to measure the performance against budget of their respective managers. However, together with the sales achieved by all the other shops operated by the business, they will be part of the total sales of the business that will be shown in the group profit and loss account. The various costs and expenses of manufacturing at a particular factory of a worldwide manufacturing company will be used to measure the performance against budget of the manager of that particular factory. They will also be incorporated in the company's group accounts. However, they may also be part of the performance measurement of the company's European Region, its UK operation, and of a particular product line that is manufactured in several different parts of the world. The essence of the requirement is to be able to analyse the same data in many different ways, a task greatly facilitated, of course, by IT systems.

It should by now be apparent that, in all but the smallest organizations, budgeting is usually a combination of several things: the delegation of responsibility, the allocation of resources, forecasting and the measurement of performance against forecast. It is also a means of influencing the behaviour of managers and provides a basis for rewarding them according to their performance. However, just as a business is itself a dynamic entity that needs to adapt to meet changing circumstances, so should budgeting systems also be adaptable. By their nature, budgets are formulated before the period to which they relate. Budgeting procedures should be sufficiently flexible to allow managers to take advantage of opportunities or react to situations that could not have been foreseen at the time the budget was prepared.

CAPITAL EXPENDITURE

As already mentioned, most budgeting systems distinguish between 'capital expenditure' and 'revenue expenditure' (or 'expense'). Capital expenditure usually has the following characteristics:

- It is money spent on long- or medium-term assets or projects.
- The amounts are substantial in the context of the organization.
- New funding is often required.

As a simple example, imagine that you wish to set up in business as a taxi driver. Your obvious item of capital expenditure is a taxi: a long-term asset costing what is, for you, a lot of money, which you would probably have to borrow. Examples of IT expenditure usually thought of as 'capital' would be most items of hardware and lump sum charges for software. See Appendix 4 for a summary of the accounting and tax rules regarding software. If software for internal use is to be developed in-house rather than bought or licensed, then the development costs would be regarded as capital.

Budget-holders often have authority to commit up to a given amount on 'capital' items; beyond that they have to obtain approval through a defined procedure. As already mentioned, some budget-holders also have authority to decide on the financing method (whether an acquisition should be leased or purchased); others do not.

REVENUE EXPENDITURE OR 'EXPENSE'

Revenue expenditure usually has the following characteristics:

- It is the consequence of earlier capital acquisitions.
- It is short term.
- It is usually funded out of day-to-day revenue.

In the taxi business, examples of revenue expenditure would be road tax, insurance, fuel and maintenance. You would expect to pay these out of the fares earned, and if you could not do so then you would have a problem. The fares should also, of course, be sufficient to cover the depreciation of the taxi and provide a reasonable profit. Examples of typical IT revenue expenditure would include power costs, insurance and personnel costs, other than those that may be regarded as 'capital' (see above), and lump-sum payments for software with an expected useful life of less than two years. They also usually include those things often described collectively as 'services'. These may be anything from training, and the maintenance of hardware and software, to the complete outsourcing of every aspect of IT. In the latter case, all IT expenditure would be regarded as expense, none as capital.

How much flexibility?

Organizations differ in their flexibility towards budgets. Some have detailed procedures and apply them rigidly, while others are more flexible. Where flexibility is permitted, some IT expenditures may be argued either way. For expenditures normally regarded as 'capital', there may be grounds for arguing that they can be treated as 'expense' and vice versa.

As an example, 'installation services' are concerned with installing IT and communications systems and making them work in a particular organization's environment. It could be argued that the cost of these services should be regarded as an integral part of the capital cost of the systems to be depreciated over their estimated useful economic lives, because without the services the systems would not work. It would follow from this argument that the total costs, including the services, should be 'capitalized' (shown as an asset on the balance sheet) and also charged against a capital budget.

On the other hand, it could be argued that the service is 'used up' as soon as it has been completed, in which case the cost should be regarded as revenue expenditure. From this argument it would follow that the expense should be charged against the profit and loss account of the period in which it is incurred, and also charged against an expense budget. None of this is intended as an incitement to transgress against accounting rules or company procedures. It is merely to point out that sometimes there are different ways of looking at things.

BUDGETS AND LEASING

Another example of differing flexibility towards budgets concerns organizations' attitudes to leasing, particularly operating leases. Payments under operating leases are, you may recall, treated as expenses for both accounting and tax purposes, being charged direct to the profit and loss account. For budgeting purposes, some organizations use this as sufficient justification for regarding operating lease payments as revenue expenditure. If the availability of the lease makes the proposed investment more affordable, then this may materially affect the decision whether to proceed.

By contrast, other organizations regard the decision about how an investment will be financed (the 'financing decision') as quite separate from the decision about whether to undertake it in the first place (the 'investment decision'). According to this view, if the investment being proposed is 'capital' by nature, then it will be regarded as 'capital' for budgeting purposes. How it is then financed, whether by operating lease or in some other way, will not affect the investment decision.

Treatment of interest

There is one other aspect of leasing that is relevant here. Already mentioned is that it is a principle of budgeting only to charge to budget-holders those costs over which they have some control. This does not usually prevent arguments about the justice or otherwise of 'cross-charges' from other departments. However, it does usually mean that only relevant items above the 'operating profit' line are charged out to budget-holders. The 'financial expenses' of the company (interest, tax and dividends) are not, at least not directly.

So, interest on funds used to purchase assets outright, out of central company funds, would usually not be charged out. Interest on leases, however, usually does get charged to the budget-holder, along with other relevant expenses, because the interest is an integral part of the lease payments. For this reason, leasing may be rejected by a budget-holder who at the same time may regard it as desirable, both operationally, and in other respects, financially. This is an example of how procedural aspects of budgeting can affect business decisions. It is an unfortunate fact of business life that an adverse effect on a departmental budget may sometimes prevent the doing of something that would in fact be for the benefit of the company as a whole and therefore of its shareholders. Where such a conflict arises it is helpful to remember that most of the shareholders neither know nor care whether the company is divisionalized or departmentalized. They have invested in the company as a whole, not in the 'sundries and miscellaneous' department, and they expect every pound, dollar or euro of their money to be spent with only one purpose: the maximization of their wealth.

Treatment of sale proceeds

While departmental budgets are charged with expenditure on capital assets, in some organizations they are not credited with any proceeds of sale. This practice, quite common in some long-established companies, often originated many years ago when most business assets were big and heavy, were expected to last a long time and to have negligible residual values. To allow inertia to let such a practice to continue today, however, can be to seriously restrict the ability of the manager of an IT, or other 'high-tech' department to manage the department's assets in an optimum way. It has to be questioned whether it is an appropriate practice with respect to IT and similar assets, whose useful lives may, for good business reasons, be short and whose residual values may be significant.

Actual versus budget

In the forgoing paragraphs we have considered budgeting as a way of planning the deployment of a company's financial resources over a period and delegating some authority to individual managers to decide how they should be used. Earlier in the book we looked in some detail at what is often known as 'capital budgeting'. This is the process of using financial methods to help decide which particular investment or project, of two or more possible alternatives, would give the best 'return'. If a project is undertaken for a customer, then the benefits will be an increase in external revenue; if it is an internal one, then the benefits are more likely to consist primarily of reduced costs.

Budgeting, of either kind, is a pointless exercise unless the actual costs and benefits are monitored and controlled against the budget. The chart in Figure 10.1 is an example of a diagrammatic way of recording actual project costs and comparing them with budgets, forecasts and, where relevant, revenues. The particular example happens to concern a project, and an external one at that, but the principle is applicable to any 'budget versus actual' situation.

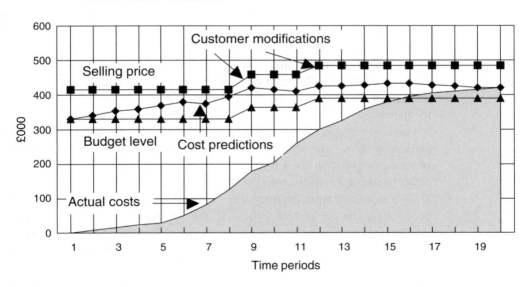

FIGURE 10.1 *A cost / profit project prediction graph*
Source: *Lock, D. (2003)* Project Management. *Gower, Aldershot.*

> **Checkpoint**
>
> So far in this chapter we have covered the first three of its objectives. In particular:
>
> - we have looked at budgeting and why it is such an important business activity, especially in departmentalized organizations, and looked at its benefits and inherent dangers;
>
> - we have considered how budgeting, sometimes called 'responsibility accounting', is often used as a motivation and measurement tool, especially in departmentalized businesses;
>
> - we have distinguished between 'capital expenditure' and 'revenue expenditure', and considered personal and business IT examples of each.

COSTING AND PRICING

In the previous section we discussed the fact that at the heart of budgeting is the process of estimating in advance the revenues likely to be achieved and the costs likely to be incurred by a business and by its various subdivisions during some future period. However, to a considerable extent we glossed over just how difficult it can sometimes be to determine what those costs might be. 'What did it cost?' A simple enough question, you might think, when applied to a recent purchase. '£15,000', you might answer in the case of a new car, or '£1' for a loaf of bread, or '£40' in the case of a PC software package. That is indeed what those items might cost us, the cost to us being the price charged by the supplier. However, the question 'what did it cost the supplier to produce the car, or the loaf of bread or the software package?' is not nearly so easy to answer.

There are several reasons why it is important to understand cost. Most obviously, if we do not know how much a product or service costs to produce or provide, then how can we know how much to charge for it in order to make a reasonable profit? Second, in a competitive world there is always pressure to reduce prices. The only way to improve or maintain profit may be to reduce costs. If we do not know which costs are attributable to which product or service, then we cannot know which costs we should try to reduce, or which products should be discontinued because they can never be profitable. Third, some businesses have a choice of making or buying certain parts or components, while most businesses can choose whether to provide certain functions in-house, for example IT, or to buy them externally, to outsource. Not knowing the cost of in-house provision would make it impossible to exercise that choice sensibly.

A very simple business

To get a taste for some aspects of this subject we shall look at some easy examples, starting with the simplest kind of business imaginable. Like Fred (see page 26), Mary sells tins of beans from a market stall. Suppose that her stall is rent free, that supplies are delivered from the supplier each day, that she sells all the tins that are delivered and that she has no other costs. Each tin costs her £1 and she sells it for £1.50, that is at a profit of 50p. Her mark-up (profit as a percentage of purchase price) is therefore 50 per cent. Probably not bad for tins of beans, but the numbers are only for illustration. Her profit margin (profit as a percentage of sales) is therefore 33.3 per cent. The more tins she sells the more profit she makes. If she sells 1,000 tins, then her cost of sales would be £1,000, her revenue would be £1,500 and her profit £500. If she sells 10,000 tins, then her cost of sales would be £10k, her revenue would be £15k and her profit £5k. Let us suppose that she actually sells 100,000 tins in a year. Her cost of sales would be £100k, her revenue would be £150k and her profit £50k.

Let us also suppose that from time to time Mary draws out some of her profit in cash to live on. The tax authorities have not yet caught up with her. For the purpose of the examples that follow we shall avoid the debate about whether proprietor's 'salary' should be a charge against profit or a distribution of profit. We shall treat it as the latter, that is as a distribution of profit, the same view that the tax authorities take. So the profit of Mary's business is indeed £50k.

VARIABLE COSTS

Why were the above calculations so easy? The reason is that all the costs of the business vary directly with the quantity of goods sold; in other words, all the costs are variable costs, in this case simply the costs of the daily supply of tins. The more Mary buys and sells, the more profit she makes, ad infinitum. A variable cost is defined as a cost that varies proportionally with a chosen unit. In this case, the unit is the number of tins sold. In a manufacturing business, the chosen unit might be the number of items manufactured; in a software house it might be number of lines of code written. The relationship between Mary's revenue, costs and profit can be represented by the chart in Figure 10.2.

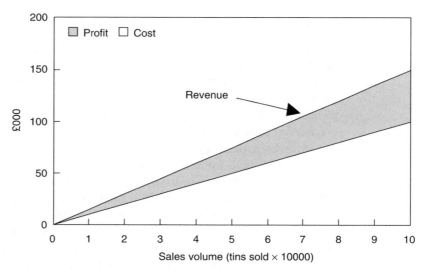

FIGURE 10.2 *Linear growth of revenue and profit*

All businesses try to reduce their costs. Suppose that Mary were able to find a new supplier who would only charge her 80p per tin instead of £1. If she were able to maintain her selling price of £1.50, then her profit per tin sold would increase from 50p to 70p. What would be the effect of all this on Mary's profit at her current volume of sales of 100,000? Her only expense (cost of sales) will be reduced by (100,000 × 20p =) £20k for her current volume of sales. What is this reduction worth to Mary's business? Since profit is the difference between revenue and expenses, and what Mary has done is to reduce her cost of sales, the benefit is to increase her profit by the same amount, that is by £20,000, but only at her current volume of sales. Halve the sales, and halve the benefit; double the sales, double the benefit, and so on.

FIXED COSTS

Now let us assume that the local council has caught up with Mary and that she is being charged £20k per year rent for her pitch. You might think that this is rather excessive, and indeed it is, but the purpose is to illustrate a point not to reflect the true economics of running a market stall. As long as Mary chooses to park her stall she must pay the £20k even if she never sells a single tin of beans. In other words, her business has joined the great majority of businesses that, in order to earn revenue, incur fixed costs as well as variable (see Figure 10.3).

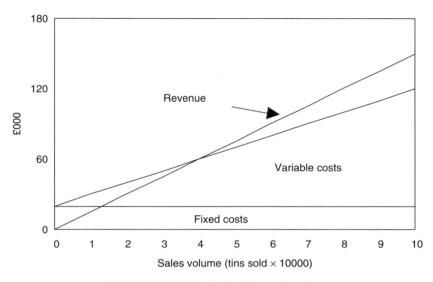

FIGURE 10.3 *Effect of introducing fixed costs*

Before, every tin of beans that Mary sold yielded a profit of 50p, which she regarded, with only the occasional glance over her shoulder at the tax authorities, as her own. Now, however, the surplus from the first few tens of thousands of tins sold does not belong to her at all, but has to go towards paying her rent. The sums are easy: each tin sold, starting with the very first, now contributes 50p towards paying the rent, the fixed cost. However, by itself the 'contribution' from selling the first tin is obviously nowhere near enough.

CONTRIBUTION

How many tins are required to make the total contribution required in this case? Well, if the rent comes to £20k and if each tin contributes 50p, then the required number is (£20k divided by 50p =) 40,000. This is the number of tins that must be sold in order that the business can just pay its fixed costs. At this level of sales Mary's business makes neither a profit nor a loss. Sales are just sufficient to cover the total costs. The business is said to 'break-even' (see Figure 10.4). Sell one tin fewer and the business makes a loss of 50p. This in turn means that Mary must pay the last 50p of the rent out of her own pocket. Sell one tin more and her business has made a profit of 50p; all subsequent tins sold add to her profit. Notice that the fixed costs represent a direct reduction in profit and the reduction is the same regardless of the level of sales. The profit had been £50k; the introduction of fixed costs of £20k has directly reduced the profit: to £30k. Had the original profit been £35k, then it would be reduced to £15k, and so on.

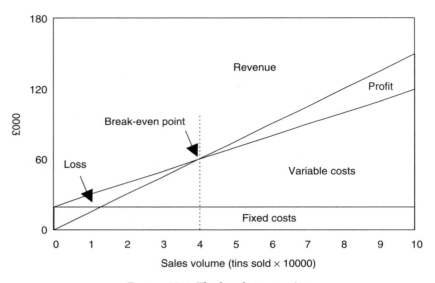

FIGURE 10.4 *The break-even point*

Suppose now that Mary complains about the amount of the rent and succeeds in having it reduced from £20k to £10k. What is the benefit of this reduction to her business? The answer is probably obvious. Precisely because fixed costs are, by definition, fixed and independent of the level of sales, the benefit of a reduction in fixed costs is an increase in profit of the same amount, regardless of the level of sales. If the fixed costs have decreased by £10k, then the profit must have increased by £10k. Furthermore, if the fixed costs are now less than they were, a correspondingly smaller contribution is required to cover them. So, the break-even point must now occur at a lower sales volume.

As before, the break-even point can be worked out arithmetically or by means of a simple diagram. How many tins must be sold in order to make the total contribution to fixed costs now required? The fixed costs (the rent) now come to £10k. Each tin sold contributes 50p; therefore the number of tins that must be sold is (£10k / 50p =) 20,000. This is now the number of tins that must be sold in order for Mary to break-even, as shown in Figure 10.5. The term 'fixed cost' is frequently used, but can be misleading. If Mary were to become really successful she might acquire another stall, at which point her fixed costs would go up, because she would have to pay rent on that too, as well as having to pay wages to someone to serve on it. Ultimately, all fixed costs become variable. We could say as a general rule that the benefit of a reduction in fixed costs is an increase in profit equal to that reduction. The amount of the benefit per year will be independent of the level of sales but only up to a certain point. Beyond that point the fixed costs may increase.

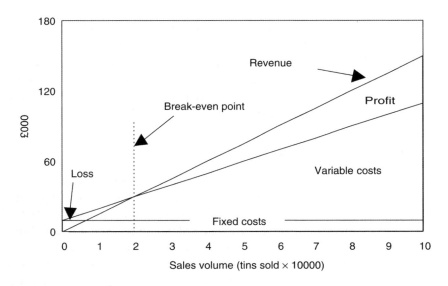

FIGURE 10.5 *Effect of reducing fixed costs*

Given the simple definition of profit to which we have reverted in this chapter, namely that it is revenue less expenses, then it follows that there are two ways of increasing profit: reducing expenses or increasing revenue. Mary has already had considerable success in reducing both her variable and fixed costs. If she wants further to increase her profit, then the only remaining option is to increase revenue, and there are two ways in which this might be done: she could sell more tins at the same price or she could increase the selling price.

Market research

Before deciding upon either approach, it would make sense for Mary to conduct a little market research, which means finding out what customers want and what they are prepared to pay for it. The fact that she already sells all of her stock every day suggests that if only she could accommodate some more stock she might well be able to sell it at the current price. Does she have space for storing more stock during the day free of charge, perhaps on the ground under her stall? If so, then she would be in the ideal position of being able to increase her sales at no extra cost other than the obvious cost of additional purchases. In particular, she would not have the awkward job of trying to forecast in advance whether she could make enough extra sales in order to recoup extra fixed costs. This would be for the good reason that no extra fixed costs would be incurred.

If, on the other hand, Mary could not find any free storage space, then her options would appear to be as follows: she may be able to sub-rent some currently unused space under a neighbouring stall or she could start a second stall. Both of these options would, however, incur additional fixed costs. In the first case she would almost certainly have to agree a contract for sub-rent payable to the other stallholder. In the second case, as already discussed, she would have to pay both rent for her second stall and the wages of an employee to run it. In either case, she would need to do a little break-even analysis in order to work out how many additional tins she would need to sell in order to recoup her additional fixed costs.

PRICE/VOLUME CALCULATIONS

Suppose on the other hand, that her market research suggests to Mary that at least most of her customers would indeed be prepared to pay more for her beans. She would now need to do a pricing exercise. Pricing simply means setting the price at which you will sell a product or service and it is about three things: cost, customers and competition. If your prices do not yield revenue that exceeds your total costs, then you make no profit. If your prices are higher than customers are prepared to pay, then you make no sales. Competition is what gives customers the choice. Suppose Mary believes that all her customers would be prepared to accept a five per cent price increase, but that if the increase were 10 per cent, then customers representing an estimated 10 per cent of her business would go elsewhere. What should she do? For what follows we revert to the original situation where the rent was £20k, as shown in Table 10.1. We can use this simple spreadsheet to test the effect of Mary's various assumptions.

TABLE 10.1 *The original price / volume situation*

		Ref	£	% of revenue
Sales volume	100,000 tins			
Revenue	100,000 × £1.50	a	150000	100.0
Variable costs	100,000 × £1.00	b	100000	66.7
Contribution	(a − b)	c	50000	33.3
Fixed costs		d	20000	13.3
Profit	(c − d)		30000	20.0

First, suppose that she were able to increase her prices by five per cent and keep all her customers. Table 10.2 shows the result: an increase in profit of £7,500 to £37,500. Now let us suppose that she were to increase her prices by 10 per cent but in so doing were to lose 10 per cent of her customers (see Table 10.3). In this case her profit, at £38,500 would be slightly more than that yielded by the price increase of only five per cent. However, she might well conclude that it would not make long-term business sense to risk losing 10 per cent of her customers for the very small short-term gain of an extra £1,000 in profit.

Table 10.2 *Increase price by 5%, keep all customers*

		Ref	£	% of revenue
Sales volume	100,000 tins			
Revenue	(100,000 × £1.50) × 1.05	*a*	157500	100.0
Variable costs	100,000 × £1.00	*b*	100000	63.5
Contribution	(*a* − *b*)	*c*	57500	36.5
Fixed costs		*d*	20000	12.7
Profit	(*c* − *d*)		37500	23.8

Table 10.3 *Increase price by 10%, lose 10% of customers*

		Ref	£	% of revenue
Sales volume	90,000 tins			
Revenue	(90,000 × £1.50) × 1.1	*a*	148500	100.0
Variable costs	90,000 × £1.00	*b*	90000	60.6
Contribution	(*a* − *b*)	*c*	58500	39.4
Fixed costs		*d*	20000	13.5
Profit	(*c* − *d*)		38500	25.9

Suppose that Mary is indeed favouring the option of raising prices by five per cent. Before deciding, however, it would make sense to revisit the option of selling more tins at the same price. The question now is 'how many extra tins would she have to sell in order to make at least the additional profit of £7,500 that she believes the five per cent price increase would produce?' Once again, you would use the spreadsheet to do the work for you. However, if you like arithmetic, here are the calculations. At the original price, the contribution made by each tin sold is 50p, or 33.33 per cent of selling price. In order to obtain an extra £7,500 of contribution, and therefore of profit, she would have to sell (£7500 / 50p =) 15,000 extra tins. If she has to pay a sub-rent of, say, £2,000 per year for her neighbour's spare space, then Mary would have to sell a further (£2000 / 50p =) 4,000 tins to cover her increased fixed costs, 19,000 extra tins in all. So, her final decision might be 'should I increase prices by five per cent with no increase in fixed costs and risk losing some customers (even though gut-feel tells me I wouldn't lose any) or should I try to increase my sales volume, but with the risk that I might possibly not even cover the additional fixed costs that I would incur?'

At this point we shall leave Mary to her decision-making, with which we can probably help her no further. Notice that all the calculations that she has done so far, and the financial statements that she has produced, have all been entirely for her own purposes, to help her manage her business and make decisions about it. They are all purely for internal consumption, and because of that, remember that there are no laws or any other rules that govern what they contain or indeed dictate that they have to be produced at all. If we did not know it already, and wanted to give a collective name to all these statements, accounts and charts that are purely for management purposes, and the process of producing and using them, then perhaps 'management accounting' might have come to mind. In fact that is the frequently used collective term for all the activities described in this chapter.

COSTING IN MANUFACTURING

For a look at another aspect of the large subject of costing we shall turn to the manufacturing industry. Think of a business that assembles PCs from bought-in components. Suppose that each PC uses £300 of components and takes one person three hours to assemble. If the cost of the person is £20 per hour, then the labour cost per PC is £60, and the cost to the business of assembling it is the materials plus the labour, a total of £360. However, is this the full cost of assembling the PC? It might be, but only if the assembly work were being done in a rent-free field, if the components found their way there automatically without being ordered or checked on delivery, if those components could be used immediately without being stored somewhere until they were needed, and if the business could somehow survive without any administration or accounting staff.

In reality, of course, the assembly work is done in a building, for which rent, insurance, power and cleaning costs have to be paid; the components have to be ordered, and checked on delivery, moved into a store and eventually issued to the production line: all by people who would quite like to be paid. Then there are other costs, more remote from the production process, but costs nevertheless: the costs of selling the product, such as advertising and sales staff; and the costs of administering the business: accounts and secretarial staff, and office costs and equipment.

All these costs are also part of the total costs of all the PCs assembled. What is the essential difference between these costs and the costs of labour and materials? The answer is that labour and material costs are obviously related directly to the assembly of the PCs, whereas the others are not. We can see the person assembling that particular PC, measure how long the work takes, and therefore easily work out the labour cost of producing it. We can see the materials being put into that particular PC and therefore, knowing what the materials cost, can easily work out the materials cost of producing it. The emphasis is deliberately on the word 'easily'. These costs, labour and materials, can easily be directly related to the product being assembled. For this reason, they are called direct costs.

Indirect costs

All the other costs that we considered are called, not surprisingly, indirect costs or sometimes overhead costs. Indirect costs or overheads are simply those costs that cannot easily be related directly to the product. Suppose that, just because it was too difficult to relate these indirect costs to an individual PC, they were simply ignored. Would we base our prices on just the direct costs? Of course not. Remember that in order to make a profit a business has to earn revenue that exceeds its total costs. Total means what it says: all costs, both direct and indirect.

'Easy', one might be tempted to say. 'At the end of the year we shall know exactly what all the costs are, indirect as well as direct, and we'll simply apportion the indirects equally among the products that have been made. If we've made 10,000 products and supposing that the total of the indirect costs is £2 million, then the proportion of indirect costs attributable to each product will be (£2 million / 10,000 =) £200. As long as wage rates and material costs remain the same, then the direct costs of each product will be £360. Each product's share of the indirect costs would be £200, so its total cost would be (£360 + £200 =) £560. Suppose we are aiming for a profit margin of 20 per cent? To achieve it, our selling price would have to be (£560 / 0.8 =) £700.'

Unfortunately, there are some fairly obvious flaws in the above argument. Chief among them is that if we wait until the end of the year to know the actual indirect costs before fixing our selling price we shall no longer have a business. It helps to have a price in order to make a sale. What is the solution to this little problem? The answer is provided by the activity described in the first section of this chapter. It is to estimate in advance, as accurately as we can, what the indirect costs will be and how many products will be made, and use the estimated or budgeted numbers. So, the budgeted indirect cost of each product would be the result of dividing the total budgeted indirect costs by the estimated number of products to be produced. For pricing purposes, such calculations might be adequate. Indeed, since pricing has to be done in advance, such calculations would usually have to be adequate.

Calculating total cost

But accounting is a continuous process. Business managers want to know as they go along what the costs and revenues of the business are and therefore what its profit is to date. So, for each product that is made, the accounting system should ideally record its total cost there and then or, rather, its total budgeted cost. Since the direct costs are, by definition, those that can easily be attributed directly to an individual product, one way of doing this would be simply to work out what percentage the indirects bear to the direct costs and apply a corresponding percentage uplift each time that direct costs are recorded. In the example above, the budgeted direct costs of each product were £360 and the budgeted indirects were £200. 200 as a percentage of 360 is 55.56 per cent. So a simple way for the accounting system to do what management requires would be always to add 55.56 per cent of the direct costs as an uplift.

So far so good, provided of course that we actually produce the estimated number of products. However, the question then becomes 'should we base the uplift on the total of the direct costs, or would it be better to base it on only one component of them?' What is wrong with using total direct costs? In some businesses, there is nothing wrong at all. However, in others, the price of materials is volatile. For example, oil prices are subject to considerable fluctuation based on both supply and, sometimes, political factors; the prices of crops, whether cocoa beans or carrots, vary according to whether the harvest has been good or bad. So, businesses manufacturing chocolate or baby food may find the price of their most important raw materials changing considerably during a year. Should the amount added for overheads fluctuate in sympathy with rises and falls in the price of materials? Of course not.

Are labour rates as volatile as the prices of some materials? Usually not. Certainly they do not usually come down, and increases are usually modest, especially in times of low inflation, and are reasonably predictable. For this reason, and because in past times direct labour accounted for the major part of product costs, direct labour is what has historically been the main basis for allocating indirect costs. In our example, direct labour costs are £60 per product. Using the same 'percentage uplift' method that we used above, the budgeted direct labour costs of each product were £60 and the budgeted indirects were £200. 200 as a percentage of 60 is 333.33 per cent. So the way the accounting system might allocate indirects on the basis of direct labour would be always to add 333.33 per cent of the direct labour costs as an uplift. However, direct labour costs now represent a much lower proportion of total costs than they once did.

Many manufacturing businesses are becoming more and more auto-mated, with machines doing much of the work previously done by people. Just as you can see a person assembling a PC, so you can see a machine doing the same thing if the assembly process has been automated. And just as the cost of employing the person to do the work is known and reasonably predictable, so is the cost of employing the machine. The purchase price of the machine is known, and its likely number of productive hours will also be known, from which a cost per hour used can be derived. Add its power costs and maintenance costs, which are also reasonably predictable, and you have an estimated total cost per machine-hour. If the machine is solely used for working on one product, then the cost of machine-hours is a direct cost attributable to that product, just as the cost of labour-hours was. If the machine is used for two hours per product and costs £15 per hour of use, then the direct machine cost attributable to each product is (£15 × 2 =) £30. If the machine is used in the manufacture of several different products, then the cost of machine-hours devoted to each product are direct costs attributable to each of the different products.

If a particular machine is used for short but varying periods on a very large number of different products, then it may be neither easy nor economically feasible to determine with sufficient precision the time spent upon each individual item. In this case, the costs of the machine no longer satisfy our criteria for being treated as direct costs, so they would be treated as indirect and be added to all the other indirect costs, to be allocated to particular products in whatever way has been determined.

ART VERSUS SCIENCE

Every different kind of business has its own particular kind of costing problems. This section should have given you an idea of some of the problems that costing tries to answer. If by now you have gained the impression that costing is a subject that is both quite complex and more art than science, then you would be right, and we have only considered quite simple examples. One thing that can be said, however, to close our brief excursion into this topic, is that the power of IT systems economically to record and analyse large amounts of individually quite small data items is helping to take just a little of the art out of costing and replace it with science.

For example, in the case of the machine, cited above, which is used for varying periods on a very large number of different products, it may now be economically feasible to allocate the costs of its use directly to the products on which it is used whereas it would not have been in earlier times. To the extent that costs previously treated as indirect, and therefore subject to some estimated basis of allocation, might now be economically treated as direct, so costing becomes more accurate. The more accurate the data used for business decision-making, the better the decisions are likely to be. In fact, that sentence could be said to represent the theme of this part of the book and is perhaps a good place at which to leave it.

Summary

The main points of this chapter, linked to its objectives, have been:
- *A budget is a financial plan setting targets for the revenues and expenditures of an organization for a specified period.*
- *In a departmental organization, budgeting is also a way of allocating financial targets and resources to departmental managers, against which performance can be measured.*

- *The characteristics of 'capital expenditure' are usually large (in context) amounts of new money spent infrequently on fixed assets; those of 'revenue expenditure' are usually frequent small amounts of money, financed from revenue, spent on replenishing current assets or on expenses.*
- *Cost accounting (or costing) is the process of analysing and classifying elements of cost for the purpose of calculating as accurately as possible the total cost of a process, product or service. Costs are categorized as either 'direct' (those, such as materials and labour, that can usually be traced to a particular unit of cost in an economically feasible way), or 'indirect' (those that cannot be so traced).*
- *Pricing is the process of determining the price that shall be charged for a product or service, usually by reference to costing information.*

Part Two

Finance Fundamentals in a Nutshell

11 Finance Fundamentals: Bringing it Together

The purpose of this chapter and the next two is to provide a brief summary of the fundamentals of finance and accounting, sufficient to enable people with no previous knowledge of the subject to understand the main part of the book. For these three chapters a 'minimalist' approach in note form has been adopted in order to conserve space in the book and to take minimum time from the reader.

Objectives

When you have studied this chapter you should be able to:
- *explain the main purpose of business, and why the concept of 'limited liability' has been vital to its development;*
- *state the three main sources of company finance;*
- *explain what a balance sheet is and why it 'balances';*
- *show how some typical business transactions affect the balance sheet;*
- *explain what a 'profit and loss account' is and how it is set out;*
- *explain what a 'cash flow statement' is and how it is set out;*
- *explain the difference between cash flow and profit.*

The main purpose of a business is to create wealth, or 'add value', for the proprietor or proprietors. It is helpful to think of a business, even a one-person business, as a separate entity from its proprietors. In the case of companies this principle is enshrined in law. A company is a separate legal entity. Its proprietors are called shareholders.

WAYS TO RUN A BUSINESS

A business may be run by an individual (a 'sole trader'), by a group of individuals working together (a 'partnership') or by a limited company.

Sole traders and partners, except those in a 'limited liability partnership', are liable for all the debts of a business. If necessary, all their personal assets can be required to pay those debts.

Limited liability partnerships are halfway between traditional partnerships and limited companies, combining the flexibility of the former with the protection of limited liability associated with the latter.

LIMITED COMPANIES

The main purpose of a limited company (and of limited liability partnerships) is to limit the liability of the proprietors to the money that they have invested in it; they may lose that, but nothing else.

Other advantages of companies over unincorporated businesses include: additional money may more easily be raised, in exchange for more shares; shares can be bought and sold; there may be tax advantages.

What follows in this chapter and the next two refers to companies, although most of the principles apply to any business.

Shareholders invest money in a company in return for 'shares'; the shareholders exercise control and are entitled to profits in proportion to the number of their shares.

The shareholders appoint 'directors' (who may also be shareholders) to run the business on their behalf and to report back to them the results and 'accounts' at least once a year.

The shareholders also appoint 'auditors' to tell them whether the accounts give a true and fair view of the state of affairs of the company and its 'profit'.

Profit means the income ('turnover' or 'revenue') earned by a business, less the expenses incurred in earning it.

Profit belongs ultimately to the shareholders, but usually only a part is paid to them each year as a 'dividend'. The rest is retained in the business to finance expansion.

It is not compulsory to pay a dividend. The directors recommend how much, if any, they think the company can afford.

Most companies are 'private limited companies', many of which are family businesses.

Public limited companies (PLCs) are companies authorized to offer their shares to members of the public. They are subject to more stringent regulations than private companies. Only the shares of PLCs may be 'listed' on a stock exchange.

Where companies obtain money

Finance means the management (the raising, custody and spending) of money.

There are three main sources of long-term finance for a company: money invested by shareholders, called 'share capital'; money borrowed from banks or other lenders, called 'loan capital', 'loans' or 'debt'; and profit retained in the business, called 'retained profit'.

The profit left after paying all expenses, including interest and tax, belongs to the shareholders, so share capital and retained profit together are known as 'shareholders' funds'. They are also known as 'shareholders' equity' or just 'equity'.

A company is thus obligated to others for all its money: to its lenders for its loan capital, to its shareholders for its share capital and for any profits made. These obligations are called 'long-term liabilities', where 'long-term' means more than one year.

Loans must usually be repaid by a fixed date. Eventually, although perhaps far into the future, when the company is 'wound up', anything left after all debts have been paid will be repaid to the then shareholders.

Meanwhile, the total long-term finance used by a company is called its 'capital employed', meaning 'money used'.

In the course of trading, a company will incur short-term liabilities as well, for example overdrafts and 'trade creditors' (suppliers from whom it has bought on credit). These must usually be paid within a year and are called 'current liabilities'.

Liabilities, whether short- or long-term, are obligations that a company owes.

What companies do with money

Some companies, for example small consultancies, need very little money in order to get started and to remain in business. All they need is people and perhaps a rented office.

Others, for example aircraft manufacturers, need a great deal of money. They have to acquire buildings and manufacturing plant. They also have to stock up with parts and components. All these things are called 'assets'.

Most companies fall somewhere in between these extremes.

Assets, like liabilities, may be long-term or short-term. Here, too, 'long-term' means more than one year. Long-term assets are called 'fixed assets'.

Most fixed assets are used up over time, as is therefore the money used to acquire them. IT equipment and motor vehicles are examples. To replace them requires more money. Not all fixed assets are used up, however. Land is an example.

Accounts usually, but not necessarily, record the using up, or 'depreciation', of fixed assets on a 'straight line' basis (as though it happened by equal amounts each year). However, other methods are permitted.

Assets do not have to be bought. Many of them, including IT assets, can be leased. Instead of a single initial cash outlay, regular payments are made during the life of the asset. Thus, leasing is a way of conserving cash.

Short-term assets are called 'current assets'. Stocks are current assets; so are 'trade debtors', which are amounts due from customers to whom goods or services have been sold on credit. Cash is also a current asset.

Current assets are used up or 'turned over', usually over short periods of less than a year. Unlike fixed assets, they are continually replenished out of money received from sales.

'Fixed capital' is a term often used to describe that part of a company's money ('capital') invested in long-term or fixed assets.

'Working capital' is a term often used to describe that part of a company's capital invested in current assets less current liabilities.

'Goodwill' is an intangible asset that may arise when one business buys another. It is the amount by which the price paid for the business exceeds the market values of the assets less liabilities acquired. It is the amount that the buyer is willing to pay for the good name or the 'know-how' of the business.

Assets, whether short- or long-term, are things that a company owns.

HOW A BUSINESS WORKS

How a business works financially is best understood by working through an example. This we shall be doing for the remainder of this chapter, considering one by one, in Example 11.1, a series of common business transactions: seeing how they are recorded and their financial effect.

To do this, we shall use as an example a small manufacturing company just starting up. Imagine that you are the only shareholder.

Getting started

You have started the company by opening a company bank account and paying in £100k of your own money in exchange for £100k worth of shares. Every transaction has two sides. For example, you sell, I buy; I lend, you borrow. Accounting systems record both sides of every transaction.

Table 11.1 is one way of showing how this first transaction has affected the company. It shows that it has acquired an asset, cash, of £100k, by incurring a corresponding liability of £100k to you for the capital that you have invested. Notice how both sides of the transaction have been recorded.

TABLE 11.1 *Balance sheet (i)*

Assets	£000	Liabilities	£000
Cash	100	Share capital	100

Table 11.1 is called a 'balance sheet'. A balance sheet is a statement of the assets and liabilities of a business at a moment in time. It is a snapshot. A balance sheet always 'balances' because both sides of every transaction are always recorded.

Suppose that in addition to your own £100k you estimate that you need a further £150k in order to get started. Friends are willing to invest, but you only accept, say, a further £80k from them in return for issuing more shares.

If the friends together had more shares than you, then you would lose control, because they could then out-vote you. Each share carries one vote. The company now has £180k in cash and owes £180k to the shareholders.

The remaining £70k you raise from the bank as a long-term loan. Table 11.2 shows what the balance sheet now looks like. The company now has £250k in cash.

TABLE 11.2 *Balance sheet (ii)*

Assets	£000	Liabilities	£000
Cash	250	Loan	70
		Share capital	180
	250		250

In most businesses, the holding of cash is a means to an end. You have set up your company in order to manufacture, so you buy a factory for £90k and some plant for £60k. You could have leased both, but we shall assume that you bought them outright.

Table 11.3 shows your balance sheet now. The company's liabilities (where its money came from) have not changed. However, what it is doing with its money has changed. In this case, it has converted part of one asset, called 'cash', into other assets, called 'factory' and 'plant'.

TABLE 11.3 *Balance sheet (iii)*

Assets	£000	Liabilities	£000
Factory	90	Loan	70
Plant	60	Share capital	180
Cash	100		
	250		250

In our balance sheets up to this point, we have shown assets and liabilities side by side. Published balance sheets used to look this, but the fashion now is for a 'vertical' format, with assets at the top and liabilities underneath. Table 11.4 shows the balance sheet rearranged in this way. It also differentiates between the long-term (fixed) and short-term (current) assets.

TABLE 11.4 *Balance sheet (iv) ('vertical' format)*

	Total £000
Fixed assets	
Factory	90
Plant	60
Current assets	
Cash	100
	250
Liabilities	
Loan	70
Share capital	180
	250

'Long-term' means more than one year; 'short-term' means one year or less.

EXAMPLE 11.1 PART 1: HOW TRANSACTIONS AFFECT THE BALANCE SHEET

The company is now ready to start business. We shall proceed through a series of simple business transactions, see how they are recorded and examine their financial effect: the changes that they cause to the balance sheet. Every business transaction causes a company's balance sheet to change, although of course a new physical balance sheet is not produced after every transaction.

The transactions, described below, are numbered 1 to 14. The effect of each transaction is recorded in a correspondingly numbered balance sheet in Table 11.5. Should you wish to work out the effects for yourself, then it is a simple matter to draw a rough version of Table 11.5 or produce a simple spreadsheet.

Look at the first column, headed (iv). It shows the balance sheet as we left it in Table 11.4 and represents the situation just before the start of trading by the company. Note that the liabilities also have been categorized into short-term, long-term and shareholders' funds. The few additional lines will be explained as we come to them.

Alternatively, simply continue reading the transactions as text, referring to the table as you do so. After each transaction in the text, there is a paragraph explaining how it was treated in the balance sheet and why.

Whether or not you attempt the answers yourself, please note especially, as you proceed, what happens to the 'cash' and 'profit' lines in the balance sheets.

Assume that there is an unlimited overdraft facility. Should it be required, any overdrawn balance will be shown as a negative number in the 'cash' line. This is only in order to avoid having yet another line in the table.

In each numbered balance sheet in Table 11.5, the boxed items are those that have changed as a result of the correspondingly numbered transaction.

The transactions

1. The company buys raw materials for £60k on credit.

Column (1) shows how transaction 1 has changed the balance sheet. A new asset, raw materials, has been acquired and a new liability incurred: a trade creditor, the obligation to pay the supplier. The balance sheet totals increase by £60k as a result.

2. Product is manufactured, using £40k of raw materials and paying wages £60k. Suppose this results in £90k of finished goods and £10k of partly-finished goods, called 'work in progress'.

Here, two kinds of asset (raw materials and cash) have been converted into two other kinds of asset (finished and partly finished goods). For the purpose of this simple example, we shall assume that no other costs have been incurred, so that the finished goods and work in progress are valued at the cost of the materials and labour that have gone into them. No extra liabilities have been incurred and none have been discharged, so the balance sheet totals are unchanged.

3. £60k worth of finished goods are sold on credit for £96k.

Finished goods have been sold at a profit of £36k. They have been converted into a higher-value asset called 'trade debtors': the right to receive payment for things sold. Why is the profit a liability? Because it belongs, ultimately, to the shareholders, and is therefore owed to them by the company. However, some subsequent transactions will cause the amount of profit to change. The balance sheet totals have increased by £36k.

4. The company pays various administrative expenses totalling £20k. Sometimes called 'overheads', these include salespeople's and admin staff's salaries (assume £10k), business rates (assume £3k) and other expenses. These details will be needed later.

You will recall from earlier in this chapter that 'profit' means income less expenses, so these expenses reduce profit by £20k. The asset 'cash' is also reduced by £20k. You will by now have noticed that where both 'sides'

TABLE 11.5 *Example 11.1, Part 1 – Balance sheets resulting from transactions (1) to (14)*

No: Boxes indicate items changed	(iv) £000	(1) £000	(2) £000	(3) £000	(4) £000	(5) £000	(6) £000	(7) £000	(8) £000	(9) £000	(10) £000	(11) £000	(12) £000	(13) £000	(14) £000
Fixed assets															
Factory	90	90	90	90	90	90	90	90	90	90	90	90	90	90	90
Plant	60	60	60	60	60	60	60	60	60	60	60	60	60	60	60
Current assets															
Stock of raw materials		60	20	20	20	20	60	60	60	20	20	20	20	60	60
Work in progress			10	10	10	10	10	10	10	10	10	10	10	10	10
Stock of finished goods			90	30	30	30	30	30	30	130	50	50	50	50	50
Trade debtors				96	96	96	96	46	45	45	173	173	173	173	64
Cash	100	100	40	40	20	-40	-40	10	10	-50	-50	-74	-114	-114	-5
	250	310	310	346	326	266	306	306	305	305	353	329	289	329	329
Current liabilities															
Trade creditors		60	60	60	60	0	40	40	40	40	40	40	0	40	40
Long-term liabilities															
Loan	70	70	70	70	70	70	70	70	70	70	70	70	70	70	70
Shareholders' funds															
Share capital	180	180	180	180	180	180	180	180	180	180	180	180	180	180	180
Profit				36	16	16	16	16	15	15	63	39	39	39	39
	250	310	310	346	326	266	306	306	305	305	353	329	289	329	329

(assets and liabilities) of the balance sheet change, so do the totals; otherwise they do not.

5. The company pays the raw materials supplier £60k.

The asset 'cash' is being used to extinguish a liability (the trade creditor). In order to do this, the company has had, for the first time, to draw on its overdraft facility. In this example we are showing this as 'negative cash', simply to avoid having an extra line. In practice, an overdraft would be shown as what it is: a current liability.

6. The company replenishes its supply of raw materials for £40k on credit.

This is similar to transaction 1. The balance sheet totals have increased by £40k.

7. The company receives £50k from its debtors.

Part of the asset 'debtors' has been converted into the asset 'cash', and the overdraft is temporarily paid off. Notice that in credit businesses profit is nearly always regarded as earned at the time a sale is made (see transaction 3), not when the customer pays. Only in cash businesses, such as market traders or taxi drivers, do the two things usually occur simultaneously.

8. The company discovers that a customer who owes £1k has gone bankrupt and will be unable to pay.

This represents a 'bad debt'. The asset 'trade debtors' is no longer worth £46k, but only £45k. The bad debt is an expense and, like any other expense, it reduces profit. Notice that it can only be recorded when it becomes apparent; no business sells to a customer knowing that they won't pay.

9. More product is manufactured, using £40k of raw materials and paying wages £60k.

This is similar to transaction 2, except that now £100k of finished product will result. Assuming that the business is now in a steady state the amount of work in progress will stay roughly the same, 'old' work in progress becoming finished product and being replaced by 'new' work in progress of a similar amount.

10. £80k worth of finished goods are sold on credit for £128k.

This is similar to transaction 3, except for the amounts. The profit is £48k and, as before, is recognized at the time the sale is made, not when the customer pays.

11. The company pays administrative expenses of £24k. Assume that this includes £12k of salespeople's and admin staff's salaries.

This is similar to transaction 4, except for the amounts.

12. The raw materials suppliers are paid in full.

This is similar to transaction 5.

13. The company replenishes its supply of raw materials for £40k on credit.

This is similar to transactions 1 and 6.

14. The remainder of the earlier customers pay their bills (£46k less the bad debt £1k), as do half (£64k) of the latest ones.

This results in a cash inflow of £(45k + 64k) = £109k, not quite enough to pay off the overdraft.

That concludes the recording of the transactions that, I think you will agree, are representative of many of the everyday transactions that occur in a real business. Indeed, since manufacturing is more complex than many businesses, you may have grappled with more complexity than was necessary.

Was the example difficult? I think not, once you had worked through a few of the transactions and grasped what it was about. With the understanding gained, you should now be able to work out the financial effect of most of the transactions that occur in your own business.

Cash and profit

At the beginning of the above exercise I suggested that you note especially what happened to the cash and to the profit as you worked through the transactions. Figure 11.1 compares the cash and profit figures shown by balance sheets 1 to 14.

The profit remains positive throughout the sequence of balance sheets, whereas the cash balance ranges between £100k and −£114k. Profit and cash are different things.

Why is this? Part of the answer is that many things have to be paid for (raw materials, wages and other expenses) before any cash is eventually received from customers for sales. The rest of the answer we shall consider shortly.

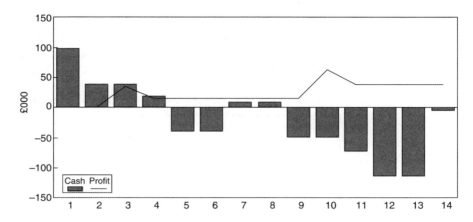

FIGURE 11.1 *Cash and profit from Table 11.5*

Whether a business is in its start-up phase, as illustrated here, or established as a going concern, it is vital that it plans its cash requirements and arranges in advance for overdraft facilities to be available as required. Profitable businesses can fail through lack of cash.

Checkpoint

So far in this chapter we have covered the first four of its objectives. In particular:

- we have discussed the purpose of business and why the concept of 'limited liability' has been vital to its development;

- we have described the three main sources of company finance;

- we have defined a balance sheet and determined why it balances;

- we have experienced building a balance sheet and have seen how it is affected by different business transactions.

We have also considered some of the reasons why cash and profit are different. We shall look at others in the next part of the chapter.

We shall now continue with Example 11.1 by considering some of the adjustments that usually have to be made to a balance sheet to try to ensure that it reflects as closely as possible the financial position of the business.

EXAMPLE 11.1 PART 2: TYPICAL ADJUSTMENTS

Suppose now that by balance sheet 14 the company has completed, say, four months of trading and that you wish to know as precisely as possible its financial position. There is nothing magic about four months; it is simply the kind of period over which the summary transactions used for illustration in Example 11.1 might have taken place.

There are usually some adjustments that the company accountant would have to make, most of which have nothing directly to do with trading. Typical such adjustments, five in all, designated (a) to (e), are described below, and their effects tabulated in Table 11.6.

TABLE 11.6 *Example 11.1, Part 2 – Typical period-end adjustments*

No:	(14) £000	(a) £000	(b) £000	(c) £000	(d) £000	(e) £000	(15) £000
Fixed assets							
Factory	90						90
Plant	60	−2					58
Current assets							
Stock of raw materials	60						60
Work in progress	10						10
Stock of finished goods	50						50
Trade debtors	64						64
Prepayments				2			2
Cash	−5						−5
	329	−2	0	2	0	0	329
Current liabilities							
Trade creditors	40						40
Other creditors			4		10	9	23
Long-term liabilities							
Loan	70						70
Shareholders' funds							
Share capital	180						180
Profit	39	−2	−4	2	−10	−9	16
	329	−2	0	2	0	0	329

This table starts with balance sheet 14, which is as we left it at the end of Part 1 except for a couple of additional lines, which will be explained as we come to them. The table ends, after all the adjustments have been made, with the final balance sheet for the period: balance sheet 15.

Once again, having glanced at the format of Table 11.6, you are recommended to try the exercise for yourself.

(a) The manufacturing plant will have depreciated with use. Suppose its estimated life is ten years and that it will be worthless at the end of that period. Assume that the depreciation is deemed to occur evenly over the ten-year period. This is known as 'straight line' depreciation.

On a 'straight line' basis the depreciation will be £6k per annum (= £60k / 10) so for four months it will be (£6k / 3 =) £2k. So, the asset value is decreased by £2k. What is the other side of this transaction? The approximate answer, adopted for the sake of simplicity in Table 11.6, is to deduct it all from profit.

However, depreciation of plant is actually another cost (together with raw materials and labour) of manufacture. In reality, therefore, the depreciation of plant should be split proportionally, as shown in Table 11.7, among all the things manufactured: work in progress, stock of finished goods and goods sold.

TABLE 11.7 *Example 11.1, Part 2 – Allocation of plant depreciation*

	Cost excl. depreciation	Depreciation	Cost incl. depreciation
	£000	£000	£000
Work in progress	10	0.1	10.1
Stock of finished goods	50	0.5	50.5
Finished goods sold ('cost of sales')	140	1.4	141.4
	200	2.0	202.0

The balance sheet values of work in progress and stock of finished goods would in practice therefore be increased by £0.1k and £0.5k respectively. Profit would only be reduced by £1.4k, the additional cost of the goods sold, not by the full £2k, as we have done. This deliberate inaccuracy has been perpetrated only for simplicity and to maintain whole numbers in the example.

There is a sense in which all expenses represent the using up of assets. For example, the expense called 'wages' represents the using up of the right to an employee's labour over a given period. Depreciation (the using up of fixed assets) is perhaps one of the more obvious illustrations of that principle.

(b) Assume you know that you owe the bank approximately £4k in interest on the loan and the overdraft so far, although it has not yet been charged. This is for illustration only: no doubt in reality interest would be charged monthly.

An expense is an expense, whether it has yet been paid in cash or not. Interest (the price to be paid for the right to use someone else's money during a given period) becomes an expense as the right is used. Our aim is to determine the true state of affairs of the company, so the £4k is an 'other creditor' and is also deducted from the profit.

It could possibly be argued that the £4k should be added to the overdraft balance. However, since it has not yet been charged by the bank that would distort the actual cash position.

(c)   In transaction 4, included in the £20k paid for expenses, all of which was deducted from profit, was £3k for business rates (local taxes). You realize now that that payment covered the whole year.

After four months, of the £3k of services paid for, only £1k-worth has yet been received. The remaining £2k-worth of services will be received over the remaining eight months of the year. £2k of the £3k paid therefore represents a payment in advance or 'prepayment'. Profit, having originally been charged with the full £3k, is correspondingly increased by £2k.

This right (to receive future services already paid for) is just as much an asset as is, for example, 'debtors' (the right to receive cash for goods already sold). After four months, only one-third of the right has been used up. The effect of the above adjustment has been that only one-third is charged as an expense.

(d)   You estimate that corporation tax payable on the profit so far will be £10k.

Tax is an expense, the price payable for making a profit, that will eventually have to be paid. So, the Inland Revenue is a creditor, not a trade creditor but an 'other creditor'. Profit is correspondingly reduced.

(e)   Assume that it has been decided that the company will pay an 'interim dividend' of 5p per share, or £9k in total. An interim dividend is a payment on account of the full dividend that a company expects to pay at the end of a year. This too is for illustration only; in reality a dividend would not usually be paid in a start-up year because of the need to conserve cash.

Dividends are not compulsory but, once decided upon, there is an obligation to pay them. This, too, is therefore an 'other creditor'. Remember that a dividend is a distribution of profit to the shareholders; it is not, as all our other examples have been, an expense deducted in arriving at profit. It nevertheless reduces the amount of profit left in the business.

Summary of Example 11.1, Parts 1 and 2

Having made the above adjustments, balance sheet 15 in Table 11.6 shows the assets and liabilities of the company and its profit to date as accurately as possible. Note, however, some of the factors that make total accuracy impossible.

For example, depreciation can only be an approximation; the amounts of interest and tax owing are also only estimates. Note also that all the above adjustments (a) to (e) have only affected the profit figure; they did not affect cash.

Introduction to Parts 3 and 4

We have seen, in the example so far, that every transaction causes the balance sheet of a company to change. A new balance sheet could be produced after every single transaction, as we have done, but to do so would be absurd. In practice, balance sheets are usually produced yearly for legal and taxation purposes, and monthly for internal use.

At the same time, summaries are prepared of all the transactions that have affected profit and cash flow respectively since the previous balance sheet or, in our example, since the start of the business. The summary of all the transactions that have affected profit is called a 'profit and loss account'; the summary of all the transactions that have affected cash is called a 'cash flow statement'.

EXAMPLE 11.1 PART 3: THE PROFIT AND LOSS ACCOUNT

A profit and loss account is a summary of all the transactions that have affected profit since the previous balance sheet or, as in this example, since the beginning of a business.

Table 11.8 shows the profit and loss account (Part 3 of Example 11.1) in a format based on that used in published accounts. It starts with 'turnover', a jargon word meaning the revenue from sales. Then, all the costs and expenses of the business are deducted, starting with those most directly related to the goods or services sold. Notice the different levels of 'profit' described.

TABLE 11.8 *Example 11.1, Part 3 – Typical format of a simple profit and loss account*

	Total £000
Note: Transaction numbers, where given, are those referred to in Example 11.1, Part 1	
Turnover	224
Less cost of sales *(as per transactions (3) and (10), plus depreciation of plant)*	142
Gross profit	82
Less administrative exps *(as per transactions (4) and (11), less prepayment, plus bad debt)*	43
Operating profit	39
Less interest	4
Profit before tax	35
Less tax	10
Profit after tax (net profit)	25
Less dividend	9
Profit retained	16

With a little effort you should be able to produce the answer for yourself. All the information you need is in the earlier descriptions of the transactions and of the adjustments. Some items are self-explanatory; explanations of the others follow.

Turnover (sales)

Turnover represents the revenue from goods (or services) sold, regardless of whether the customers have yet paid for them. Similarly, the items described under the two following headings represent costs incurred, whether or not they have yet been paid for.

Confusingly, 'turnover' has another meaning also. It refers to the rate at which assets, or particular classes of asset, such as stock, are used and replenished ('turned over') in the process of achieving sales. This meaning is discussed in Chapter 13.

Cost of sales

These are the costs directly related to getting the goods or services sold during the period to a saleable state and location. In this simple example these consist of raw materials and labour costs of the goods actually sold, plus depreciation of the manufacturing plant. Remember that in the interests of keeping things simple we have charged the full £2k of depreciation as part of cost of sales, whereas in practice it would have been split between cost of sales, stock of finished goods and work in progress.

'Gross profit' is what is left after deducting cost of sales from turnover.

Administrative expenses

These are the other expenses of running or 'operating' the business, excluding interest and other finance-related expenses. They are sometimes called 'administrative overheads' or just 'overheads'.

Operating profit

This is the profit made from running or 'operating' the business. Because it is the profit before deducting any finance-related expenses, it facilitates comparison between businesses whose operations are similar but which are financed in different ways.

Profit after tax

Sometimes called 'net profit', this is what finally belongs to the shareholders after all the expenses have been paid. It is the fund out of which dividends may be paid.

EXAMPLE 11.1 PART 4: THE CASH FLOW STATEMENT

A cash flow statement is a summary of all the transactions that have affected the cash position since the previous balance sheet or, as in our example, since the beginning of a business. Its purpose is similar to that of a profit and loss account, but it deals with cash rather than profit.

Table 11.9 shows the cash flow statement resulting from our example, in a format based on one that is used in published accounts. It sets out the main headings under which cash has been received or paid out, together with the amounts applicable to each heading. These should be self-explanatory, except for 'capital expenditure', which means money spent on long-term assets.

If you wish to try it for yourself, all the information you need is in the descriptions of the transactions given earlier in Part 1 of the example. It is not necessary to refer to the adjustments in Part 2 because none of them affected cash.

Remember to include all the items that affect cash, right from the very beginning of the company, before you had paid your £100k into its newly opened bank account.

Note that we included interest, tax and dividends in the profit and loss account, because they represented expenses incurred; they are excluded from the cash flow statement because they have not yet been paid.

TABLE 11.9 *Example 11.1, Part 4 – Typical format of a simple cash flow statement*

	Total £000
Net cash flows from:	
Operating activities *	−105
Interest paid and received	0
Tax paid or refunded	0
Capital expenditure	−150
Dividends paid to shareholders	0
Raising or repaying long-term finance	250
Incr / decr in cash *(since previous balance sheet or, in this case, since start of company)*	−5
* *Cash flow from operating activities made up as follows:*	
Cash received from customers	159
Cash paid to suppliers of goods and services	−122
Cash paid to employees *(incl. manufacturing wages and selling and admin salaries)*	−142
	−105

RELATING CASH FLOW TO PROFIT

We have discussed the fact that, in all except purely cash businesses, cash and profit are different things. Nevertheless, they both concern the same business activities. It should therefore be possible to draw up a statement that relates the two. Table 11.10 is such a statement.

TABLE 11.10 *Example 11.1, Part 4 – Relating cash flow to profit*

	Ref	Total £000
Operating profit		39
Depreciation charges (add) *(an expense not represented by a cash payment)*		2
Increase in stocks (deduct) *(items not yet charged against profit as 'cost of sales' but for which cash paid or payable – see (b))*	a	−120
Increase in trade debtors and prepayments (deduct) *(sales for which cash not yet received, and cash paid, for which services not yet received)*		−66
Increase in trade creditors (add) *(that part of (a) not yet paid in cash)*	b	40
Net cash flow from operating activities		−105

Note: This form of analysis of 'net cash flow from operating activities' may be used instead of the one shown in the cash flow statement in Table 11.9.

Note that this table is simply another way of arriving at the 'net cash flow from operating activities'. This approach is often adopted rather than the one shown in Table 11.9. This is because all the data can be obtained by reference to the profit and loss account and balance sheet. With the first method this may not be the case. Brief explanations of each item follow.

Depreciation charges

These are expenses deducted in arriving at profit but not represented by cash payments.

Increase in stocks

These are items for which cash has been or will be paid (see 'increase in trade creditors' below), but which have not yet been charged against profit as part of 'cost of sales'.

Increase in trade debtors and prepayments

These are sales for which cash has not yet been received, and cash paid, for which services have not yet been received.

Increase in trade creditors

That part of the 'increase in stocks' (above) not yet paid for in cash.

PUBLISHED ACCOUNTS

What would our results typically look like in a set of published accounts? Table 11.11 shows our balance sheet, very similar in form to the working version that we have been using, as it might appear in a company's Annual Report. The profit and loss account is more or less in the form in which we have already considered it, as would be the cash flow statement, which is not shown. Notice that the balance sheet, however, has a few presentational differences from the 'working' version that we have used thus far. The references are simply navigation aids. The main differences are:

- Current liabilities are shown as a deduction from the current assets, the net total being described as 'net current assets'. This is simply a way of facilitating the comparison of like things: short-term assets with short-term liabilities, and long-term with long-term. If, as would be expected in a manufacturing business, current assets exceed current liabilities, the excess represents the extent to which short-term assets are being financed with long-term money. This difference between current assets and current liabilities is also sometimes called 'net working capital', although strictly this term means not the net current assets themselves, but that part of the company's money being used to finance them.

- The other major difference between the two formats is that another of the five main sections of the balance sheet (the long-term liabilities) has been transplanted from the 'liabilities side' of the balance sheet and shown as a deduction from the 'assets side'. This leaves only 'shareholders' funds' remaining on the liabilities side. The reasoning behind this presentational method is that the company belongs to the shareholders and that it is therefore useful to highlight, as the bottom line, 'total shareholders' funds' (the money that belongs to them and is invested in the total net assets: the total assets less all the external liabilities).

The other presentational differences are as follows:

- Note the italicized headings representing the five main sections into which the items on a balance sheet can always be divided. These are as already described, and in summary are: fixed assets, current assets, current liabilities, long-term liabilities and shareholders' funds. However, note that the terms 'current liabilities' and 'long-term liabilities' are shown in published accounts by the more long-winded descriptions 'creditors: amounts falling due within one year' and '... after one year' respectively.

- The overdraft of £5k is now shown as what it is: a current liability, rather than as negative cash.

Notes to the accounts

In real Accounts, not all the information required by law can be given on the face of the balance sheet, profit and loss account and cash flow statement. In a typical published Annual Report there are many pages of notes that provide more detail.

Consolidated accounts

Many businesses consist not just of one company but of several companies in what is known as a group. Typically, there is one overall company, known as the 'holding company', that owns all or a majority of the shares in the others, which are known as 'subsidiaries'. If Annual Reports had to contain full accounts of all the companies in the group, the reports would in some cases run to hundreds of pages.

So, for the purpose of reporting only, groups are permitted to produce 'consolidated' or 'group' accounts. These are simply the accounts of all the individual companies in the group combined or consolidated into a single balance sheet, profit and loss account and cash flow statement. In published Annual Reports it is usually consolidated accounts that you will be looking at. This is because most public companies are groups. The principles of consolidated accounts are the same as those that we have considered in this chapter, except that 'inter-company transactions' within the group are eliminated to avoid double counting.

There are situations where one company has a significant minority shareholding and therefore exercises significant influence in another company. In this case, the other company is called an 'associate' or 'associated undertaking' of the investing company.

Different kinds of business

In this chapter we have used a manufacturing business to illustrate accounting principles. This is because it provided examples of all the main kinds of commercial transaction. The knowledge gained should enable you to understand the accounts of any company. However, the more you know about the nature and jargon of the particular business, the greater your understanding of its accounts is likely to be. The next chapter describes the financial characteristics of different kinds of business, with examples of published Accounts. Appendix 3 includes a UK-specific example of the published Accounts of a UK Local Authority, mainly to indicate their similarity to commercial Accounts.

What does it all mean?

The presentational style of balance sheets, profit and loss accounts and cash flow statements has evolved to the point where it is difficult to see how any greater clarity could be achieved. Despite that, many people

TABLE 11.11 *Example 11.1 – Typical published format of balance sheet and profit and loss account*

	Ref	Ref	Totals
			£000
Balance sheet at . . .			
Fixed assets			
Factory			90
Plant			58
		a	148
Current assets			
Stocks			120
Trade debtors			64
Prepayments			2
Cash			0
		b	186
Creditors: amounts falling due within one year			
Overdraft			5
Trade creditors			40
Other creditors			23
		c	68
Net current assets	(b − c)	d	118
Total assets less current liabilities	(a + d)	e	266
Creditors: amounts falling due after more than one year			
Loan		f	70
Total net assets	(e − f)		196
Capital and reserves			
Called up share capital			180
Profit and loss account			16
Total shareholders' funds			196
Profit and loss account for the period ended . . .			
Turnover			224
Cost of sales			142
Gross profit			82
Administrative expenses			43
Operating profit			39
Interest			4
Profit before tax			35
Tax			10
Profit after tax			25
Dividend			9
Profit retained			16

would say that these documents are static and by themselves, tell us little about the dynamics of a business.

The answer to this understandable criticism is that the dynamics are there, but that a bit of searching is necessary in order to find them. How to do this searching is the subject of the next chapter but one.

Summary

The main points covered in this chapter, linked to its objectives, have been the following:

- *The main purpose of a business is to increase the wealth of its proprietors: in a company, the shareholders. Without 'limited liability', modern business would be impossible, because all the personal assets of proprietors would be at risk.*
- *The three main sources of company finance are shareholders, lenders and profit retained in the business.*
- *A balance sheet is a snapshot of the assets and liabilities of a business at a moment in time. All business transactions affect the balance sheet. A balance sheet balances because every transaction has two sides and both sides are always recorded.*
- *A profit and loss account is a summary of all the transactions that have affected profit since the last balance sheet or, as in our example, the start of the business.*
- *A cash flow statement is a summary of all the transactions that have affected cash since the last balance sheet or the start of the business.*
- *In all but 'cash only' businesses, profit will always be different from cash flow. Some reasons are: timing differences between sales and getting paid, and between incurring expenses and paying for them; and depreciation, an accounting adjustment that affects profit but not cash flow.*

12 Different Kinds of Business and their Financial Characteristics

---

Objectives

When you have studied this chapter you should be able to:

- *summarize the main typical financial characteristics of manufacturing, buying and selling, and service businesses, especially those offering IT consultancy services;*
- *interpret published Accounts with particular reference to those characteristics;*
- *describe some of the typical items in published Accounts that are additional to the 'core' items discussed in the previous chapter.*

In this chapter we shall look at three main categories of business that have contrasting financial characteristics and requirements:

- Manufacturing businesses, which sell products that have been converted into a different form from those that they bought.
- Buying and selling businesses, whether retail or wholesale, which sell products that are, generally, unchanged from those that they bought.
- Service businesses, which usually do not sell tangible products at all.

We shall consider each kind of business in turn and examine the Accounts of a company typical of each category, gaining in the process further insights into the meaning of accounts. Since we have already spent much of the previous chapter considering manufacturing, we shall start with that.

MANUFACTURING BUSINESSES

Manufacturing businesses usually, but not necessarily, have the following financial characteristics:

- They have a requirement for fixed assets, such as buildings, plant and machinery.
- They carry substantial holdings of stocks, of three main kinds: raw materials or bought-in parts, work in progress and finished goods.

- Most or all of what they sell is sold on credit, so they usually carry substantial debtors.

- They have a long cash cycle. Cash has to be spent over possibly long design and production periods before there are products available to sell. Because products are usually sold on credit, there is a further delay before cash is finally received.

- Their current assets would usually exceed their current liabilities, subject to the relative amounts of cash and short-term borrowings. This is because their often high levels of stocks and debtors would usually exceed the amounts owed to suppliers for things bought on credit.

As a focus for discussing these characteristics in a little more detail and for exposing the work we did in the previous chapter to the cold light of reality, we shall refer to extracts from the 2004 Group Accounts of Aga Foodservice Group plc, a British manufacturing company. Aga Foodservice Group plc is a long-established producer of premium range cookers and refrigerators for the domestic, commercial and bakery markets and is a home interiors retailer. Its consumer brands include Aga, Rayburn, La Cornue, Rangemaster, Fired Earth, Divertimenti, Grange, Domain and Waterford Stanley. Its total turnover in 2004 was £435 million. I have chosen the Aga Foodservice plc Accounts for several reasons:

- The balance sheet illustrates the typical financial characteristics of a manufacturing company, outlined above.

- The balance sheet, profit and loss account and cash flow statement illustrate clearly the basic formats of these documents that we have already considered.

- All three main documents contain a sufficient number of items that did not occur in those basic examples to make them interesting and to provide material for further learning.

The balance sheet, profit and loss account and cash flow statement are reproduced, with permission, in Figures 12.1–12.3. The full 2004 Annual Report of Aga Foodservice Group plc can be found at the Company's website (www.agafoodservice.com). The Notes to the Accounts occupy more than 20 pages and are not reproduced here. However, where appropriate, information from them is provided in the following paragraphs, which are in the same sequence as the items to which they refer. We shall start with the balance sheet, shown in Figure 12.1

Balance sheets

As at 31st December

	Notes	Group 2004 £m	Group 2003 £m	Company 2004 £m	Company 2003 £m
Fixed assets					
Intangible assets	11	136.8	140.7	–	–
Tangible assets	12	76.6	73.2	–	–
Investments	13	6.5	5.8	855.9	498.7
Total fixed assets		221.9	219.7	855.9	498.7
Current assets					
Stocks	14	70.2	61.3	–	–
Debtors	15	107.2	102.7	289.5	627.7
Cash at bank and in hand	17	49.8	52.0	31.2	33.3
Total current assets		227.2	216.0	320.7	661.0
Creditors – amounts falling due within one year					
Operating creditors	16	(102.6)	(88.9)	(565.5)	(530.8)
Borrowings	17	(23.1)	(2.2)	(22.6)	(1.2)
Tax and dividends payable	16	(9.4)	(9.5)	(7.3)	(6.5)
Total amounts falling due within one year		(135.1)	(100.6)	(595.4)	(538.5)
Net current assets / (liabilities)		92.1	115.4	(274.7)	(122.5)
Total assets less current liabilities		314.0	335.1	581.2	621.2
Creditors – amounts falling due after more than one year					
Creditors	16	(0.1)	(2.2)	–	–
Borrowings	17	(1.6)	(20.2)	–	(18.6)
Provisions for liabilities and charges	19	(28.6)	(30.4)	(17.4)	(18.8)
Total net assets employed		283.7	282.3	563.8	583.8
Capital and reserves					
Called up share capital	20	31.5	32.4	31.5	32.4
Share premium account	21	60.9	59.9	60.9	59.9
Revaluation reserve	21	2.1	2.4	–	–
Capital redemption reserve	21	36.0	35.0	36.0	35.0
Profit and loss account	21	153.0	152.2	435.4	456.5
Total shareholder's funds		283.5	281.9	563.8	583.8
Equity minority interests	22	0.2	0.4	–	–
Total funds		283.7	282.3	563.8	583.8

The accounts on pages 31 to 58 were approved by the board of directors on 18th March 2005 and were signed on its behalf by:

W B McGrath   Chief Executive

S M Smith   Finance Director

Notes to the accounts are on pages 36 to 58.

FIGURE 12.1 *Aga Foodservice Group plc – Balance Sheets as at 31 December 2004*

Balance Sheet

As explained at the end of the last chapter, most public companies are 'groups' consisting of a holding company and one or more subsidiaries. In published Accounts it is usually 'consolidated' or 'group' Accounts that you will be looking at, as in the two left-hand columns of the Aga Foodservice balance sheet. For our purposes we shall ignore the 'Company' balance sheet on the right, except to note that it is the balance sheet of the holding company, which usually does no trading, and it is a legal requirement that it be shown. The Group balance sheet shows clearly the five main sections of any balance sheet, namely:

- fixed assets
- current assets
- current liabilities ('creditors – amounts falling due within one year')
- long-term liabilities ('creditors – amounts falling due after more than one year')
- capital and reserves or 'total shareholders' funds'.

Whenever you look at a new balance sheet, think of these headings as landmarks to help you find your way in unfamiliar territory.

Intangible assets

Note 11, not reproduced here, tells us that of the intangible assets of £136.8 million, all but about £3 million consists of 'goodwill'. This term is used to describe the amount by which the price paid for a business exceeds the market value of the other assets less liabilities acquired. It therefore only arises where a company has taken over one or more other businesses. By way of illustration, think about your local corner shop. Let us assume that it has been there for many years, that it has a good reputation and that its loyal customers travel some distance to it because they appreciate the personal service that it has always provided. If you wanted to buy the shop as a going concern, then you would, I think, expect the purchase price to be more than just the total of the values of the shop and its stock less any bills outstanding. You would expect to have to pay something extra for its loyal customer base and its reputation, built up over many years. That 'something extra' is what would be called the goodwill of the business. Once you have bought the business, then the goodwill purchased will be an asset on your balance sheet, together with the other assets acquired.

Goodwill may be an intangible asset, but it is an asset nevertheless, and like most other assets it depreciates over time. Five or ten years from now, the reputation of the shop is going to be largely down to you, for better or worse. Your predecessor will be forgotten. Like other fixed assets, the depreciation of goodwill has to be recorded over its expected useful life. If you were buying, not the corner shop, but a large company, then, in addition to the customer base and the reputation, you might also be buying such valuable intangible assets as brands, trademarks and patents, a loyal and trained labour force and intellectual property.

Tangible fixed assets

As you might expect, Aga Foodservice Group's tangible fixed assets (Note 12) consist almost entirely of land and buildings, and plant, machinery and equipment, in roughly equal quantities.

Investments

These represent the interest of the company in an 'associated under-taking'. As described in the previous chapter, an associated undertaking is another company in which a company has a substantial minority share holding and therefore exercises significant influence. Because the invest-ing company does not have a controlling interest and the other company is therefore not a subsidiary, different accounting rules apply, the details of which need not concern us here.

Stocks

Note 14 tells us that the total stocks of £70.2 million comprise the following:

- raw materials and consumables £16.6 million
- work in progress £10.0 million, and
- finished goods and goods for resale £43.6 million.

'Consumables' are things such as tools and spare parts. You will recall that stocks, far from earning money for a business, cost money until they are sold or are transformed into goods that are sold. Therefore, raw materials and finished goods are held in the minimum quantities necessary to ensure that production is not held up for want of materials, and sales are not lost for want of finished products.

Debtors

Aga Foodservice plc has substantial debtors, because it sells on credit. Of the total debtors of £107.2 million, £65.3 million represents trade debtors.

Creditors – amounts falling due within one year

Of the total 'operating creditors' of £102.6 million, £64 million represents trade creditors. Although the similarity of the numbers is coincidental, comparison with the previous paragraph highlights how free credit helps to oil the wheels of industry and commerce. Because we obtain free credit from our suppliers, we in turn can afford to extend free credit to our customers.

Net current assets

Notice that, as would normally be expected of a manufacturing company, Aga Foodservice plc did indeed have current assets substantially in excess of its current liabilities, both in 2004 and 2003. They would be said to have 'positive net working capital'.

Provisions for liabilities and charges

A provision is an amount set aside for a known liability the amount of which cannot be determined with substantial accuracy. A typical 'provision' in many companies would be for bad debts. They know from experience that on average a proportion of their customers will not pay, but they cannot know precisely what proportion. Aga Foodservice's provisions include, for example, product warranties, deferred tax liabilities and possible costs associated with divested businesses.

Capital and reserves

These represent money that belongs to the shareholders. 'Capital' in this context means the nominal or face value of the shares multiplied by the number of shares issued and for which payment has been demanded ('called up'). 'Reserve' means all the money that belongs to the shareholders over and above their share capital. For example, 'profit and loss account' means the reserve representing the total of accumulated retained profit, which, generally speaking, is the only reserve out of which dividends can be paid.

Share premium account

Usually the nominal or face value of a company's shares does not change. However, the price at which a successful company's shares trade on a stock exchange will tend to increase over time. As new shares are issued in order to finance expansion, those who buy them would obviously expect to pay close to the market price of the shares at the time. The difference between the nominal value and the issue price is called the 'share premium'. The 'share premium account' is a reserve representing the accumulated sum of share premiums.

Revaluation reserve

It is permitted, but not mandatory, for a company to revalue assets, such as land, the value of which may have increased substantially since it was acquired. Remembering that all transactions are two-sided, the revaluation reserve is the other side of such a transaction. If the asset subsequently falls in value, then the reduction would be set against the revaluation reserve.

Capital redemption reserve

This is a technicality, included here for the sake of completeness but which can safely be skipped if you wish. 'Preference shares' are shares in a company that entitle the holder to a fixed rate of interest rather than a variable dividend, but usually carry no voting rights. When preference shares are 'redeemed' or cancelled, their face value is paid back to their holders. However, in order to replenish the capital redeemed (paid out), an amount equivalent to the nominal value of the shares redeemed must be transferred from the 'profit and loss account' reserve to a 'capital redemption reserve', which is not available for the payment of dividends. It follows that in the past Aga Foodservice Group has redeemed preference shares.

Total shareholders' funds

This is the proportion of the total money invested in the company that belongs to the group's ordinary or equity shareholders.

Equity minority interests

This is the proportion of the total money invested in the company that belongs to shareholders outside the group.

Profit and loss account

As explained earlier, in published Accounts it is usually group or consolidated Accounts that you will be looking at. Unlike the balance sheet, there is no requirement to show a profit and loss account for the holding company, not least because holding companies do not usually do any trading. The profit and loss account for a period shows, in summarized form, all those things that have contributed to the profit, or loss, made during the period since the last balance sheet was published or, as with our earlier example, since the business started.

As with the balance sheet, the group profit and loss account of Aga Foodservice Group (Figure 12.2) shows clearly most of the landmark items that we became familiar with in that earlier example. Whenever you look at a new profit and loss account, noting these landmarks will help you find your way around. There is one landmark, however, that is often not shown in published profit and loss accounts (although it is usually shown in a note), and that is gross profit.

Continuing operations

One of the main objectives of the rules governing published Accounts is comparability between the Accounts of different years. It follows that, where a company has acquired or divested itself of one or more businesses the results of the 'continuing' part of the business should be clearly discernible. That is why, all the way down to 'Profit before interest and tax', items relating to acquisitions and discontinued operations are shown separately.

Group profit and loss account

For the year ended 31st December

Turnover	Notes	2004 £m	2003 £m
Continuing operations		427.9	
Acquisitions		7.1	
Total continuing operations		435.0	390.3
Discontinued operations		–	2.1
Total turnover	2 & 3	**435.0**	392.4
Operating profit			
Continuing operating profit before goodwill amortisation		37.5	33.7
Goodwill amortisation		(8.0)	(8.0)
		29.5	25.7
Continuing operations		29.5	25.7
Acquisitions	3	–	–
Total continuing operations		29.5	25.7
Discontinued operations	3	–	(0.5)
Group operating profit	2 & 3	**29.5**	25.2
Share of profit from associate		0.5	–
Total operating profit		**30.0**	25.2
Disposal of businesses	23	–	1.8
Profit before interest and tax		**30.0**	27.0
Net interest receivable	6	0.6	0.9
Profit on ordinary activities before tax		**30.6**	27.9
Tax on profit on ordinary activities	7	(7.1)	(5.6)
Profit on ordinary activities after tax		**23.5**	22.3
Equity minority interests	22	(0.1)	(0.1)
Profit attributable to shareholders		23.4	22.2
Dividends	9	(10.4)	(9.3)
Profit retained	21	**13.0**	12.9
Earnings per share	10	p	p
Basic		18.4	17.2
Diluted		18.3	17.1
Basic - before goodwill amortisation		24.7	23.3

Notes to the accounts are on pages 36 to 58.

FIGURE 12.2 *Aga Foodservice Group plc – Group profit and loss account for the year ended 31 December 2004*

Operating profit

Remember that, precisely because it excludes financial charges, operating profit allows comparison between different businesses at the operational level, regardless of how they are financed. It is also an important number when broken down to the departmental level of a business. Usually only the non-financial expenses of a business are charged out or allocated to departments, such as an IT department. The principle is that departmental managers should only be charged with expenses that they are capable of influencing. Matters such as tax, and the extent to which a company borrows money, are not the responsibility of non-financial departmental managers.

Goodwill amortization

In the above discussion of goodwill it was noted that it depreciates like most other assets. Note 11 in the published Accounts (not reproduced here) states that it is Aga Foodservice Group's policy to depreciate goodwill over 20 years. You no doubt recall that the word amortization is used to describe the depreciation of intangible assets.

Share of profit from associate

This is the part of the operating profit of the associate company attributable to Aga Foodservice Group.

Equity minority interests

Just as it is necessary in the balance sheet to identify the proportion of the total money invested in the company that belongs to shareholders outside the group, so is it equally important in the profit and loss account to show how much of the profit after tax is attributable to them.

Dividends

As already mentioned, dividends are not compulsory, but most established companies pay a dividend. The amount is typically between 25 and 50 per cent of the profit after tax.

Profit retained

Retained profit is what is left after any dividend has been taken into account. As a business grows, so does the amount of money that it needs to finance that growth. The best source of additional money, at least for steady year-by-year expansion as distinct from discontinuities such as takeovers or mergers, is that which has been generated internally, namely retained profit. In deciding upon the amount of dividend, a balance has to be struck between satisfying the expectations of the shareholders and retaining enough of the money represented by profit for expansion.

Basic earnings per share

As already mentioned, because the number of shares in issue by a company varies from time to time, an additional view of the company's performance, over and above the absolute number representing profit is given by 'earnings per share'. This is the profit after tax and minority interest attributable to ordinary shareholders (for Aga Foodservice Group, £23.4 million) divided by the weighted average number of shares in circulation during the year.

Diluted earnings per share

In addition to shares actually in circulation during the year, there may be additional shares that could have been issued if certain events had taken place or if certain rights had been exercised. For example, a company may grant employees options to buy its shares, usually at a price less than the market price. At the accounting date, the company will calculate how many shares would be in circulation had all employees exercised their options to the fullest extent. Obviously, the greater the number of shares in circulation, the less the earnings per share. One could say that the earnings per share would have been diluted to a smaller number had these additional shares actually been issued, hence the term 'diluted earnings per share'.

Basic earnings per share before goodwill amortization

The amortization of goodwill is the consequence of acquiring another business. It is not, like the depreciation of plant and machinery, a direct consequence of normal business activity. So companies will often, as here, seek to emphasize the effect of normal business activity.

Supplementary statements

Not reproduced here, but following any published profit and loss account there is always a supplementary statement in several parts that 'reconciles' the 'profit retained' in the profit and loss account with 'total shareholders' funds' in the balance sheet. 'Reconciliation' when used by an accountant simply means how you get from one number to another.

Cash flow statement

The first part of the Aga Foodservice Group's cash flow statement (Figure 12.3) is very similar to our simple example shown in Table 11.9, although different words are used to describe the main items. The only additional item, which is self-explanatory, is 'acquisitions and disposals'.

The second part of the statement is called 'Reconciliation of net cash flow to movement in net cash'. This particular reconciliation describes how we get from the 'decrease in cash in the year' (£2 million) to the 'closing net cash' (£25.1 million), which, as detailed in Note 17 in the

Group cash flow statement

For the year ended 31st December

	Notes	2004 £m	2004 £m	2003 £m	2003 £m
Net cash inflow from operating activities			32.9		23.9
Returns on investments and servicing of finance			0.6		0.9
Tax paid			(5.5)		(5.2)
Capital expenditure and product development			(9.6)		(20.5)
Acquisitions and disposals	23		(4.6)		(16.1)
Equity dividends paid			(9.6)		(8.1)
Net cash inflow / (outflow) before financing			4.2		(25.1)
Financing					
- issue of ordinary share capital	24	1.1		0.1	
- loan to associated undertaking	24	(0.3)		–	
- purchase of own shares	24	(9.4)		–	
- increase / (decrease) in debt	24	2.4		(1.7)	
Net financing outflow			(6.2)		(1.6)
Decrease in cash in the year	25		(2.0)		(26.7)
Reconciliation of net cash flow to movement in net cash					
Decrease in cash in the year	25	(2.0)		(26.7)	
(increase) / decrease in debt	24	(2.4)		1.7	
Change in net cash resulting from cash flows	25		(4.4)		(25.0)
Borrowings acquired with acquisitions			–		(0.4)
Exchange adjustments	25		(0.1)		(0.5)
Decrease in net cash			(4.5)		(25.9)
Opening net cash			29.6		55.5
Closing net cash			25.1		29.6

This statement should be read in conjunction with the reconciliations on page 35.

Notes to the accounts are on pages 36 to 58.

FIGURE 12.3 *Aga Foodservice Group plc – Group cash flow statement for the year ended 31 December 2004*

published Accounts (not reproduced here), is the net of the balance sheet items 'cash at bank and in hand' (£49.8 million) and the total of short-term and long-term borrowings (£24.7 million).

That completes our review of the financial characteristics of manufacturing companies in the context of the 2004 published Accounts of Aga Foodservice Group plc.

BUYING AND SELLING BUSINESSES

Buying and selling businesses include wholesalers, department stores, supermarkets and small shops. This section concentrates on supermarkets, which usually, but not necessarily, have the following financial characteristics:

- They have a requirement for fixed assets, such as buildings, fixtures and delivery vehicles.
- They carry substantial stocks of goods for resale, both in stores and depots.
- They typically sell for cash and so usually carry negligible debtors.
- They have a very short, or even 'negative' cash cycle. Because they buy on credit and sell for cash, in respect particularly of food products having a short shelf life, they may receive the cash for sales before they have to pay cash for purchases.
- Due to the combined effects of the previous two points, their current liabilities often exceed their current assets. To the extent that this is so, supermarkets are generally in the happy position of, in effect, having their fixed assets financed to some extent by free credit from the company's suppliers.

As a focus for illustrating these characteristics we shall refer to the balance sheet from the 2005 Group Accounts of Tesco plc, the British supermarket chain. The principal activity of the Group, as stated in its 2005 Annual Report, is the operation of food stores and associated activities in the UK, Republic of Ireland, Hungary, Poland, Czech Republic, Slovakia, Turkey, Thailand, South Korea, Taiwan, Malaysia and Japan. During the year, the Group entered into a Joint Venture in China. Its turnover in its 2005 financial year was £33,974 million.

One profit and loss account is much like another. Cash flow statements are also pretty similar. Of the three main accounting documents, it is the balance sheet that reveals the distinctive characteristics of the industry in which a company operates, so for our remaining two examples of published Accounts we shall confine ourselves to balance sheets. The balance sheet of Tesco plc, like that of Aga Foodservice Group plc, illustrates well the financial characteristics of its industry, the supermarket industry, and our examination of it will be mostly confined to those aspects, plus any other items of interest that have not already been covered. It is reproduced, with permission, in Figure 12.4. The full 2005 Annual Report of Tesco plc can be found on the Company's website (www.tescocorporate.com/investor_centre).

Balance sheets   26 February 2005

	note	£m	2005 £m	£m	Group 2004 restated £m	Company 2005 £m	Company 2004 £m
Fixed assets							
Intangible assets	12		1,044		965	–	–
Tangible assets	13		15,495		14,094	–	–
Investments	14		7		6	9,421	9,077
Investments in joint ventures	14						
Share of gross assets		4,280		2,006		–	–
Less: Share of gross liabilities		(4,037)		(1,712)		–	–
Goodwill		145		15		–	–
			388		309	145	143
Investments in associates	14		19		21	–	–
			16,953		15,395	9,566	9,220
Current assets							
Stocks	15		1,309		1,199	–	–
Debtors	16		1,002		826	2,702	1,624
Investments	17		346		430	150	99
Cash at bank and in hand			800		670	–	–
			3,457		3,125	2,852	1,723
Creditors:							
falling due within one year	18		(6,072)		(5,516)	(3,152)	(2,456)
Net current liabilities			(2,615)		(2,391)	(300)	(733)
Total assets less current liabilities			14,338		13,004	9,266	8,487
Creditors:							
falling due after more than one year	19		(4,531)		(4,368)	(4,037)	(3,950)
Provisions for liabilities and charges	22		(750)		(593)	–	–
Net assets			9,057		8,043	5,229	4,537
Capital and reserves							
Called up share capital	24		389		384	389	384
Share premium account	25		3,704		3,470	3,704	3,470
Other reserves	25		40		40	–	–
Profit and loss account	25		4,873		4,104	1,136	683
Equity shareholders' funds			9,006		7,998	5,229	4,537
Minority interests			51		45	–	–
Total capital employed			9,057		8,043	5,229	4,537

Accounting policies and notes forming part of these financial statements are on pages 38 to 63.

Terry Leahy
Andrew Higginson
Directors
Financial statements approved by the Board 11 April 2005.

FIGURE 12.4 *Tesco plc – Balance sheets as at 26 February 2005*

Balance Sheet

Intangible assets

From Note 12 , this is all goodwill, except for £2 million.

Tangible assets

Of these, £13,175 million represents land and buildings, the remaining £2,320 being plant, equipment, fixtures and fittings, and motor vehicles.

Joint ventures

A joint venture is defined as an undertaking by which its participants expect to achieve some common purpose or benefit, controlled jointly by two or more parties or 'venturers'.

Stocks

These are all goods for resale, except for £3 million representing development property (land awaiting development).

Debtors

None of these are described as trade debtors.

Investments (short-term)

These are 'money market deposits', which are short-term deposits of temporarily surplus cash.

Creditors – falling due within one year

£2,819 million of these represent trade creditors.

Net current liabilities

Notice that, as would normally be expected of a supermarket company, Tesco plc did indeed have current liabilities substantially in excess of its current assets, both in 2005 and 2004. They would be said to have 'negative net working capital'.

The remainder of the balance sheet consists of items similar to those already covered earlier and do not call for particular comment. That completes our brief review of the financial characteristics of supermarket companies in the context of the 2005 published Accounts of Tesco plc.

Other buying and selling businesses (wholesalers in general, and some kinds of retailer, for example department stores) sell wholly or partly on credit, the obvious result being that they carry debtors. This, together with the fact that they would typically turn their stocks over rather less rapidly than supermarkets, would mean a greater likelihood of current assets exceeding current liabilities.

IT SERVICES

Businesses providing 'know-how', such as IT consultancies, usually have the following financial characteristics:

- Their requirements for fixed assets is often limited primarily to IT and communications equipment, and premises.

- They carry negligible tangible stocks.

- Their services are sold on credit, but in the case of long contracts their clients may be required to make stage payments, some of them in advance, so that they may have substantial amounts of both accrued revenue (work done but not yet invoiced) and deferred revenue (work paid for but not yet done).

As a focus for illustrating these characteristics we shall refer to the balance sheet from the 2004 Group Accounts of LogicaCMG plc, the consultancy company. As stated in its 2004 Annual Report, LogicaCMG plc is a major international force in IT services and wireless telecoms. It provides management and IT consultancy, systems integration and outsourcing services to clients across diverse markets including telecoms, financial services, energy and utilities, industry, distribution and transport and the public sector. Its turnover in 2004 was £1,669 million.

The balance sheet of LogicaCMG plc, like the others that we have looked at, illustrates well the financial characteristics of its sector. Our examination of it will be mostly confined to those aspects, plus any other items of interest that have not already been covered. It is reproduced, with permission, in Figure 12.5. The full 2004 Annual Report of LogicaCMG plc can be found on the Company's website at www.logicacmg.com (search for 'annual report'). The following paragraphs should be read with reference to the LogicaCMG plc balance sheet. They are in the same sequence as the items to which they refer.

Balance sheet

Intangible assets

The Notes to the Accounts tell us that this consists entirely of goodwill.

Tangible assets

These comprise land and buildings £32.1 million, and equipment and plant £46.9 million. No doubt much of the latter would be computer and communications equipment.

Stocks

Negligible.

Consolidated balance sheet

31 December 2004

	Note	2004 £'m	2004 £'m	Restated 2003 £'m	Restated 2003 £'m
Fixed assets					
Intangible assets	12		333.5		358.6
Tangible assets	13		79.0		84.1
Share of net assets of joint venture			–		1.1
Trade investments			–		0.5
			412.5		444.3
Current assets					
Stock		1.2		3.3	
Debtors	15	640.5		604.8	
Investments – liquid resources		1.8		2.3	
Cash at bank and in hand		104.8		132.4	
		748.3		742.8	
Creditors – amounts falling due within one year					
Borrowings	16	(25.3)		(1.2)	
Other creditors	17	(405.9)		(426.6)	
		(431.2)		(427.8)	
Net current assets			317.1		315.0
Total assets less current liabilities			729.6		759.3
Creditors – amounts falling due after more than one year					
Convertible debt	16	(211.2)		(208.6)	
Other borrowings	16	(64.6)		(102.3)	
			(275.8)		(310.9)
Provisions for liabilities and charges					
Deferred tax	8		(41.7)		(6.5)
Other	18		(24.4)		(20.1)
Net assets			387.7		(421.8)
Capital and reserves					
Called-up equity share capital	19		75.1		75.0
Share premium account	20		707.3		705.9
Other reserves	20		4.0		2.5
Profit and loss account	20		(399.8)		(364.1)
Merger reserve	20		(1.3)		(1.3)
Shareholders' funds	21		385.3		418.0
Equity minority interests			2.4		3.8
Total capital employed			387.7		421.8

FIGURE 12.5 *LogicaCMG plc – Consolidated balance sheet as at 31 December 2004*

Debtors

Of these, £269.5 million are trade debtors, which you will recall represent work that has been invoiced to clients but not yet paid for. Within 'debtors', prepayments and accrued income are grouped together at £119.6 million. Also included is 'amounts recoverable on contracts' £175.8 million. This concerns long-term contracts and represents the excess of the value of work carried out to date over cumulative payments on account received. It, too, therefore represents accrued income, but with specific reference to long-term contracts that extend beyond the current year. A summary of UK long-term contract accounting rules is provided in Appendix 5.

Creditors – amounts falling due within one year

These include trade creditors £75.1 million and 'payment received on account on contracts' £54.3 million. This represents the obligation to do work that has been paid for, sometimes described as 'deferred revenue' or 'deferred income'.

Net current assets

As previously discussed, whether current assets exceed current liabilities or vice versa depends on the mix of stock, trade debtors and trade and other creditors. It also depends on the relative amounts of cash and short-term borrowings. Reference to the Notes is always necessary.

That completes our review of the financial characteristics of IT service companies in the context of the 2004 published Accounts of LogicaCMG plc.

The purpose of this chapter has been to show how the characteristics of very different businesses are represented in their published Accounts using the fundamental principles that we have considered hitherto. If you have given some study to the exposition of those principles, then, with a little understanding of the nature of the particular business and with reference to the Notes to the Accounts, you should be able to understand much of what any set of published Accounts is telling you, with a few possible exceptions. Some businesses, for example banks and insurance businesses, are so specialized that anyone uninitiated in the particular business and its jargon would be able to understand rather less of their Accounts than those of other companies. We shall not consider them here; nevertheless, the principles on which they are based remain the same.

THE PUBLIC SECTOR

All the examples of published Accounts reproduced in this chapter have been taken from the commercial world and the principles that they illustrate are applicable in most countries. In the UK, since 1998, public sector accounting principles are now in most respects the same as those applicable to business and commerce. For those interested in the public sector, Appendix 3 contains, as an example and with permission, extracts from the published Accounts of a UK Local Authority, Hampshire County Council.

Summary

The main points of this chapter, linked to its objectives, have been:

- *We have summarized the typical financial characteristics of manufacturing, buying and selling, and service businesses, especially those offering IT consultancy services.*
- *We have examined the published Accounts of three major UK companies with particular reference to those characteristics.*
- *By reference to those Accounts we have encountered some of the typical items in published Accounts that are additional to the 'core' items discussed in the previous chapter.*

13 Finance Fundamentals: Pulling it Apart

Objectives

When you have studied this chapter you should be able to:
- *explain the limitations on the amount of useful information about a business or other organization that can be conveyed by a single set of accounts in isolation;*
- *describe some of the most commonly used financial ratios;*
- *list the various contexts that give them meaning;*
- *explain what is meant by 'shareholder value added' (SVA) as applied to a company as a whole.*

FINANCIAL ANALYSIS

At the end of Chapter 11 I suggested that balance sheets and profit and loss accounts are a bit dull. Heresy for a finance person, you might think. In this chapter we shall see how financial ratios can bring accounts to life and reveal some of the dynamics of a business. Again I have adopted a minimalist approach in note form.

One important caution is necessary before we start. Accounts can be misleading, ratios can be misleading. Even trends, at least short-term trends, can be misleading. It is necessary always to think of as many reasons as possible why a particular number, a particular ratio or a particular trend might be as it is.

For example, it costs money to hold stocks. Therefore, it is usually the case that the smaller the amount of stocks for a given quantity of production or sales, the better. However, the accounting year-end of a seasonal business, such as a toy manufacturer, might happen to coincide with its slack period. This might be precisely the time at which the business has to stock up, ready for its busy period. In this case, high stock might be evidence of prudent preparation for peak business, not as evidence of poor stock control.

Ratios in everyday life

Ratios are simply relationships between numbers. We use them in everyday life and have come to recognize those that are useful for our purposes. Speed is one. Gradient is another (height gained or lost relative to horizontal distance) and it can be expressed in different ways. A steep hill can be described as 'one in four' or '1 : 4' or '25%'.

Business people also recognize that the relationships between some numbers in balance sheets and profit and loss accounts are useful. In various contexts, listed below, they can reveal how the business is doing. For example, 'gross margin' is the relationship of gross profit to sales. It too can be expressed in different ways. If turnover is 100, and gross profit is 25, then gross margin could be expressed as '1 : 4' or '25%' or '0.25'.

There is no universal agreement on which financial ratios are useful. Neither is there any universal agreement on the names or even the components of some of them. For example, one person's 'gearing ratio' might be another's 'borrowing ratio'. In this chapter I have included a selection of the ratios that would probably appear on most people's 'useful' list. I have also tried to follow what I believe to be the majority taste in terms of their names and components.

Whenever you see a financial ratio being referred to, find out what numbers comprise it and, if one ratio is being compared with another, for example this year against last year, make sure that like is being compared with like.

Contexts

As with, for example, crime figures and interest rates, so a single ratio is virtually meaningless. Ratios only come to life in a context, where they can provide comparisons or reveal trends. For example, two companies in the same industry might both show a gross margin this year of 30 per cent. However, for one company this might be part of a declining trend; for the other, part of an improving trend. The ratio itself would tell a potential investor very little about either company; the trend would provide valuable information. Useful contexts include the following:

- previous years;
- earlier forecasts;
- industry norms;
- competitors.

Even in context, the need to use judgement in interpreting ratios is worth reiterating.

Interested parties

Who is interested in business results and ratios? They may be:

- shareholders, actual or potential;

- lenders, actual or potential;
- managers and employees;
- suppliers and customers;
- salespeople (concerning a customer or prospect);
- auditors, tax authorities, financial analysts and stockbrokers.

Categories of ratio

It is sometimes convenient to group commonly used ratios together into categories. As with the ratios themselves there is no rule and some ratios really belong in more than one category. Categories often used, and that we shall use, are as follows:

- profitability;
- activity, also sometimes called 'capital productivity';
- liquidity;
- gearing;
- stockmarket;
- others.

We shall work through these categories in the sequence given above.

In what follows, the word 'turnover' is restricted to the second of its two meanings given in the glossary; namely, the rate at which assets, or particular classes of asset, are used in the process of achieving sales. Its other meaning (as a synonym for the revenue from sales) is rendered by, simply, 'sales'. The reason is to avoid confusion between the two related meanings.

Some people suggest rule-of-thumb 'right' values for some ratios. However, these can be misleading and, in any case, can vary greatly from industry to industry. They are not shown here, with one exception: the 'quick ratio'.

EXAMPLE 13.1: A SAMPLE COMPANY

As with the business transactions that we considered in Chapter 11, it will be helpful to use a contrived example for the financial ratios that we are considering in this one. There are two particular advantages to be had from adopting this approach. First, we can choose to concentrate on the core items of any balance sheet and profit and loss account, thus avoiding unnecessary complications and allowing us to see more clearly the principles involved. A second advantage is that we can choose numbers that are easy to work with. The business whose fortunes we followed in Chapter 11 has so far, you may recall, only existed for four months. In considering ratios it would be more helpful to use a well-established business as an example. The accounts of such a business are set out in

Table 13.1. They are in the now familiar format and have numbers that are easy to work with.

TABLE 13.1 *Example company – Balance sheet and profit and loss account*

	This yr	Last yr
	£m	£m
Balance sheet at . . .		
Fixed assets		
Factory	20	20
Plant	7	5
	27	25
Current assets		
Stocks	15	18
Trade debtors	10	9
Prepayments	0	0
Cash	3	4
	28	31
Creditors: amounts falling due within one year		
Overdraft	0	0
Trade creditors	12	11
Other creditors	3	4
	15	15
Net current assets	13	16
Total assets less current liabilities	40	41
Creditors: amounts falling due after more than one year		
Loan	15	18
Total net assets	25	23
Capital and reserves		
Called up share capital	20	20
Profit and loss account *(£3m from earlier years, plus £2m from this year)*	5	3
Total shareholders' funds	25	23
Profit and loss account for the period ended . . .		
Turnover	60	58
Cost of sales	48	45
Gross profit	12	13
Administrative expenses	7	7
Operating profit	5	6
Interest	1	1
Profit before tax	4	5
Tax	1	1
Profit after tax	3	4
Dividend	1	1
Profit retained	2	3
Earnings per share (pence)	15	20

The only item that we have not already considered is the one at the bottom of the profit and loss account called 'earnings per share'. This is simply the profit after tax divided by the number of shares in circulation. Suppose that the company has issued 20 million shares of £1 each (rather than, say, 40 million shares of 50 pence each). Profit after tax is the amount by which the book value of shareholders' funds has increased during the year covered by the accounts. It varies from year to year. In most companies, the number of shares in circulation will also vary from year to year. This ratio provides a common measure: the amount of profit after tax attributable to each share.

Table 13.2 shows, as an addendum to the accounts, all the ratios that we shall be considering in the remainder of this chapter, cross-referenced to the items that comprise them. The two last items, dividend per share and assumed share price, do not form part of a published profit and loss account. They are memorandum items used in working out some of the financial ratios. You may wish to refer to Table 13.2 throughout this chapter. In what follows, each paragraph about a particular ratio consists of the following parts:

- the name of the ratio;
- its usual components;
- its meaning (the information conveyed by it);
- the relevant extract from Table 13.2 (this year's result, followed by last year's in brackets);
- brief comments.

Two years' results could hardly be called a trend. However, in referring to the ratios in Table 13.2 I shall use the word as a convenient shorthand when commenting on the results. Where I suggest that further analysis would need to be done, I am usually referring to analysis that could only be done by people within the company, using the detailed information to which only they would have access.

PROFITABILITY RATIOS

These represent different ways of showing how profitable a business is, by which I mean how much profit it has made relative either to sales or to the financial resources used in the business. The ratios in this category that we shall consider are:

- gross margin;
- operating margin;
- return on capital employed;
- return on equity.

TABLE 13.2 *Example company – Summary of some commonly used financial ratios*

	Ref	This yr	Last yr		Ref	This yr	Last yr
		£m	£m			£m	£m
Balance sheet at . . .				**Financial ratios**			
Fixed assets				*Profitability*			
Factory		20	20	Gross margin	*k/j* %	20.0	22.4
Plant		7	5	Operating margin	*m/j* %	8.3	10.3
		27	25	Return on capital	*m/(h+f)* %	12.5	14.6
				Return on equity	*p/h* %	12.0	17.4
Current assets							
Stocks	*a*	15	18				
Trade debtors	*b*	10	9	*Activity*			
Prepayments		0	0	Capital productivity	*j/(h+f)*	1.5	1.4
Cash		3	4	Stock turnover	*j/a*	4.0	3.2
	c	28	31	Debtor days	365(*b/j*)	61	57
Creditors: falling due within one year							
Overdraft	*d*	0	0	*Liquidity*			
Trade creditors		12	11	Current ratio	*c/e*	1.9	2.1
Other creditors		3	4	Quick ratio	(*c−a*)/*e*	0.9	0.9
	e	15	15				
Net current assets		13	16	*Gearing*			
Total assets less current liabilities		40	41	Debt/equity	(*f+d*)/*h* %	60	78.3
				Interest cover	*m/n*	5	6
Creditors: falling due after > one year							
Loan	*f*	15	18	*Stock market*			
Total net assets		25	23	Dividend yield	*s/t* %	2.5	1.7
				Price/earnings	*t/r*	13.3	15.0
Capital and reserves							
Called up share capital	*g*	20	20				
Profit and loss account		5	3				
Total shareholders' funds	*h*	25	23				

	Ref	This yr	Last yr	
Profit and loss account for the year ended . . .				**Note**
Turnover	*j*	60	58	Remember that there is no universal agreement
Cost of sales		48	45	on the names of ratios; on whether they are
Gross profit	*k*	12	13	expressed as ratios, percentages or ordinary
Administrative expenses		7	7	numbers; or, in some cases, on their precise
Operating profit	*m*	5	6	components.
Interest	*n*	1	1	
Profit before tax		4	5	
Tax		1	1	
Profit after tax	*p*	3	4	
Dividend	*q*	1	1	
Profit retained		2	3	

	Ref	This yr	Last yr	
Earnings per share (*p/g*)	*r*	15	20	pence
Dividend per share (*q/g*)	*s*	5	5	*pence*
Assumed share price	*t*	200	300	*pence*

Gross margin

Ratio: Gross profit : sales
Meaning: Shows what percentage of sales is left after all the costs
                of getting a product or service to a saleable state have
                been deducted. The higher the better.
Table 13.2:   20% (22.4%)

Trend bad. Further analysis would be needed to show to what extent this is
due to lower sales volumes, lower selling prices or higher cost of sales.
Comparisons with competitors and industry averages would provide
further insights, a comment that is applicable to all the ratios that we shall
discuss.

Operating margin

Ratio: Operating profit : sales
Meaning: Shows what percentage of sales is left after deducting
                all the costs including the expenses of selling and
                delivering to the customer, and administering the
                business, but excluding the 'financial costs' (interest,
                tax and dividend). The higher the better.
Table 13.2:   8.3% (10.3%)

Trend bad. Because operating profit is arrived at before deducting the
'financial' charges (interest, tax and dividends) this ratio is useful for
comparison with other companies, whose businesses may be similar, but
which may be financed in different ways. This is one of the two ratios
often called 'secondary ratios'. The other is 'capital productivity' (see
below).

Return on capital employed (ROCE)

Ratio: Operating profit : capital employed (usually equity plus
                long-term debt)
Meaning: Shows the percentage 'return' made from using the
                long-term money employed in the business. It allows
                comparison with other possible uses of that money.
                The higher the better.
Table 13.2:   12.5% (14.6%)

Trend bad. Sometimes called the 'primary ratio', this ratio is closely related
to two other ratios (operating margin and capital productivity), which are
sometimes therefore called the 'secondary ratios'. The precise relationship
we shall consider shortly.

Would it not be more accurate to use as the figure for capital employed
the average during the year rather than, as I have done, the capital

employed at the end of the year? The answer is 'yes, it would'. However, in practice many people do not do so. This is for two reasons:

- It is quicker and simpler to use all numbers from a single year.
- Trends and comparisons are what ratios should be used for. Revealed trends are likely to be the much same whichever method is used, provided it is used consistently.

Similar remarks apply to other balance sheet numbers used in the following examples.

Return on equity

Ratio:	Profit after tax : shareholders' funds (equity)
Meaning:	Shows the profit that belongs to the shareholders, as a percentage of the funds that belong to them. The higher the better.
Table 13.2:	12% (17.4%)

Trend bad. Remember that shareholders' funds include both share capital and the profit that has been retained in the business. The reason why this ratio has shown such a sharp decline is that the profit after tax is smaller but the shareholders' funds have increased.

ACTIVITY (OR CAPITAL PRODUCTIVITY) RATIOS

These ratios relate sales to all or some of the assets being used or 'turned over' in generating sales; or (the other side of the same coin) how productively the capital invested in those assets is being used, hence the alternative name.

Capital productivity

This is one of the two ratios often called the 'secondary ratios'. The other is 'operating margin'. See below for an explanation of the connection between these ratios and the so-called 'primary ratio': the return on capital employed.

Ratio:	Sales : net assets (total assets less current liabilities) or capital employed (shareholders' funds plus long-term debt)
Meaning:	Shows the relationship between sales and the total resources used by the business. The higher the better. The 'total resources' can be thought of as either the net assets (total assets less current liabilities) being used or the long-term capital employed in financing them. The number, £40 million in this case, is of course the same.
Table 13.2:	1.5 (1.4)

Trend good. The additional insight gained from this ratio is that we appear to be getting more effective at using our assets to generate sales, but (from the profitability ratios) less effective at generating profit from those sales. The principle, used in this ratio to relate total net assets to sales, can also be applied to particular classes of asset: fixed assets, for example, or stock and debtors (see below).

Stock turnover or 'stockturn'

Ratio:	Sales : stocks
Meaning:	Shows how rapidly the business is using or 'turning over' its stock. The ratio can be applied to stock as a whole or to its components (raw materials, work in progress and finished goods). The higher the turnover the better. The following example illustrates a use of this ratio.
Table 13.2:	4.0 (3.2)

Trend good. The more rapid the stock turnover for a given amount of sales, the lower the average level of stock held. Most stocks are expensive to hold. Depending upon the kind of stocks, holding costs include interest on the money invested in them, and storage costs (people and space, insurance, deterioration and pilferage). The less stock a business can operate with, the lower the holding costs.

Illustration

The stockturn this year is 60 / 15 = 4, which means that for £60 million of sales £15 million of stock is carried. Suppose the industry average to be a stockturn of 5. If we could equal this average it would mean that, for the same level of sales, we would only be carrying £12 million (60 / 5) of stock, a reduction of £3 million. Supposing our stockholding costs to be, say, 20 per cent of stock value, not at all unusual, then the annual saving in holding costs would be 20 per cent of £3 million = £600k. If you were a manager pressing for a more efficient stock control system or a salesperson proposing such a system, would this not be useful information with which to help make your case?

Applications that result in a reduction of stock-holding are typical IT applications. This is an example of how simple financial analysis could be used to obtain a broad initial idea of the likely benefit to a business of a proposed major application.

Debtor days

Debtors means money earning interest in customers' bank accounts rather than in ours. The sooner customers pay their bills, the better. This ratio shows how long, on average, they are taking.

Ratio:	Debtors : average daily sales
Meaning:	Shows how effective the business is on average at getting its customers to pay their bills. Allows comparison with the company's terms of trade. Obviously, the figure for credit sales only should be used if known. The fewer days, the better.
Table 13.2:	61 days (57 days)

Illustration

Trend bad. Our debts are currently outstanding on average for 61 days. Suppose our terms of trade require payment in 30 days. If these terms were to be adhered to there would on average be only approximately half the amount of debts, £5 million, outstanding. If our cost of money is 10 per cent, then the annual saving from such a reduction, in terms of interest payable, would be 10% × £5 million = £500k. The numbers used are, of course, for illustration only. Such a large reduction in debtor days would be regarded by most businesses as optimistic.

The converse of debtor days is 'creditor days'. This is worked out in a similar way, but is usually the ratio of trade creditors to daily sales. The answer is an approximation to the number of days that a company is, on average, taking to pay its creditors. A company should usually take advantage of any discounts offered for early payment, otherwise pay on the due date. Ideally the comparison should be not with sales but with credit purchases. However, the latter figure is not usually determinable directly from published accounts, although it may be possible to derive an approximation to it.

More on the 'primary' and 'secondary' ratios

Having now covered the so-called primary and secondary ratios, a digression will be worthwhile in order to examine the relationship between them. Summarizing what we know of them:

- Operating margin is operating profit over sales.
- Capital productivity is sales over capital employed (or net assets).
- Return on capital employed (ROCE) is operating profit over capital employed.

Expressing these relationships algebraically we can obtain the following expression:

$$\frac{\text{operating profit}}{\text{sales}} \times \frac{\text{sales}}{\text{capital employed}} = \frac{\text{operating profit}}{\text{capital employed}}.$$

Giving each term its usual name, we obtain the following:

$$\text{operating margin} \times \text{capital productivity} = \text{ROCE}$$

We can now see why operating margin and capital productivity are sometimes called the 'secondary ratios'. It is because they are the components of the primary ratio (ROCE). For our company the relevant numbers are:

$$8.33\% \times 1.5 = 12.5\%.$$

Figure 13.1 represents this relationship diagrammatically. What happens on the left-hand side of the diagram concerns the profit and loss account. What happens on the right-hand side concerns the balance sheet. Note how 'sales' represents the link between them. Figure 13.2 simply shows the relevant numbers from our company superimposed on the diagram.

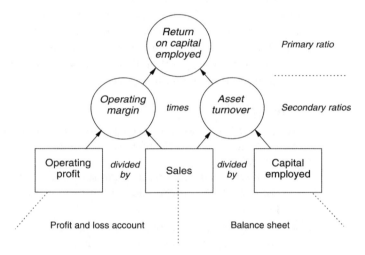

FIGURE 13.1 *The primary and secondary ratios*

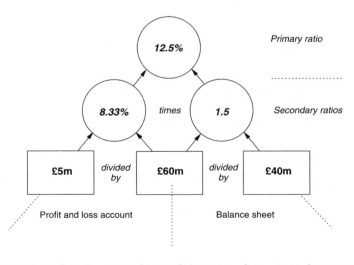

FIGURE 13.2 *The primary and secondary ratios of our example company*

Using the primary and secondary ratios

So what? As an example, suppose that our major competitor, of similar size and with a similar sales figure, consistently delivers a return on capital employed of 15 per cent, compared with our 12.5 per cent. The competitor would appear to be 'doing better' than us. The ROCE by itself says nothing about how they are achieving this, but its two components do.

Suppose that the competitor's capital productivity or asset turnover is much the same as ours, at 1.5. In that case, their profit margin must be higher, and we would look to a more detailed comparison of the respective profit and loss accounts to discover why.

Suppose, on the other hand, that the competitor's profit margin is much the same as ours, namely 8.3 per cent. In that case their capital productivity must be greater, and we would look to a more detailed comparison of the respective balance sheets to discover why. Depending on the kind of business, this more detailed analysis would usually include consideration, among other things, of two particular assets, stocks and debtors, which we have already done.

> ### Checkpoint
> So far in this chapter we have covered the first and third objectives, and have done some work toward the achievement of the second. In particular:
> - we have discussed why a single set of business accounts in isolation conveys little information about how the business is actually performing;
> - we have worked through examples of some commonly used ratios concerning profitability and activity;
> - we have considered the various contexts in which ratios have meaning.

LIQUIDITY (OR CASH MANAGEMENT) RATIOS

Liquidity means the extent to which a business has cash and other assets that could readily be turned into cash. Liquidity is primarily about whether a business can fulfil its obligations as they fall due. The analysis is usually done with two ratios, the first being rather a broad one.

Current ratio

Ratio: Current assets : current liabilities
Meaning: Shows to what extent current assets are adequate to meet current liabilities or, putting it another way, the extent to which current assets are financed by current liabilities.
Table 13.2:   1.9 (2.1)

Current assets, collectively, are the only fund out of which current liabilities could be paid. If fixed assets had to be sold to pay the bills, then the business would be in trouble. However, the key word above is 'adequate' and this only has meaning in the context of a particular industry. The components, and relative proportions, of current assets and current liabilities vary greatly from industry to industry. The main use of this ratio is to prompt investigation of any significant trends either way, and as a comparison with other companies and with industry averages.

Quick or 'acid test' ratio

Ratio: (Current assets less stocks) : current liabilities
Meaning: Gives an indication of the business's ability to pay its
                bills as they fall due.
Table 13.2:   0.9 (0.9)

Similar to the current ratio except that, by excluding stocks, it removes the one current asset that is not usually convertible into cash other than through the usual processes of the business. The others are mainly either cash or debtors. Debtors can be turned into cash immediately by 'factoring' or 'invoice discounting' (selling debtors to a specialist company for an immediate discounted cash lump sum). A quick ratio of approximately 1 (as in this example) is usually regarded as a satisfactory indication of liquidity.

GEARING RATIOS

These ratios concern the relationship between shareholders' money and borrowed money. For us as individuals, borrowing can be a good thing, but only up to a point because the higher the borrowing, the more the interest payable. The same is true of businesses and other organizations. The higher the proportion of borrowed money, the higher 'geared' the company is said to be. The equivalent US term is 'leveraged'.

Gearing (or debt/equity) ratio

Ratio: Borrowing (interest-bearing debt) : shareholders' funds
                (equity)
Meaning: Provides a measure of the amount of debt relative to the
                amount of equity.
Table 13.2:   60.0 (78.3)

Borrowing usually means all interest-bearing debt, including overdrafts if applicable. On a bicycle, changing to a higher gear means that you travel further for each turn of the pedals, but only up to a point. If the gearing is too high for the conditions, then you come to a stop. The higher the gearing in a business, the more it can do (because it has more money) without diluting the control of the existing shareholders, but only up to a point. If the gearing becomes too high, then the business may come to a stop because the interest burden is too great. We can see, from the balance sheet that the main reason for the fall in this ratio from last year to this is that £3 million of the loan has been repaid.

Interest cover

Ratio: Operating profit : interest payable
Meaning: Is the business making enough profit to cover the interest on its borrowings?
Table 13.2:   5 (6)

Compares the amount of profit before interest with the interest payable. The higher the better. However, the interest cover that might satisfy a potential lender would vary from industry to industry, and from company to company. The more volatile or speculative the industry, the higher the cover would need to be.

Summary of ratios considered so far

Table 13.2 summarizes the ratios that we have considered so far, cross-referenced to the balance sheet and profit and loss account from which they were derived. The list is representative rather than exhaustive, but the ratios it contains are among the most commonly used. It should serve to give an idea of what financial analysis is about.

STOCK MARKET RATIOS

All the ratios discussed so far are derived solely from numbers in a company's balance sheet and profit and loss account. However, there is an external factor that is of considerable significance to companies whose shares are quoted on a stock exchange, and to their shareholders. This is the price at which the company's shares are traded: the 'share price'.

The better a company's prospects are deemed to be, the greater will be the demand for its shares, and therefore the higher will be the share price. But prospects of what? The answer is 'future earnings or profits'. Again referring to our company, examples of two commonly used stock market ratios are as follows:

Dividend yield

From its profit and loss account, it is apparent that our company has declared a dividend of £1 million. This represents five pence per share.

Ratio: Latest dividend : current share price

Meaning:	This is the latest dividend per share compared with the current share price, expressed (usually) as a percentage.
Table 13.2:	2.5% (1.7%)

Whether a dividend yield is 'good' or 'bad' depends on several things. For example, an investor seeking primarily dividend income might regard a high yield as good. However, if the high yield has been achieved by retaining insufficient profit in the business for expansion, then in the longer term it may prove to be bad, because additional borrowings may be necessary, the interest on which will deplete profit in later years.

Price/earnings (P/E)

Suppose that the market price of our shares stands at £2 (or 200 pence) per share.

Ratio:	Current share price : latest earnings per share (EPS)
Meaning:	A measure of how optimistic or otherwise the market is about the future prospects of a company. The higher the P/E ratio, the more optimistic the market.
Table 13.2:	13.3 (15.0)

The price at which shares change hands is governed by supply and demand. If the market thinks that a company is going to produce better than average profits in future, then demand for its shares will increase and the price will go up; and vice versa. The higher the P/E ratio, the higher the market's regard for a share. The P/E ratio is also useful because it takes into account, via the earnings per share, all of the profit that belongs to the shareholders, not just that part of it that is paid to them as dividend.

OTHER RATIOS

Probably the most important other class of ratio almost universally used is the one that concerns those important assets that do not usually appear on company balance sheets: people. Among the most widely used are sales per employee and operating profit per employee, but many others are possible. Other ratios are specific to particular industries. For example, supermarkets measure sales per square foot or square metre; airlines and other transport undertakings measure revenue per passenger/kilometre and (for freight) revenue per ton/kilometre.

SHAREHOLDER VALUE ADDED

Shareholder value added, sometimes shortened to SVA, is an old idea rediscovered, developed and packaged. The purpose of a business is to create wealth, or 'add value', for the proprietor or proprietors (in a company, the shareholders).

Shareholders require as a minimum from their investment a return at least as great as that obtainable from investments generally with an equivalent level of perceived risk. They would actually like a greater return: the higher the better. However, if they do not earn at least this minimum return, then they have no motivation to keep their money invested. They will take it out and put it elsewhere. Any return in excess of that minimum is 'value added' to the shareholders.

The cost of equity

This minimum return is usually called, rather confusingly, a company's 'cost of equity'. Dividends are optional. Some companies never pay a dividend; some refrain from doing so in hard times. Shareholders gain their 'return' from a combination of dividends and capital growth (increase in share price). Both of these depend, in different ways, on profit. Dividends can only be paid out of profit, while capital growth will only happen if the market believes that the company will in the medium-term do better in profit terms than the expectation for companies in that industry generally.

So, in its simplest form, the question is: 'of the profit after tax (the profit that belongs to the shareholders) how much, if any, is left after deducting the minimum return required by the shareholders (the "cost of equity")?' Table 13.3 shows an example that illustrates the point.

TABLE 13.3 *A simple example of shareholder value added (SVA)*

		£ million
The data		
Profit after tax		3.0
Equity at beginning of year		23.0
Assumed return expected by shareholders (the 'cost of equity')	10%	
A simple 'shareholder value added' calculation is as follows:		
Profit after tax		3.0
Return expected by shareholders (10% × £23 million)		2.3
Value added to shareholders		0.7

In Table 13.3 I have used as the equity number the equity at the beginning of the year. I have stated earlier in this chapter that most people use end-of-year numbers for other ratios, so why the apparent inconsistency here? The reason is that the SVA calculation is analogous to the investor putting money into a bank or building society and seeing if the interest earned after a year is greater than the 'going rate' for investments of that kind. In order for the argument to make sense, the investment obviously has to have been in place for a year. So, the shareholder capital on which the return is worked out should be the capital at the beginning of the year.

What does the answer mean?

In this particular year, the company has added £0.7 million of value to its shareholders. This is the amount by which the profit after tax has exceeded their minimum expectation from their investment. Had the final number been negative it would mean that value had been taken away from the shareholders. Notice that the amount of dividend actually paid is ignored in the calculation. This is because all the profit after tax belongs to the shareholders, whether it is paid to them as dividend or not.

I have glossed over the question of how the 'cost of equity' is actually worked out. It is not a particularly complicated calculation, but the arguments needed to justify it are lengthy and unnecessary for our purpose. If your company is into shareholder value added, then you will no doubt be able to find out (a) the particular way in which they apply it, and (b) what percentage cost of equity is currently assumed.

Some companies use a 'weighted average cost of capital' or WACC in their SVA calculations instead of a cost of equity. If they do, they will add back the cost of any interest paid to debt holders to their profit after tax (they will also increase the tax charged by the amount of tax saved by paying the interest). In the accountant's jargon the resultant figure is called profit before interest and after tax. For our SVA example we have used the simpler 'cost of equity' approach, which is also commonly used (particularly in the financial services industry).

The implications of shareholder value added

What are the implications of shareholder value added? If the ultimate aim of a company is to add value to its shareholders, then it follows that every division and department of the company should, if possible, achieve the same end. This is why, in some companies, a way of managing based on SVA, sometimes also called 'value-based management', is being used:

- as a yardstick by which divisions and departments are measured;
- as a basis for incentives for managers.

The principle of SVA may also be used as a method of evaluating investment opportunities such as IT proposals. Ways of doing so are explored in Chapter 5.

This has been a brief outline of shareholder value added as applied to a company as a whole. It has proponents among finance professionals, and applications of the SVA idea are generally well accepted. Some people have taken the basic idea and made it considerably more sophisticated.

One organization that has done this is Stern Stewart, the New York consultancy firm. They have developed a large number of suggested adjustments to normal accounting numbers in order that accountants might do a better job of showing the economic reality of companies. They have trademarked their particular approach under the name Economic Value Added (EVA®). One purpose of the various attempts at sophistication is to explore the use of the SVA idea as a vehicle for correcting some of the perceived shortcomings of conventional accounting methods and to assist in the process of reconciling the differences in methods between countries.

Summary

The main points covered in this chapter, linked to its objectives, have been the following:

- *A balance sheet is a snapshot. A profit and loss account only covers a single period. To determine the progress of a business it is necessary to look at relationships between key numbers in a set of accounts, and at trends and comparisons.*
- *The following are the ratios covered in this chapter as commonly categorized:*
    - *Profitability: gross margin, operating margin, return on capital employed, return on equity.*
    - *Activity: capital productivity, stock turnover, debtor days.*
    - *Liquidity: current ratio, quick ratio.*
    - *Gearing: debt / equity, interest cover.*
    - *Stock market: earnings per share, dividend yield, price / earnings.*
- *The following contexts usually give meaning to ratios: past years, previous forecasts, industry norms, competitors.*
- *Shareholder value added is the amount, if any, left after deducting from profit after tax the cost of the capital used to earn it.*

Appendices

Appendix 1: Discount Tables

The tables in this appendix are referred to in the text. Following each table are brief descriptions, the formula from which it is derived and a numeric example.

THE PRESENT VALUE OF A LUMP SUM

Table A1.1 gives the present value (PV) of a lump sum of £1 receivable or payable n years in the future discounted at rate i.

$$PV = \frac{1}{(1+i)^n} = (1+i)^{-n}$$

Example

The present value of a lump sum of £1 receivable or payable three years in the future discounted at eight per cent is given by

$$PV = (1 + 0.08)^{-3} = £0.7938$$

THE PRESENT VALUE OF AN ANNUITY

An annuity is a series of equal annual receipts or payments, such as amounts due under leases. In practice, the term is also sometimes applied to non-annual regular periods. Table A1.2 gives the present value (PV) of a series of amounts of £1 receivable or payable for n years starting one year in the future, discounted at rate i.

$$PV = \frac{1 - (1+i)^{-n}}{i}$$

Example

The present value of an annuity of a series of amounts of £1 receivable or payable for three years starting one year in the future discounted at eight per cent is given by

$$PV = \frac{1 - (1 + 0.08)^{-3}}{0.08} = £2.5771$$

ANNUAL EQUIVALENT ANNUITY

'Annual equivalent annuity' is the annuity required to give a present value of £1 for various rates of interest and numbers of years. In practice the term is sometimes also applied to non-annual regular periods. Table A1.3 shows the annual equivalent annuity (AEA) over n years at rate i that gives a present value of £1.

$$\text{AEA} = \frac{i}{1 - (1 + i)^{-n}}$$

Example

A lump sum today of £1 is equivalent to an annuity over three years starting one year in the future discounted at eight per cent of

$$\frac{0.08}{1 - (1 + 0.08)^{-3}} = £0.388$$

TABLE A1.1 *Present value of a lump sum of £1 receivable or payable n periods from today at discount rate i*

n	1	2	3	4	5	6	7	8	9	10	11	12	13	14	15	16	17	18	19	20
i																				
5	0.9524	0.9070	0.8638	0.8227	0.7835	0.7462	0.7107	0.6768	0.6446	0.6139	0.5847	0.5568	0.5303	0.5051	0.4810	0.4581	0.4363	0.4155	0.3957	0.3769
6	0.9434	0.8900	0.8396	0.7921	0.7473	0.7050	0.6651	0.6274	0.5919	0.5584	0.5268	0.4970	0.4688	0.4423	0.4173	0.3936	0.3714	0.3503	0.3305	0.3118
7	0.9346	0.8734	0.8163	0.7629	0.7130	0.6663	0.6227	0.5820	0.5439	0.5083	0.4751	0.4440	0.4150	0.3878	0.3624	0.3387	0.3166	0.2959	0.2765	0.2584
8	0.9259	0.8573	0.7938	0.7350	0.6806	0.6302	0.5835	0.5403	0.5002	0.4632	0.4289	0.3971	0.3677	0.3405	0.3152	0.2919	0.2703	0.2502	0.2317	0.2145
9	0.9174	0.8417	0.7722	0.7084	0.6499	0.5963	0.5470	0.5019	0.4604	0.4224	0.3875	0.3555	0.3262	0.2992	0.2745	0.2519	0.2311	0.2120	0.1945	0.1784
10	0.9091	0.8264	0.7513	0.6830	0.6209	0.5645	0.5132	0.4665	0.4241	0.3855	0.3505	0.3186	0.2897	0.2633	0.2394	0.2176	0.1978	0.1799	0.1635	0.1486
11	0.9009	0.8116	0.7312	0.6587	0.5935	0.5346	0.4817	0.4339	0.3909	0.3522	0.3173	0.2858	0.2575	0.2320	0.2090	0.1883	0.1696	0.1528	0.1377	0.1240
12	0.8929	0.7972	0.7118	0.6355	0.5674	0.5066	0.4523	0.4039	0.3606	0.3220	0.2875	0.2567	0.2292	0.2046	0.1827	0.1631	0.1456	0.1300	0.1161	0.1037
13	0.8850	0.7831	0.6931	0.6133	0.5428	0.4803	0.4251	0.3762	0.3329	0.2946	0.2607	0.2307	0.2042	0.1807	0.1599	0.1415	0.1252	0.1108	0.0981	0.0868
14	0.8772	0.7695	0.6750	0.5921	0.5194	0.4556	0.3996	0.3506	0.3075	0.2697	0.2366	0.2076	0.1821	0.1597	0.1401	0.1229	0.1078	0.0946	0.0829	0.0728
15	0.8696	0.7561	0.6575	0.5718	0.4972	0.4323	0.3759	0.3269	0.2843	0.2472	0.2149	0.1869	0.1625	0.1413	0.1229	0.1069	0.0929	0.0808	0.0703	0.0611
16	0.8621	0.7432	0.6407	0.5523	0.4761	0.4104	0.3538	0.3050	0.2630	0.2267	0.1954	0.1685	0.1452	0.1252	0.1079	0.0930	0.0802	0.0691	0.0596	0.0514
17	0.8547	0.7305	0.6244	0.5337	0.4561	0.3898	0.3332	0.2848	0.2434	0.2080	0.1778	0.1520	0.1299	0.1110	0.0949	0.0811	0.0693	0.0592	0.0506	0.0433
18	0.8475	0.7182	0.6086	0.5158	0.4371	0.3704	0.3139	0.2660	0.2255	0.1911	0.1619	0.1372	0.1163	0.0985	0.0835	0.0708	0.0600	0.0508	0.0431	0.0365
19	0.8403	0.7062	0.5934	0.4987	0.4190	0.3521	0.2959	0.2487	0.2090	0.1756	0.1476	0.1240	0.1042	0.0876	0.0736	0.0618	0.0520	0.0437	0.0367	0.0308
20	0.8333	0.6944	0.5787	0.4823	0.4019	0.3349	0.2791	0.2326	0.1938	0.1615	0.1346	0.1122	0.0935	0.0779	0.0649	0.0541	0.0451	0.0376	0.0313	0.0261
21	0.8264	0.6830	0.5645	0.4665	0.3855	0.3186	0.2633	0.2176	0.1799	0.1486	0.1228	0.1015	0.0839	0.0693	0.0573	0.0474	0.0391	0.0323	0.0267	0.0221
22	0.8197	0.6719	0.5507	0.4514	0.3700	0.3033	0.2486	0.2038	0.1670	0.1369	0.1122	0.0920	0.0754	0.0618	0.0507	0.0415	0.0340	0.0279	0.0229	0.0187
23	0.8130	0.6610	0.5374	0.4369	0.3552	0.2888	0.2348	0.1909	0.1552	0.1262	0.1026	0.0834	0.0678	0.0551	0.0448	0.0364	0.0296	0.0241	0.0196	0.0159
24	0.8065	0.6504	0.5245	0.4230	0.3411	0.2751	0.2218	0.1789	0.1443	0.1164	0.0938	0.0757	0.0610	0.0492	0.0397	0.0320	0.0258	0.0208	0.0168	0.0135
25	0.8000	0.6400	0.5120	0.4096	0.3277	0.2621	0.2097	0.1678	0.1342	0.1074	0.0859	0.0687	0.0550	0.0440	0.0352	0.0281	0.0225	0.0180	0.0144	0.0115

TABLE A1.2 *Present value of an annuity of £1 receivable or payable in arrear for n periods at discount rate i*

n	1	2	3	4	5	6	7	8	9	10	11	12	13	14	15	16	17	18	19	20
5	0.9524	1.8594	2.7232	3.5460	4.3295	5.0757	5.7864	6.4632	7.1078	7.7217	8.3064	8.8633	9.3936	9.8986	10.3797	10.8378	11.2741	11.6896	12.0853	12.4622
6	0.9434	1.8334	2.6730	3.4651	4.2124	4.9173	5.5824	6.2098	6.8017	7.3601	7.8869	8.3838	8.8527	9.2950	9.7122	10.1059	10.4773	10.8276	11.1581	11.4699
7	0.9346	1.8080	2.6243	3.3872	4.1002	4.7665	5.3893	5.9713	6.5152	7.0236	7.4987	7.9427	8.3577	8.7455	9.1079	9.4466	9.7632	10.0591	10.3356	10.5940
8	0.9259	1.7833	2.5771	3.3121	3.9927	4.6229	5.2064	5.7466	6.2469	6.7101	7.1390	7.5361	7.9038	8.2442	8.5595	8.8514	9.1216	9.3719	9.6036	9.8181
9	0.9174	1.7591	2.5313	3.2397	3.8897	4.4859	5.0330	5.5348	5.9952	6.4177	6.8052	7.1607	7.4869	7.7862	8.0607	8.3126	8.5436	8.7556	8.9501	9.1285
10	0.9091	1.7355	2.4869	3.1699	3.7908	4.3553	4.8684	5.3349	5.7590	6.1446	6.4951	6.8137	7.1034	7.3667	7.6061	7.8237	8.0216	8.2014	8.3649	8.5136
11	0.9009	1.7125	2.4437	3.1024	3.6959	4.2305	4.7122	5.1461	5.5370	5.8892	6.2065	6.4924	6.7499	6.9819	7.1909	7.3792	7.5488	7.7016	7.8393	7.9633
12	0.8929	1.6901	2.4018	3.0373	3.6048	4.1114	4.5638	4.9676	5.3282	5.6502	5.9377	6.1944	6.4235	6.6282	6.8109	6.9740	7.1196	7.2497	7.3658	7.4694
13	0.8850	1.6681	2.3612	2.9745	3.5172	3.9975	4.4226	4.7988	5.1317	5.4262	5.6869	5.9176	6.1218	6.3025	6.4624	6.6039	6.7291	6.8399	6.9380	7.0248
14	0.8772	1.6467	2.3216	2.9137	3.4331	3.8887	4.2883	4.6389	4.9464	5.2161	5.4527	5.6603	5.8424	6.0021	6.1422	6.2651	6.3729	6.4674	6.5504	6.6231
15	0.8696	1.6257	2.2832	2.8550	3.3522	3.7845	4.1604	4.4873	4.7716	5.0188	5.2337	5.4206	5.5831	5.7245	5.8474	5.9542	6.0472	6.1280	6.1982	6.2593
16	0.8621	1.6052	2.2459	2.7982	3.2743	3.6847	4.0386	4.3436	4.6065	4.8332	5.0286	5.1971	5.3423	5.4675	5.5755	5.6685	5.7487	5.8178	5.8775	5.9288
17	0.8547	1.5852	2.2096	2.7432	3.1993	3.5892	3.9224	4.2072	4.4506	4.6586	4.8364	4.9884	5.1183	5.2293	5.3242	5.4053	5.4746	5.5339	5.5845	5.6278
18	0.8475	1.5656	2.1743	2.6901	3.1272	3.4976	3.8115	4.0776	4.3030	4.4941	4.6560	4.7932	4.9095	5.0081	5.0916	5.1624	5.2223	5.2732	5.3162	5.3527
19	0.8403	1.5465	2.1399	2.6386	3.0576	3.4098	3.7057	3.9544	4.1633	4.3389	4.4865	4.6105	4.7147	4.8023	4.8759	4.9377	4.9897	5.0333	5.0700	5.1009
20	0.8333	1.5278	2.1065	2.5887	2.9906	3.3255	3.6046	3.8372	4.0310	4.1925	4.3271	4.4392	4.5327	4.6106	4.6755	4.7296	4.7746	4.8122	4.8435	4.8696
21	0.8264	1.5095	2.0739	2.5404	2.9260	3.2446	3.5079	3.7256	3.9054	4.0541	4.1769	4.2784	4.3624	4.4317	4.4890	4.5364	4.5755	4.6079	4.6346	4.6567
22	0.8197	1.4915	2.0422	2.4936	2.8636	3.1669	3.4155	3.6193	3.7863	3.9232	4.0354	4.1274	4.2028	4.2646	4.3152	4.3567	4.3908	4.4187	4.4415	4.4603
23	0.8130	1.4740	2.0114	2.4483	2.8035	3.0923	3.3270	3.5179	3.6731	3.7993	3.9018	3.9852	4.0530	4.1082	4.1530	4.1894	4.2190	4.2431	4.2627	4.2786
24	0.8065	1.4568	1.9813	2.4043	2.7454	3.0205	3.2423	3.4212	3.5655	3.6819	3.7757	3.8514	3.9124	3.9616	4.0013	4.0333	4.0591	4.0799	4.0967	4.1103
25	0.8000	1.4400	1.9520	2.3616	2.6893	2.9514	3.1611	3.3289	3.4631	3.5705	3.6564	3.7251	3.7801	3.8241	3.8593	3.8874	3.9099	3.9279	3.9424	3.9539

TABLE A1.3 *Annual equivalent annuity of £1 after n years*

n	1	2	3	4	5	6	7	8	9	10	11	12	13	14	15	16	17	18	19	20
i																				
5	1.0500	0.5378	0.3672	0.2820	0.2310	0.1970	0.1728	0.1547	0.1407	0.1295	0.1204	0.1128	0.1065	0.1010	0.0963	0.0923	0.0887	0.0855	0.0827	0.0802
6	1.0600	0.5454	0.3741	0.2886	0.2374	0.2034	0.1791	0.1610	0.1470	0.1359	0.1268	0.1193	0.1130	0.1076	0.1030	0.0990	0.0954	0.0924	0.0896	0.0872
7	1.0700	0.5531	0.3811	0.2952	0.2439	0.2098	0.1856	0.1675	0.1535	0.1424	0.1334	0.1259	0.1197	0.1143	0.1098	0.1059	0.1024	0.0994	0.0968	0.0944
8	1.0800	0.5608	0.3880	0.3019	0.2505	0.2163	0.1921	0.1740	0.1601	0.1490	0.1401	0.1327	0.1265	0.1213	0.1168	0.1130	0.1096	0.1067	0.1041	0.1019
9	1.0900	0.5685	0.3951	0.3087	0.2571	0.2229	0.1987	0.1807	0.1668	0.1558	0.1469	0.1397	0.1336	0.1284	0.1241	0.1203	0.1170	0.1142	0.1117	0.1095
10	1.1000	0.5762	0.4021	0.3155	0.2638	0.2296	0.2054	0.1874	0.1736	0.1627	0.1540	0.1468	0.1408	0.1357	0.1315	0.1278	0.1247	0.1219	0.1195	0.1175
11	1.1100	0.5839	0.4092	0.3223	0.2706	0.2364	0.2122	0.1943	0.1806	0.1698	0.1611	0.1540	0.1482	0.1432	0.1391	0.1355	0.1325	0.1298	0.1276	0.1256
12	1.1200	0.5917	0.4163	0.3292	0.2774	0.2432	0.2191	0.2013	0.1877	0.1770	0.1684	0.1614	0.1557	0.1509	0.1468	0.1434	0.1405	0.1379	0.1358	0.1339
13	1.1300	0.5995	0.4235	0.3362	0.2843	0.2502	0.2261	0.2084	0.1949	0.1843	0.1758	0.1690	0.1634	0.1587	0.1547	0.1514	0.1486	0.1462	0.1441	0.1424
14	1.1400	0.6073	0.4307	0.3432	0.2913	0.2572	0.2332	0.2156	0.2022	0.1917	0.1834	0.1767	0.1712	0.1666	0.1628	0.1596	0.1569	0.1546	0.1527	0.1510
15	1.1500	0.6151	0.4380	0.3503	0.2983	0.2642	0.2404	0.2229	0.2096	0.1993	0.1911	0.1845	0.1791	0.1747	0.1710	0.1679	0.1654	0.1632	0.1613	0.1598
16	1.1600	0.6230	0.4453	0.3574	0.3054	0.2714	0.2476	0.2302	0.2171	0.2069	0.1989	0.1924	0.1872	0.1829	0.1794	0.1764	0.1740	0.1719	0.1701	0.1687
17	1.1700	0.6308	0.4526	0.3645	0.3126	0.2786	0.2549	0.2377	0.2247	0.2147	0.2068	0.2005	0.1954	0.1912	0.1878	0.1850	0.1827	0.1807	0.1791	0.1777
18	1.1800	0.6387	0.4599	0.3717	0.3198	0.2859	0.2624	0.2452	0.2324	0.2225	0.2148	0.2086	0.2037	0.1997	0.1964	0.1937	0.1915	0.1896	0.1881	0.1868
19	1.1900	0.6466	0.4673	0.3790	0.3271	0.2933	0.2699	0.2529	0.2402	0.2305	0.2229	0.2169	0.2121	0.2082	0.2051	0.2025	0.2004	0.1987	0.1972	0.1960
20	1.2000	0.6545	0.4747	0.3863	0.3344	0.3007	0.2774	0.2606	0.2481	0.2385	0.2311	0.2253	0.2206	0.2169	0.2139	0.2114	0.2094	0.2078	0.2065	0.2054
21	1.2100	0.6625	0.4822	0.3936	0.3418	0.3082	0.2851	0.2684	0.2561	0.2467	0.2394	0.2337	0.2292	0.2256	0.2228	0.2204	0.2186	0.2170	0.2158	0.2147
22	1.2200	0.6705	0.4897	0.4010	0.3492	0.3158	0.2928	0.2763	0.2641	0.2549	0.2478	0.2423	0.2379	0.2345	0.2317	0.2295	0.2278	0.2263	0.2251	0.2242
23	1.2300	0.6784	0.4972	0.4085	0.3567	0.3234	0.3006	0.2843	0.2722	0.2632	0.2563	0.2509	0.2467	0.2434	0.2408	0.2387	0.2370	0.2357	0.2346	0.2337
24	1.2400	0.6864	0.5047	0.4159	0.3642	0.3311	0.3084	0.2923	0.2805	0.2716	0.2649	0.2596	0.2556	0.2524	0.2499	0.2479	0.2464	0.2451	0.2441	0.2433
25	1.2500	0.6944	0.5123	0.4234	0.3718	0.3388	0.3163	0.3004	0.2888	0.2801	0.2735	0.2684	0.2645	0.2615	0.2591	0.2572	0.2558	0.2546	0.2537	0.2529

Appendix 2: Lease Accounting Rules

Until the mid-1980s payments under leases of all kinds were regarded as expenses for accounting purposes. They were charged directly to the profit and loss account of the lessee (the customer). The leased asset did not appear on the lessee's balance sheet, even though the asset may have been the company's main source of revenue. New accounting rules were defined in most countries during the 1980s and have continued to evolve since then. In parallel, international standards have been developed (see below) and there is an accelerating trend towards the adoption of these standards.

The main purpose of the leasing standards is make accounts reflect more the economic substance of business transactions rather than necessarily their legal form. The details and the terminology differ from country to country. However, the essential feature in most countries and in the international standard is that if a lease transfers substantially all the risks and rewards of ownership to the lessee then the leased asset should appear on the lessee's balance sheet. The corresponding obligation to pay for it should be shown as a liability. Such a lease is called a finance lease in the UK and a capital lease in the USA. If the lease does not transfer substantially all the risks and rewards of ownership, then payments under it continue, as before, to be treated as expenses and charged straight to the profit and loss account of the lessee. Such a lease is called an operating lease.

This is an area in which you may wish to seek specialist help. However, for reference, summarized below are the relevant sets of rules most likely to affect organizations in the UK and the EU. There is also a pointer to the rules governing US corporations.

INTERNATIONAL ACCOUNTING STANDARDS

In most countries at the time of writing (December 2005), the accounting rules on leasing (and most other things) are in a state of transition towards the eventual adoption of International Accounting Standards, although it is likely to be some years before full international standardization is achieved. However, recent EU legislation on the subject is of immediate importance to companies in countries that are members of the European Union, including of course the UK. The main relevant EU and UK legislation is as follows:

- Regulation (EC) No. 1606/2002 of the European Parliament and of the Council of 19 July 2002 on the application of International Accounting Standards (the 'IAS Regulation');
- The Companies Act 1985 (International Accounting Standards and Other Accounting Amendments) Regulations 2004.

As already stated (page 113) the combined effect of the above regulations for UK companies is that as from accounting periods beginning on or after 1 January 2005:

- publicly traded companies (PLCs in the UK) governed by the law of a Member State of the European Union are **required** to prepare their consolidated (or group) accounts using International Accounting Standards (IASs), instead of national accounting standards;
- publicly traded companies in the UK are **permitted** to use IASs in their individual accounts or to continue using UK accounting standards;
- non-publicly traded companies (non-PLCs) in the UK are **permitted** to use IASs in both their individual and consolidated accounts or to continue using UK accounting standards.

In respect of the last two items above, once a company has prepared its accounts using IASs for a financial year, it cannot then switch back to UK standards in subsequent financial years.

Notice that the first item above is mandatory, whereas the last two are permissive. Some UK companies to which the permissive paragraphs apply are planning to adopt International Accounting Standards from 2005; others will continue to use UK Standards. It happens that the main UK accounting standard for leasing (SSAP 21, see below) is very close to the international standard (IAS 17, also below) and contains the words '… compliance with SSAP 21 will ensure compliance with IAS 17 in all material respects'.

RULES GOVERNING UK COMPANIES

International Accounting Standard No. 17 (IAS 17): Accounting for Leases

The following extracts[1] from definitions in IAS 17 are relevant in determining whether or not a leased asset has to be shown on the balance sheet of the lessee.

---

[1] Extracts from International Accounting Standard No. 17 (IAS 17) are reproduced by kind permission of the International Accounting Standards Board.

A lease is classified as a *finance lease* if it transfers substantially all the risks and rewards incident to ownership. All other leases are classified as *operating leases*. Classification is made at the inception of the lease.

IAS 17 paragraph 4

Whether a lease is a finance lease or an operating lease depends on the substance of the transaction rather than the form. Situations that would normally lead to a lease being classified as a finance lease include the following:
- The lease transfers ownership to the lessee by the end of the lease term.
- The lessee has the option to purchase the asset at a price that is expected to be sufficiently lower than fair value at the date the option becomes exercisable that, at the inception of the lease, it is reasonably certain that the option will be exercised.
- The lease term is for the major part of the economic life of the asset, even if title is not transferred.
- At the inception of the lease, the present value of the minimum lease payments amounts to at least substantially all of the fair value of the leased asset; and
- The leased assets are of a specialized nature such that only the lessee can use them without major modifications being made.

IAS 17 paragraph 10

UK Statement of Standard Accounting Practice 21 (SSAP 21)

The following extracts[2] from definitions in SSAP 21 are relevant in determining whether or not a leased asset has to be shown on the balance sheet of the lessee.

Finance lease

A *finance lease* is a lease that transfers substantially all the risks and rewards of ownership of an asset to the lessee. It should be presumed that such a transfer of risks and rewards occurs if at the inception of a lease the present value of the minimum lease payments, including any initial payment, amounts to substantially all (normally 90 per cent or more) of the fair value of the leased asset. The present value should be calculated by using the interest rate implicit in the lease. If the fair value of the asset is not determinable, an estimate thereof should be used.

SSAP 21 paragraph 15

---

[2] Extracts from Accounting Standards 2005/2006 are reproduced by kind permission of the Accounting Standards Board Limited. For further information please visit www.frc.org.uk/asb.

Fair value

> *Fair value* is the price at which an asset could be exchanged in an arm's length transaction less, where applicable, any grants received towards the purchase or use of the asset.
>
> **SSAP 21 paragraph 25**

In practice this would usually mean its purchase price.

Operating lease

> An *operating lease* is a lease other than a finance lease.
>
> **SSAP 21 paragraph 17**

Hire purchase

> A *hire purchase* contract is a contract for the hire of an asset, which contains a provision giving the hirer an option to acquire legal title to the asset upon fulfilment of certain conditions stated in the contract.
>
> **SSAP 21 paragraph 18**

In practice the main condition is normally the payment of an agreed number of instalments.

An asset leased under a finance lease or hire purchase must be shown on the balance sheet of the lessee and depreciated in the usual way. Payments under operating leases are charged as expenses to the profit and loss account of the lessee.

Compliance with International Accounting Standard No. 17: Accounting for leases (IAS 17)

> The requirements of International Accounting Standard No. 17 'Accounting for leases' accord very closely with the content of the United Kingdom and Irish Accounting Standard No. 21 'Accounting for leases and hire purchase contracts' and accordingly compliance with SSAP 21 will ensure compliance with IAS 17 in all material respects.
>
> **SSAP 21 paragraph 69**

UK Local Authority accounting for leases now generally follows the same (SSAP 21) rules (as described in Section J (Leases) of 'Guidance Notes for Practitioners for 2004/2005 Accounts', part of the CIPFA Code of Practice on Local Authority Accounting in the UK – Statement of Recommended Practice). For further information please visit www.cipfa.org.uk.

Financial Reporting Standard 5 (FRS 5)

A more recent UK accounting standard is FRS 5 – 'Reporting the substance of transactions'. Its main purpose was to try to ensure that accounting represents the substance of business transactions in general, rather than (necessarily) their legal form and to make 'creative accounting' harder. While it has relevance to leasing among other things, it complements rather than supersedes SSAP 21 and in most situations it is probable that the provisions of SSAP 21 will continue to be the primary determinants of the accounting treatment of leases. However, as stated above, this is an area in which you are likely to wish to seek specialist help.

RULES GOVERNING US CORPORATIONS

The rules governing US corporations are contained within US Financial Accounting Standards Board Statement 13 – Accounting for Leases (FASB 13). As with the International and UK Accounting Standards described above, a distinction is made between two fundamentally different kinds of lease, in this case *capital leases* and *operating leases*. An asset leased under a capital lease has to be capitalized, that is shown on the balance sheet of the lessee, whereas payments under operating leases are charged as expenses to the income statement (profit and loss account) of the lessee. However, the detailed rules (and associated definitions) for classifying a lease as either a capital lease or an operating lease are quite complex, and readers are advised to refer, preferably with specialist help, direct to The Financial Accounting Standards Board website at www.fasb.org/st.

Appendix 3: Example of UK Local Government Accounts

In Chapter 12 we looked at the financial characteristics of different kinds of business in the context of the published Accounts of companies in various industries. For some years now, UK public sector accounting principles have been in most respects similar to those applicable in the private sector. To illustrate the similarity, in this Appendix are reproduced, with permission, extracts from the 2005 published Accounts of a UK Local Authority: Hampshire County Council.

Hampshire County Council is one of the largest county councils in the United Kingdom and one of the largest employers in the country, with about 37,000 employees, both full-time and part-time. The Council has responsibility for the provision and maintenance of education, social services, highways, roads and transport, and cultural, environmental and planning services. Of these, education accounts for by far the greatest proportion (approximately 60 per cent) of total expenditure. Most of the County Council's income comes from general Government grant and a share of local taxes on both businesses and individuals (called respectively 'national business rates' and 'council tax'). The remainder of local taxes are used to fund lower tiers of local government (district, town and parish councils), the police, and the fire and rescue service. In addition, specific Government grants pay directly for certain services, and fees are charged to customers for some services.

The 2005 balance sheet of Hampshire County Council is reproduced in Figure A3.1. The main balance sheet difference between Local Authorities and companies is that Local Authorities do not have shareholders. Instead they are financed on a year-by-year basis by general Government and by local taxes, as described above. However, they do maintain reserves, much as companies do, and in the balance sheet these reserves occupy the place that would be occupied by 'capital and reserves' in company accounts.

Consolidated balance sheet	31 March 2004 £ '000	note		£ '000	31 March 2005 £ '000
	2,403,831	1	Tangible fixed assets	2,646,278	
	2,068	2	Deferred charges	–	
	54,142	3	Long-term debtors	51,221	
	2,460,041		**Total long-term assets**		**2,697,499**
			Current assets		
	2,536	4	Stocks and work in progress	3,031	
	43,665	5	Debtors	49,920	
	6,553		Payments in advance	8,159	
	65,395	6	Short-term investments	108,210	
	9,419	7	Cash in hand	6,703	
	127,568			**176,023**	
			Current liabilities		
	10,058	8	Deposits	23,029	
	99,750	9	Creditors	120,475	
	35,471	10	Receipts in advance	35,315	
	95,488	11	Borrowing repayable within one year	117,542	
	12,229	12	Cash overdrawn	19,753	
	252,996			**316,114**	
	125,428		**Net current liabilities**		**140,091**
	2,334,613		**Total assets less current liabilities**		**2,557,408**
	208,000	13	Long-term borrowing	243,000	
	209,753	14	Deferred contributions and Government grants	280,004	
	25,067	15	Developers' contributions	27,483	
	10,988	16	Provisions	7,709	
	453,808				**558,196**
	405,300	26	Net liability related to defined benefit pension schemes		**597,030**
	1,475,505		**Total net assets**		**1,402,182**
			Financed by:		
	1,535,918	17	Fixed asset restatement account	1,633,394	
	265,778	18	Capital financing account	272,420	
	–405,300	26	Pensions reserve	–597,030	
	66,506	19	Earmarked reserves	75,711	
	4	20	Other balances	66	
	12,599	27	Revenue account	17,621	
	1,475,505		**Total net worth**		**1,402,182**

FIGURE A3.1 *Hampshire County Council – Consolidated balance sheet as at 31 March 2005*

Because Local Authorities are not profit-making, the term 'profit and loss account' would be inappropriate. The term 'consolidated revenue account' is used instead. Hampshire County Council's consolidated revenue account is reproduced in Figure A3.2 and its cash flow statement in Figure A3.3. The full 2005 Statement of Accounts of Hampshire County Council can be found on the Council's website (www.hants.gov.uk). Search for 'Statement of Accounts 05'.

Consolidated revenue account

Expenditure and income

2003/04 Net Expenditure £'000		Gross Expenditure £'000	Specific Grants £'000	Other Income £'000	Total £'000	2004/05 Net Expenditure £'000
2,258	Central services to the public	3,814	299	1,269	1,568	2,246
93,422	Cultural, environmental and planning services	114,313	346	16,340	16,686	97,627
660,531	Education services	866,867	83,315	91,498	174,813	692,054
67,848	Highways, roads and transport services	84,436	1,793	5,314	7,107	77,329
210,532	Social services	385,037	77,235	48,816	126,051	258,986
268	Court services (note 2)	1,110	-	681	681	429
10,451	Corporate and democratic core	11,987	-	-	-	11,987
1,311	Non-distributed costs (note 10)	1,897	-	-	-	1,897
-	Exceptional item (note 15)	−439	-	-	-	−439
−119	Reduction in provisions (note 6)	−3,469	-	-	-	−3,469
1,046,502	**Net cost of continuing services**	**1,465,553**	**162,988**	**163,918**	**326,906**	**1,138,647**
4,722	Magistrates' courts (note 2)	15,318	9,479	834	10,313	5,005
1,051,224	**Net cost of services**	**1,480,871**	**172,467**	**164,752**	**337,219**	**1,143,652**
41,205	Contribution to Hampshire Fire and Rescue Authority (note 4)					-
−1,202	Internal trading accounts (note 16)					−761
−75,529	Asset management revenue account (note 12)					−84,562
24,780	Pensions interest cost and expected return on pensions assets (note 9)					22,830
1,040,478	**Net operating expenditure**					**1,081,159**
37,887	Revenue contribution to capital expenditure					24,245
−2,354	Contribution from other authorities (note 22)					−2,277
−15,862	Contribution from capital financing account (note 13)					−14,819
−14,117	Deferred charges written down					−19,145
−24,190	Contribution to/(from) pension reserve					−32,320
4,780	Contribution to/(from)other reserves (note 14)					9,205
1,026,622	**Amount to be met from Government grant and local taxpayers**					**1,046,048**
−295,397	Revenue support grant					−334,004
−332,574	National business rates					−311,621
−401,219	Precept					−402,458
−2,915	Surplus on collection funds					−2,987
−5,483	**(Increase)/reduction in revenue account balance for the year**					**−5,022**
−7,606	Balance brought forward 1 April					−12,599
−13,089	**Balance at 31 March**					**−17,621**
490	less transfer to Hampshire Fire and Rescue Authority (note 2)					-
−12,599	**Balance carried forward at 31 March**					**−17,621**

FIGURE A3.2 *Hampshire County Council – Consolidated revenue account for the year ended 31 March 2005*

Cash flow statement

	2003/04	2004/05
	£'000	£'000
Revenue activities		
Cash outflows		
Cash paid to and on behalf of employees	738,351	775,091
Other operating costs	536,860	541,614
	1,275,211	**1,316,705**
Cash inflows		
Rents	–3,769	–4,346
Precepts	–401,219	–402,458
National business rates	–332,574	–313,904
Revenue support grant	–295,397	–332,926
Collection fund surpluses	–2,915	–2,987
Charges for goods and services	–72,855	–77,186
Specific Government grants	–155,841	–172,468
Other income	–93,184	–80,591
	–1,357,754	**–1,386,866**
Net cash inflow from revenue activities (note 1)	**–82,543**	**–70,161**
Returns on investments and servicing of finance		
Cash outflows - Interest paid	14,051	14,652
Cash inflows - Interest received	–3,025	–3,009
Net cash outflow from servicing of finance activities	**11,026**	**11,643**
Capital Activities		
Cash outflows		
Fixed assets	139,463	181,796
Deferred charges	13,522	17,077
	152,985	**198,873**
Cash inflows		
Sale of fixed assets	–16,508	–18,817
Capital grants (note 2)	–34,550	–41,972
Other income	–23,112	–55,087
	–74,170	**–115,876**
Net cash outflow from capital activities	**78,815**	**82,997**
Net cash outflow before financing (notes 3 and 4)	**7,298**	**24,479**
Financing		
Borrowing repayable over periods of one year or more		
Repayments	4,000	8,000
New loans	–34,000	–39,000
Borrowing repayable within one year		
Repayments	427,132	412,361
New loans	–439,603	–438,415
Net cash inflow	**–35,173**	**–32,575**

FIGURE A3.3 *Hampshire County Council – Cash flow statement for the year ended 31 March 2005*

Appendix 4: UK Software Tax and Accounting Rules

The tax and accounting treatment of software has evolved over many years. At the time of writing (2005), in the UK the relevant legislation is Section 67A of the Capital Allowances Act 1990 and Section 68 of the Finance (No. 2) Act 1992. In the interpretation and application of this legislation, assistance may be found in Revenue Interpretation 56 (RI 56) published in Inland Revenue Tax Bulletin, Issue F, November 1993.

Revenue Interpretations (and Tax Bulletins) do not have the force of law, but explain how the HM Revenue and Customs (formerly Inland Revenue) interpret and intend to operate legislation. All Inland Revenue and Customs publications are available on the HM Revenue and Customs website (www.hmrc.gov.uk). The following is a summary of the main UK rules from the viewpoint of the user organization.

MONTHLY OR OTHER PERIODIC LICENCE AND MAINTENANCE CHARGES

These are expenses and are charged straight to the profit and loss account. They reduce the profit (or increase the loss) and therefore, like any other normal business expense, reduce the amount of corporation tax payable or (if a loss) increase the amount reclaimable.

LUMP SUM PAYMENTS FOR SOFTWARE

The Finance (No. 2) Act 1992, Section 68, which amends the Capital Allowances Act 1990, simplified the taxation treatment of lump sum payments for software. Section 68 removes any distinction for tax purposes between payments to acquire software outright and payments made to use software under licence. They are now both treated the same, in accordance with the guidance set out in the Tax Bulletin article referred to above, on which the remainder of this Appendix is based. In either case, the question to be asked is whether the software (licensed or owned) is a capital asset in the trade of the user company. This depends upon its expected 'useful economic life' in the business.

Useful life is less than two years

If the expected life is less than two years, then HM Revenue and Customs will accept treatment of the lump sum as an expense. This means that its full cost can be deducted in arriving at taxable profit according to normal accounting rules. For example, assume that £24k is paid at the beginning of an accounting year for software expected to have a useful economic life of 18 months. £16k would be treated as a tax-deductible expense in that year, the remaining £8k in the following year. A recent example of 'short-life' software could be software that was acquired specifically to assist in the preventing or solving of 'millennium bug' problems.

Useful life is two years or more

If, as would usually be the case, the expected life of software is two years or more, then for tax purposes it would be treated as a capital asset, just like hardware. It would be regarded as 'plant and machinery', on which capital allowances could be claimed, usually at 25 per cent on the reducing balance. In this case, only £6k (25% × £24k, the first-year capital allowance) would be treated as a tax-deductible expense in the first year. The remainder of the cost would be treated according to the capital allowance rules outlined in Chapter 6.

Self-developed software

Where organizations develop software for themselves for use in their own business, the Inland Revenue will apply the same rules as for licensed or bought software (see above) to determine whether the costs, including the salaries of the in-house writers, shall be treated as expense or capital.

Equipment and software acquired as a package

Where the package is acquired for a single payment, the guidance is that the expenditure should be apportioned between hardware and software. Capital allowances under the normal rules will be given on the hardware portion. The treatment of the software element, whether licensed or bought outright, will be determined according to the rules set out above. However, the main purpose of the rules is to prevent payments being treated as 'expense' that should more properly be treated as 'capital'. Therefore, where the user wishes to treat the whole package as 'capital', apportionment might not in practice be necessary.

SUMMARY

In summary, the effect of the above rules is to bring software assets into line with other business assets in the way they are treated for tax. The tax treatment corresponds with generally accepted accounting treatment.

Appendix 5: UK Long-term Contract Accounting Rules

A contract is regarded as long term if the time taken to complete it falls into different accounting periods. A contract requiring to be accounted for as 'long term' will usually extend for a period exceeding one year. However, shorter contracts may fall within the requirement where not to do so would lead to distortion of the results. I would concede that the detailed accounting for long-term contracts belongs in 'deep accounting' territory, and the rules governing it are set out later in this Appendix. However, the following few paragraphs are intended to summarize the main principles for the non-specialist.

Obviously the precise financial outcome of a long-term contract will only be known on its completion. However, to await completion before taking into account any revenue (and resulting profit or loss) during the intervening years, during which costs will be incurred, would distort the accounts of those years. The main purpose of the accounting rules is to ensure that the accounts in any year show, as accurately as possible, the revenue and costs attributable to long-term contracts, and the resulting profit or loss.

The most important rule is that no profit should be attributed to a long-term contract until the outcome of it can be assessed with reasonable certainty. Where the outcome can be assessed with reasonable certainty, and assuming that costs and contract activity accrue evenly over time, then usually:

1. Cumulative contract turnover to date is taken as the proportion of total contract price relating to work actually done to date. In years other than the first year of a contract, turnover for the year is thus the cumulative turnover to date less the corresponding figure at the end of the preceding year. You will no doubt recall from earlier parts of the book that turnover (revenue earned) has nothing to do with whether stage payments have or have not been received.

2. Cumulative contract cost of sales to date is usually taken as the same proportion as in (1) of total expected contract costs, plus full provision for any expected losses (see (3) below). Cost of sales for the

year is thus the cumulative cost of sales to date less the corresponding figure at the end of the preceding year.

3. Any losses, for example excess costs or penalties, expected to arise on the contract must be provided for (i.e. taken into account by adding to cost of sales) at the time that they are foreseen. The full amount of the expected loss must be provided for, not just the amount of the loss that has arisen to date.

4. Contract gross profit for the year is the difference between contract turnover and contract cost of sales.

RULES GOVERNING UK COMPANIES

The accounting rules governing long-term contracts in the UK are contained in Statement of Standard Accounting Practice 9 (SSAP 9): Stocks and long-term contracts. The relevant international standard is International Accounting Standard No. 11 (IAS 11): Accounting for construction contracts. SSAP 9 is very close to the international standard and contains the words '... compliance with SSAP 9 will ensure compliance with ... IAS 11 in all material respects'. SSAP 9 should be studied in detail if a comprehensive understanding of the rules is required. However, the following extracts* from SSAP 9 contain the main accounting rules for determining how a long-term contract should be accounted for by the contractor.

> **Long-term contracts should be assessed on a contract by contract basis and reflected in the profit and loss account by recording turnover and related costs as contract activity progresses. Turnover is ascertained in a manner appropriate to the stage of completion of the contract, the business and the industry in which it operates.**
>
> **SSAP 9 paragraph 28**

> **Where it is considered that the outcome of a long-term contract can be assessed with reasonable certainty before its conclusion, the prudently calculated attributable profit should be recognised in the profit and loss account as the difference between the reported turnover and related costs for that contract.**
>
> **SSAP 9 paragraph 29**

> Long-term contracts should be disclosed in the balance sheet as follows:
>
> (a) The amount by which recorded turnover is in excess of payments on account should be classified as 'amounts recoverable on contracts' and separately disclosed within debtors;
>
> (b) The balance of payments on account (in excess of amounts (i) matched with turnover, and (ii) offset against long-term contract balances) should be classified as payments on account and separately disclosed within creditors;
>
> (c) The amount of long-term contracts, at costs incurred, net of amounts transferred to cost of sales, after deducting foreseeable losses and payments on account not matched with turnover, should be classified as 'long-term contract balances' and separately disclosed within the balance sheet heading 'Stocks'. The balance sheet note should disclose separately the balances of:
>
>   (i) net cost less foreseeable losses, and
>
>   (ii) applicable payments on account;
>
> (d) The amount by which the provision or accrual for foreseeable losses exceeds the costs (after transfers to cost of sales) should be included within either provisions for liabilities and charges or creditors as appropriate.
>
> SSAP 9 paragraph 30

Illustration of accounting for long-term contracts

The following example, quoted in full from Appendix 3 of SSAP 9*, provides illustrations of all the accounting principles set out in the above paragraphs. Thus far in this book it has been possible to delve quite deeply into finance and accounting without any mention of those rather confusing terms 'debit' and 'credit'. However, they do make an appearance (in their abbreviated forms 'DR' and 'CR' on the first page of the example), it being a condition of the permission to use it that the example be reproduced exactly as given. As used in the example, 'DR' simply means 'asset' and 'CR' means 'liability'. More information on 'debit' and 'credit' is provided in Appendix 7.

---

* Extracts from Accounting Standards 2005/2006 are reproduced by kind permission of the Accounting Standards Board Limited. For further information please visit www.frc.org.uk/asb.

TABLE A5.1 *Illustration of accounting for long-term contracts*

	Project Number					Balance Sheet Total	Profit & Loss Account
	1	2	3	4	5		
Recorded as turnover – being value of work done	145	520	380	200	55		1,300
Cumulative payments on account	(100)	(600)	(400)	(150)	(80)		
Classified as amounts recoverable on contracts	45				50	95DR	
Balance (excess) of payments on account		(80)	(20)		(25)		
Applied as an offset against long-term contract balances – see below		60	20		15		
Residue classified as payments on account		(20)	–		(10)	(30)CR	
Total costs incurred	110	510	450	250	100		
Transferred to cost of sales	(110)	(450)	(350)	(250)	(55)		(1,215)
	–	60	100	–	45		
Provision/accrual for foreseeable losses charged to cost of sales				(40)	(30)		(70)
		60	100		15		
Classified as provision/accrual for losses				(40)		(40)CR	
Balance (excess) of payments on account applied as offset against long-term contract balances		(60)	(20)		(15)		
Classified as long-term contract balances		–	80		–	80DR	
Gross profit or loss on long-term contracts	35	70	30	(90)	(30)		15

Table continues ...

TABLE A5.1 *Continued*

PROJECT 1
Profit and Loss Account – cumulative

Included in turnover	145
Included in cost of sales	(110)
Gross profit	35

Balance Sheet
The amount to be included in debtors under 'amounts recoverable on contracts' is calculated as follows:

Cumulative turnover	145
Less cumulative payments on account	(100)
Included in debtors	45

In this case, all the costs incurred to date relate to the contract activity recorded as turnover and are transferred to cost of sales, leaving a zero balance in stocks.
Note that if the outcome of the contract could not be assessed with reasonable certainty, no profit would be recognized. If no loss is expected, it may be appropriate to show as turnover a proportion of the total contract value using a zero estimate of profit.

PROJECT 2
Profit and Loss Account – cumulative

Included in turnover	520
Included in cost of sales	(450)
Gross profit	70

Balance Sheet
As cumulative payments on account are greater than turnover there is a credit balance, calculated as follows:

Cumulative turnover	520
Less cumulative payments on account	(600)
Excess payments on account	(80)

This credit balance should firstly be offset against any debit balance on this contract included in stocks and then any residual amount should be classified under creditors as a payment received on account as follows:

Total cost incurred to date	510
Less cumulative amounts recorded as cost of sales	(450)
	60
Less excess payments on account (above)	(80)
Included in creditors	(20)

The amount to be included in stocks is zero and the credit balance of 20 is classified as a payment received on account and included in creditors.

The balance sheet note on stocks should disclose separately the net cost of 60 and the applicable payments on account of 60.

Table continues ...

TABLE A5.1 *Continued*

PROJECT 3
Profit and Loss Account – cumulative

Included in turnover	380
Included in cost of sales	(350)
Gross profit	30

Balance Sheet

As with Project 2, cumulative payments on account are greater than turnover and there is a credit balance, calculated as follows:

Cumulative turnover	380
Less cumulative payments on account	(400)
Excess payments on account	(20)

This credit balance should firstly be offset against any debit balance on this contract included in stocks and the residual amount, if any, should be classified under creditors as a payment received on account.

The amount to be included in stocks under long-term contract balances is calculated as follows:

Total cost incurred to date	450
Less cumulative amounts recorded as cost of sales	(350)
	100
Less excess payments on account (above)	(20)
Included in long-term contract balances	80

The balance sheet note on stocks should disclose separately the net cost of 100 and the applicable payments on account of 20.

PROJECT 4
Profit and Loss Account – cumulative

Included in turnover	200
Included in cost of sales	(290)
Gross loss	90

Balance Sheet

The amount to be included in debtors under 'amounts recoverable on contracts' is calculated as follows:

Cumulative turnover	200
Less cumulative payments on account	(150)
Included in debtors	50

The amount to be included as a provision/accrual for foreseeable losses is calculated as follows:

Total cost incurred to date		250
Less transferred to cost of sales	(250)	
Foreseeable losses on contract as a whole	(40)	
		(290)
Classified as provision/accrual for foreseeable losses		(40)

Note that the credit balance of 40 is not offset against the debit balance of 50 included in debtors.

Table continues ...

TABLE A5.1 *Continued*

PROJECT 5
Profit and Loss Account – cumulative

Included in turnover	55
Included in cost of sales	(85)
Gross loss	(30)

Balance Sheet

As cumulative payments on account are greater than turnover there is a credit balance, calculated as follows:

Cumulative turnover	55
Less cumulative payments on account	(80)
Excess payments on account	(25)

The credit balance should firstly be deducted from long-term contract balances (after having deducted foreseeable losses) and the residual balance included in creditors under payments received on account as follows:

Total cost incurred to date		100
Less transferred to cost of sales	(55)	
Foreseeable losses on contract as a whole	(30)	
		(85)
		15
Less excess payments on account (above)		(25)
Included in creditors		(10)

The balance sheet note on stocks should disclose separately the net cost of 15 and the applicable payments on account of 15.

Appendix 6: UK Value Added Tax (VAT): IT Aspects

This Appendix is a brief guide to some aspects of VAT in the United Kingdom that are particularly relevant to IT, starting with a review of its main principles, some of its jargon and the various categories of 'supply'. VAT is a complex subject and readers are recommended to consult the numerous explanatory booklets published by HM Revenue and Customs, starting with 'The VAT Guide'. This is a guide to the main VAT rules and procedures, and it contains a list of other VAT publications. All VAT publications are available on the HM Revenue and Customs website (www.hmrc.gov.uk).

WHAT IS VAT?

VAT is a tax on consumer expenditure on most goods and services, including second-hand goods. It is administered by HM Revenue and Customs. It was introduced in 1973 as a condition of the UK joining the EU.

Disregarding those businesses whose turnover is below the VAT registration threshold, and disregarding the cases where transactions are exempt from VAT (see below), VAT is charged on every business supply of goods and services, at rates currently ranging from zero per cent to 17.5 per cent in the UK. Every VAT-registered business has to account quarterly for the difference between the VAT that it has charged and the VAT that it has paid. In this way the actual burden of VAT is borne by the first person down a chain of transactions who cannot offset the VAT charged to him/her against VAT that he/she has received: essentially the ultimate consumer.

DEFINITIONS

Supplies Goods or services sold to others.
Output tax VAT that a VAT-registered business must charge on its supplies.
Inputs Goods or services bought from others.

Input tax VAT that a business pays on its inputs.

CATEGORIES OF SUPPLY

Standard Supplies on which the seller charges VAT at the standard rate. This category covers most goods and services. The seller can usually recover all or part of the input tax paid.

Zero-rated Supplies on which VAT is charged at zero per cent. The seller can usually recover input tax as above. Examples of zero-rated supplies are food, books and transport.

Exempt Supplies that are exempt from VAT. The seller does not charge output tax and cannot generally recover input tax on inputs related to those supplies (but see 'partial exemption' and the 'Capital Goods Scheme' below). Examples of exempt supplies are banking, most kinds of insurance, education and health goods and services.

Partial exemption If inputs (such as IT equipment and software) are used towards the provision of both exempt and non-exempt supplies, then a proportion of input tax is recoverable.

To avoid double taxation, non-recoverable VAT is a deductible expense in calculating corporation tax.

PURCHASE AND LEASE COMPARED

Purchase and hire purchase

For VAT purposes, purchase and hire purchase are both regarded as methods of acquiring ownership of goods. Input tax is paid on the purchase price. On any eventual sale, output tax is charged to the buyer and must be paid over to HM Revenue and Customs in the usual way.

Leasing

For VAT purposes, leases other than hire purchase are regarded as payments for the provision of services. Output tax is charged by the lessor to the lessee on the lease payments.

When a finance-leased asset is sold, the proceeds being shared between lessor and lessee, output tax is charged to the buyer in the usual way. However, only tax on the proportion of sales proceeds retained by the lessor has to be paid over to HM Revenue and Customs. The lessee retains its proportion of proceeds including the output tax. The lessee's proportion of sale proceeds is regarded for VAT purposes as a refund of payments already made.

THE VAT CAPITAL GOODS SCHEME

This scheme, described fully in VAT leaflet 706/2, applies to certain IT assets and to land and buildings. The main features of the scheme as it applies to IT assets are as follows.

The Scheme was introduced in 1990 in recognition of the inequity of input tax on short-life assets, in particular IT equipment, being totally irrecoverable by businesses providing exempt supplies, however short the time that the assets may be used in the business. The main features of the scheme, as applicable to businesses making only exempt supplies, are:

- The scheme only applies to 'computers and items of computer equipment' (not software) with a VAT-exclusive value of £50,000 or more. This minimum value applies to individual items of equipment; smaller amounts cannot be aggregated as a way round the limit.

- For the purposes of the scheme, the equipment is deemed to have a five-year life. A proportion of input VAT is recoverable in respect of assets sold in years 1, 2, 3 or 4, as shown in Table A6.1.

TABLE A6.1 *Proportion of input VAT recoverable*

Year of disposal	Proportion of input VAT recoverable (but see limit below)
1	80%
2	60%
3	40%
4	20%
5	0%

- The total amount recoverable may not exceed the amount of the output VAT charged on the sale of the asset; so if the asset is scrapped then no input tax is recoverable

Example

Assume that a single item of computer equipment is bought in Year 1 for £100k by a company, all of whose supplies are VAT-exempt. The equipment is sold during Year 3 for £25k. For this example, and to keep the arithmetic simple, assume a VAT rate of 20 per cent.

In Year 1 the company would pay input tax of £20k on acquisition of the equipment (20% × £100k). For the sale in Year 3, the company would invoice the buyer for £25,000, plus £5,000 output tax. The maximum amount of input tax recoverable under the Scheme would be 40 per cent of £20k, which is £8k. However, this would be restricted to £5k, the amount of output tax on the sale. This would be retained by the company instead of being paid to HM Revenue and Customs.

More complex arithmetic applies to partially exempt businesses (see leaflet 706/2 or visit the website mentioned above).

Appendix 7: Debit and Credit

Having got this far in the book, then I believe that you will have understood the essential simplicity of financial concepts, and of accountancy, which is nothing more than the means whereby the application of those concepts is recorded. If so, you will have done so without any mention of the terms 'debit' and 'credit', except (briefly) in Appendix 5. However, you might be interested in how those terms came about.

It happens that in the United Kingdom, and in some other countries, balance sheets are today usually set out as described in Chapter 11. Assets are shown at the top, liabilities at the bottom, and this is sometimes referred to as the 'vertical format'. However, in former times, when accounting was done by hand rather than by computer, and in some countries still today, balance sheets were set out differently, being divided into two columns. Assets were shown on the left-hand side and liabilities on the right: the 'horizontal format'. The same was true of profit and loss accounts. Instead of the vertical format often used today, the horizontal format was used for them too. Expenses were shown on the left-hand side and revenues on the right.

This was all a natural consequence of the way in which, in those days, individual transactions were recorded in a book, often a beautifully bound book, that was called a 'journal'. For example, the two sides of the transaction representing the sale of goods to J Bloggs for £10 would have been recorded in the journal of the selling business, inessential details being omitted, as shown in Table A7.1. People to whom goods or services were sold, and who therefore owed a debt to the business (the obligation to pay for them) were called 'debitors', different by only one letter from the word used today. Those to whom a business owed a debt (in this example, the obligation to deliver goods) were called creditors, as they still are. By convention, the debitors were always shown in the left-hand column, the creditors on the right. Over time, 'debitor' and 'creditor' became abbreviated to 'debit' and 'credit', and eventually to 'dr' and 'cr'. Notice from the example that, even in those more leisurely days, the intermediate recording as a 'creditor' of the obligation of the seller to actually deliver the goods would have been omitted, the transaction being instead immediately 'credited' to sales.

TABLE A7.1 *Illustration of an entry in a journal*

Date	Details of transaction	Debitor £	Creditor £
November 25	*J Bloggs, for goods sold*	*10.00*	
	Sales		*10.00*

Because the two-column format was obviously a convenient way of recording two-sided transactions, it came to serve as the medium for recording all transactions, not just those involving actual debitors and creditors. So, all assets came to be recorded as 'debits', and all liabilities as 'credits'. It was then only a small step also to use the 'debit' column to record expenses (the using up of assets, you will recall) and the 'credit' column to record revenues, the money earned when the obligation to actually deliver goods or services had been fulfilled.

Thus it was that generations of finance and accountancy students came to be told that 'assets and expenses are debits, while liabilities and revenues are credits'. This might possibly have contributed to understanding if it had been explained to those same students that expenses were used-up assets and that revenues represented money earned when a liability (the obligation to deliver) had been fulfilled. Often, there was no such explanation.

Some Relevant Financial Definitions

Where appropriate, US equivalent terminology is also shown.

accounting rate of return (ARR) or **return on investment (ROI)** Average annual profit generated by a project as a percentage of the capital employed in it.

accrued expense or **accrual** A service received or expense incurred for which payment has not yet been made.

accrued income or **accrued revenue** Work done for which payment has not yet been received.

acid test ratio Same as *quick ratio*.

administrative expenses In a published profit and loss account, the sum of all the non-financial expenses of the business except cost of sales.

allocation A charge made by one division or department of an organization to another. Also called 'cross-charge'.

amortization Depreciation of intangible assets such as property leases and goodwill.

annual accounts Financial statements of a business produced annually to comply with statutory obligations.

asset Something of value that is owned or to which an individual or business has a right, that may be tangible or intangible, long-term (*fixed* or *capital asset*) or short-term (*current asset*).

asset turnover See *capital productivity*.

associated undertakings Other companies, of whose shares a company holds a significant minority, usually at least 20 per cent.

auditor A person appointed to report to the shareholders of a company on the accuracy of its annual accounts.

bad debt (*US – uncollectible*) A debt, owed by a customer, that is unlikely or certain not to be paid, written off to the profit and loss account as an expense.

balance sheet (*US – statement of financial position*)   A summary of the assets and liabilities of a business at a point in time.

bankruptcy   The state of being unable to pay one's debts; a legal procedure for giving public notice of that fact.

book value   The value at which an asset appears on the balance sheet; for fixed assets, usually cost less accumulated depreciation.

break-even   Same as *payback*; also the sales volume at which the revenue from sales exactly equals the fixed costs plus the variable costs.

budget   A financial plan setting targets for the revenues and expenditures of an organization or department for a specified period.

business case   A recommendation regarding a particular investment opportunity, giving reasons that include a summary of the financial case.

capital   Money contributed by the proprietors of a business to enable it to function.

capital allowances   Tax relief on capital expenditure (UK).

capital assets   Same as *fixed assets*.

capital employed   Usually all the long-term money (proprietors' capital and long-term loans) being used in a business.

capital expenditure   Money spent on fixed assets.

capital productivity or **asset turnover**   Sales divided by capital employed; a measure of the sales being generated by the long-term capital employed in the business.

cash flow   A movement of cash into or out of a business; also the net total of such movements during a period.

cash flow statement   A summary of cash inflows and cash outflows during a period of time, usually a year.

Companies Acts 1985 and 1989   The main Acts of Parliament regulating companies in the UK.

company (*US – corporation*)   A corporate enterprise that has a legal identity separate from that of its members.

consolidated or **group accounts**   Combined accounts of a group of companies.

contribution   What is left from revenue after deducting the variable costs of earning it.

corporation tax   Tax on company profits.

cost accounting or **costing**   The process of analysing and classifying elements of cost for the purpose of calculating as accurately as possible the total cost of a process, product or service.

cost–benefit analysis A method of deciding whether or not a particular project or investment should be undertaken, by comparing its attributable likely costs and benefits over its estimated lifetime.

cost of capital The return expected by the providers of capital; in a company, the weighted average of the costs of equity and debt.

cost of sales The total costs of getting goods or services sold during a period to a saleable state.

creditor A person or business to whom a debt is due.

cross-charge Same as *allocation*.

current assets or **circulating assets** Short-term assets that are turned over (used and replenished) frequently, usually within one year, in the course of business; mainly stocks, debtors and cash.

current liabilities Short-term obligations to be discharged within a year; mainly trade creditors and overdrafts.

current ratio Current assets divided by current liabilities.

debt/equity or **gearing ratio** Usually the total of interest-bearing debt (long-term borrowing plus overdrafts) divided by equity (total capital and reserves), expressed as a percentage.

debtor A debt due to a business or individual.

debtor days Trade debtors divided by (credit sales / 365); the number of days, on average, that credit customers are taking to pay their bills.

deferred income or **deferred revenue** Cash received in advance of goods or services delivered.

depreciation An accounting technique for charging the cost of a fixed asset as an expense over its expected useful economic life.

diluted earnings per share What the earnings per share would have been if the exercise of certain options or the occurrence of certain events had resulted in more shares being in circulation.

direct costs Costs, for example materials and labour, that can be traced to a particular unit of cost, for example a product, a batch of products or a process or a service in an economically feasible way.

director A person appointed by the shareholders of a company to run the business on their behalf.

discounted cash flow (DCF) Two related methods for comparing the values of cash flows occurring at different times, by taking into account the time value of money: net present value (NPV) and internal rate of return (IRR).

discounted payback The application of the payback method to discounted cash flows.

dividend   That part of the profit of a company paid to its shareholders in cash.

dividend yield   The dividend per share divided by the current share price, expressed as a percentage.

drawings   Amounts drawn out of an unincorporated business by the proprietor or proprietors.

earnings per share (*US – earnings per share of common stock*)   Profit attributable to ordinary equity shareholders of a company, or of the parent company if a group, divided by the weighted average number of ordinary shares outstanding during the period.

equity   Same as *shareholders' funds.*

equity dividends   Dividends on ordinary or equity shares.

equity shares (*US – common shares* or *common stock*)   The ordinary shares of a company.

exceptional item   Something falling within the ordinary activities of a business but which is a 'one-off occurrence' or sufficiently unusual to warrant being shown separately.

exempt supply   A supply on which the seller does not charge UK value added tax (VAT).

expense   The extent to which an asset has been used up during a period of time, shown as a charge against profit in the profit and loss account; also the everyday meaning of the term.

extraordinary item   An item possessing a high degree of abnormality that arises from events outside the ordinary activities of a business that are not expected to recur, for example natural disasters.

factoring or **invoice discounting**   Buying the trade debts of a company in return for a discounted lump sum.

financial accounting   The process of recording the transactions of an organization and preparing its annual Accounts.

finance   Money resources.

finance lease (*US – capital lease*)   A lease that transfers all or substantially all the risks and rewards of ownership of an asset to the lessee.

financial case   A tabulation, designed to aid decision-making, of the estimated financial costs and benefits of an investment opportunity over a chosen period.

financing   The process of obtaining the money resources for something that it is wished to acquire or have the use of.

fixed assets, also **capital assets**   Long-term assets likely to last more than one year.

fixed capital   That part of a company's capital that is invested in fixed assets.

fixed costs   Costs that stay the same regardless of the quantity of goods manufactured or sold.

full payout finance lease (*US – full payout capital lease*)   A lease under which the lessee, during the primary period, pays the lessor the full cost of the leased asset plus interest; a lease whose residual value is zero.

gearing (*US – leverage*)   The relationship between the amount of borrowed money and the amount of proprietors' money in a business.

gearing ratio   See *debt/equity ratio.*

gilt-edged securities or **gilts**   UK Government stocks or bonds on which a fixed rate of interest is usually paid.

goodwill   The amount by which the price paid for a business exceeds the market value of the assets less liabilities acquired.

gross profit   The difference between turnover (sales) and cost of sales.

group accounts   Same as *consolidated accounts.*

group of companies   A holding or parent company together with its subsidiaries.

hire purchase   A lease with a purchase option.

holding company or **parent company**   A company that holds all or a majority of the shares of other companies, which it then controls, and that are then known as subsidiaries.

holiday   A period, usually at the beginning of a lease, during which no cash payments are required.

hurdle rate   The minimum rate of return that a proposed project is required to deliver; usually refers to internal rate of return (IRR) or return on investment (ROI).

indirect costs   Costs that cannot be traced to a particular unit of cost, for example a product, a batch of products, a process or a service, in an economically feasible way.

input   UK value added tax (VAT) term meaning goods or services bought from others.

input tax   UK value added tax (VAT) term meaning VAT that a business pays on its inputs, and that most businesses can reclaim.

interest cover   Operating profit divided by interest payable; the extent to which profit is available to cover interest payable.

internal rate of return (IRR)   The rate of return earned by the money invested in a project; the percentage discount rate i that must be applied in the present value formula to a series of cash flows if the net present value of the series is to equate to zero.

investment   The acquisition of assets or the depositing of money with a primary view to financial return, either as income or capital gain.

joint venture   An undertaking by which its participants expect to achieve some common purpose or benefit, controlled jointly by two or more venturers.

lease   A contract under which the owner of an asset (the lessor) permits someone else (the lessee) to use it during a defined period in return for agreed payments.

liability   Something that is owed; an obligation.

limited company, also **limited liability company**   A company whose members are legally responsible only to a specified amount for its debts.

liquid assets   Cash and things easily convertible into cash.

loan capital   The long-term money provided to a company by lenders.

loss (or profit) on disposal   The difference between the book value of an asset and its proceeds of sale or trade-in.

management accounting   The process of using financial information as a way of helping management to manage an organization rather than to satisfy statutory reporting requirements, including but not limited to budgeting, costing and pricing.

manufacturing overheads or **indirect production costs**   Manufacturing costs, for example factory insurance, heating and cleaning costs that cannot be traced to a particular unit of cost in an economically feasible way.

mark-up   With respect to goods bought and sold, profit as a percentage of purchase price.

materiality   The state of having sufficient significance to require separate disclosure in a company's accounts.

minority interest   In a group of companies, the proportion of group capital and group profits or losses attributable to shareholders outside the group.

multiple   Same as *price/earnings (P/E) ratio.*

negative equity   Of the situation where an asset has a market value less than the outstanding loan borrowed to purchase it.

net cash flow   The sum, positive or negative, of a series of cash flows.

net current liabilities or **net current assets**   The difference between total current assets and total current liabilities.

net present value (NPV)   The sum of a series of positive and negative present values.

net worth   What is left when the external liabilities have been deducted from the value of the assets of an individual or a business.

nominal or **par value**   The face value of a share.

off balance sheet   Of an operating lease, descriptive of the fact that neither the leased asset nor the obligation to make payments appears on the balance sheet of the lessee.

operating lease   A lease other than a finance lease (US – a lease other than a capital lease); usually a lease that includes a guaranteed residual value.

operating margin or **return on sales**   Operating profit over sales, expressed as a percentage.

operating profit (*US – operating earnings*)   The difference between gross profit and administrative expenses; the profit from business operations before interest and tax.

opportunity cost   The benefit lost by not employing an economic resource in the most profitable alternative activity.

ordinary or **equity share** (*US – common share* or *common stock*)   Part ownership in a company that confers a legal right to a proportionate part of the company's profits or losses and to a proportionate share of the proceeds if the company is wound up.

output tax   UK value added tax (VAT) term meaning VAT that a VAT-registered business must charge on its non-exempt supplies.

outsourcing   The arranging of work to be done by an outside contractor, rather than in-house.

overheads   Administrative expenses not directly attributable to the production of goods or the provision of services.

partnership   An association of two or more people carrying on a business.

payback or **break-even**   The length of time that it will take for the net cash inflows of a project to equal the initial cash outlay.

payable   US term meaning the same as *trade creditor*.

peppercorn   The nominal periodic payment usually required from a lessee in the secondary period of a full payout finance lease.

plc   See *public limited company*.

preference share   A share in a company that entitles the holder to a fixed rate of interest rather than a variable dividend, but usually carries no voting rights.

prepayment or **payment in advance**   Payment made for goods or services before they have been received.

present value   The value derived by applying the present value formula to a future cash flow.

present value formula $F(1 + i)^{-n}$ represents the present value of a cash flow (F), receivable or payable n periods in the future, discounted at a required rate of return i.

price/earnings (P/E) ratio or **multiple**   The market price of a share divided by the earnings per share of the company.

pricing   The process of determining the price at which a product or service is to be sold.

private limited company   A company that is not a public limited company.

profit or **loss**   The difference between the earnings and expenses of a business.

profitability index   Usually the total present value of the future net cash flows of a project, divided by the present value of the net initial investment.

profit after tax or **net profit** (*US – net income*)   The profit that, subject in group accounts to any necessary adjustment for minority interests, belongs to the shareholders.

profit and loss account (*US – statement of earnings*)   In a balance sheet, the reserve representing the amount of accumulated profits and losses of a business to date after dividends or drawings; also an account showing how the profit or loss during a year was arrived at.

profit margin   With respect to goods bought and sold, profit as a percentage of selling price.

project risk   The risk of the extent to which estimates of the benefits and costs of a project may be wrong.

provision   An amount set aside for a known liability, the amount of which cannot be precisely determined.

public limited company (plc)   A company that is authorized to offer shares to the public either directly or by trading on a stock exchange.

quick or **acid test ratio**   Usually the sum of all current assets except stock, divided by current liabilities.

receivable   US term meaning the same as *trade debtor*.

rental   Payments for the use of an asset, often but not necessarily characterized by the lack of any direct connection, visible to the user, between the cost of the asset and the payments required.

reserve   Anything that is part of shareholders' funds other than share capital.

residual value   An amount, based on the expected value of an asset at the end of a lease, deducted by the lessor from the asset's value in determining the payments due.

retained profit   Profit that belongs to the shareholders but has not yet been paid to them as dividends.

return   The yield or profit from an investment.

return on capital employed (ROCE)   Profit (usually operating profit) divided by capital employed (usually all the long-term money used in a business), expressed as a percentage.

return on equity (ROE)   The profit that belongs to the shareholders (profit after tax) divided by the equity or capital that belongs to them (the total capital and reserves), expressed as a percentage.

return on investment (ROI)   Same as *accounting rate of return*.

return on sales   Same as *operating margin*.

revaluation reserve   The increase in capital represented by an upward revaluation in the balance sheet of one or more of a company's assets.

revenue or **turnover**   Earnings from the sale of goods or services.

risk capital   A term used to describe money invested in ordinary or equity shares because with the right to a share of profits comes the risk of a share of losses.

rolling debt   The practice of adding debt from the early termination of one lease to the amount financed by a subsequent one.

share   See *ordinary share* and *preference share*.

share capital   The capital contributed by the shareholders of a company.

share certificate   A document that is evidence of ownership of shares in a company.

shareholder (*US – stockholder*)   Owner of shares in a limited company.

shareholders' funds (*US – total stockholders' equity*)   Share capital plus total reserves.

shareholder value added (SVA)   At its simplest, the amount, if any, left after deducting from profit after tax the cost of the capital used to earn it.

share premium   The amount by which the price at which a share is issued by a company exceeds the nominal or par value of the share.

share premium account   A reserve representing the accumulated sum of share premiums.

sole trader   An individual who is the sole owner or proprietor of a business.

stock exchange   A place where stocks and shares are bought and sold, prices being determined by supply and demand.

stocks (*US – inventory*)   Things held temporarily pending the purpose for which they are intended.

stock turnover or **stock turn**   Sales divided by stocks; a measure of the sales being generated relative to the stocks held.

subsidiary company   A company controlled by another that holds all or a majority of its shares.

sunk cost   Money already spent that cannot be recouped, and that therefore should not affect financial decision-making.

supplies   UK value added tax (VAT) term meaning goods or services sold to others.

systematic risk   The risk represented by unpredictable factors in the economy such as interest rates, taxation and consumer demand.

taxable profit   Turnover less allowable expenses and capital allowances; the amount on which tax is payable.

tax book value   A UK term meaning the cost of a fixed asset less capital allowances claimed to date.

tax loss   The result of allowable expenses and capital allowances exceeding revenue in a year.

time value of money   A term descriptive of the fact that money received or paid in the future is worth less than money received or paid today.

trade creditors (*US – accounts payable* or *payables*)   Suppliers of goods and services to whom money is owed in the ordinary course of trade.

trade debtors (*US – accounts receivable* or *receivables*)   Customers who owe money for goods and services supplied in the ordinary course of trade.

transaction   A piece of business done, especially commercial business.

turnover (*US – revenues*)   Same as *revenue*; also used to describe the rate at which assets, or particular classes of assets, are used and replenished, or 'turned over'.

value added tax (VAT)   A tax levied on goods and services at every point at which value is added; ultimately borne by consumers.

variable costs   Costs that vary directly with the quantity of goods manufactured or sold.

working capital That part of a company's capital that is invested in net current assets.

work in progress Partly manufactured goods or partly performed services.

zero-rated supplies UK value added tax (VAT) term meaning supplies on which VAT is levied at zero per cent.

Further Reading

Angel, J. (General editor) (2003) *Technology Outsourcing – A Practitioner's Guide.* The Law Society, London.[1]

Black, A., Wright, P. and Bachman, J. E. (2001) *In Search of Shareholder Value – Managing the Drivers of Performance.* Financial Times / Prentice Hall, in association with PricewaterhouseCoopers, London.

Brett, M. (2003) *How to Read the Financial Pages – A Simple Guide to the Way Money Works and the Jargon.* Random House, London.[1]

Burnett, R. (2005) *Outsourcing – The Legal Contract.* The Faculty of Information Technology, The Institute of Chartered Accountants in England and Wales, London.[1]

Dixon, R. (1994) *Investment Appraisal – A Guide for Managers.* Kogan Page, in association with the Chartered Institute of Management Accountants, London.[1, 2]

Hanan, M. (2004) *Consultative Selling*™. Amacom, New York.[1]

Helfert, E. A. (2002) *Techniques of Financial Analysis.* McGraw-Hill Professional, Columbus, Ohio.

Hogbin, G. and Thomas, D. V. (1994) *Investing in Information Technology – Managing the Decision-making Process.* McGraw-Hill, Maidenhead.[1, 2]

Horngren, C. T., Foster, G. and Datar, S. M. (2002) *Cost Accounting – A Managerial Emphasis* (International Edition). Prentice Hall, New Jersey.

More, L. (2003) *IT Outsourcing – Management and Technical Considerations.* The Faculty of Information Technology, The Institute of Chartered Accountants in England and Wales, London.[1]

Ogier, T., Rugman, J. and Spicer, L. (2004) *The Real Cost of Capital – A Business Field Guide to Better Financial Decisions.* Financial Times / Prentice Hall, www.pwc.com/costofcapital.

Rice, A. (2003) *Accounts Demystified.* Prentice Hall, London.[1]

Sparrow, E. (2003) *Successful IT Outsourcing: From Choosing a Provider to Managing the Project.* Springer-Verlag, London.[1]

Steward, C. (2005) *Smith's Taxation.* Perfect Cover Ltd, Bridgwater.[1]

Walsh, C. (2005) *Key Management Ratios – How to Analyse, Compare and Control the Figures that Drive Company Value.* Financial Times / Prentice Hall, London.[1]

---

[1] Suitable for the non-financial reader.
[2] Out of print but worth seeking a library copy.

Index

Other books from BCS that you might enjoy

Our topical, informed and readable books span the boundaries of IT and management – essential reading for anyone in business!

Practical Data Migration

John Morris

Techniques and strategies for ensuring data migration projects achieve maximum return on investment. This practical guide contains: original methods; ideas on rescuing ailing projects; and a model of best practice to be used as a starting point for implementation of the methods. All blended with real life examples and clear definitions of commonly used jargon.

1-902505-71-9 (ISBN 13: 978-1-902505-71-8).
Cover Price: £30.
Paperback: 220pp.
Approx published: May 2006. **www.bcs.org/books/datamigration**

A Manager's Guide to IT Law

Jeremy Newton and Jeremy Holt (Editors)

This comprehensive guide to the IT-related legal issues explains, in plain English, the most relevant legal frameworks, with examples from actual case law used to illustrate the kinds of problems and disputes that most commonly arise. Contents include: IT contracts; systems procurement contracts; avoiding employment problems; instructing an IT consultant; intellectual property law; escrow; outsourcing; data protection.

1-902505-55-7 (ISBN 13: 978-1-902505-55-8).
Cover price: £25.
Paperback: 180pp.
Published: July 2004. **www.bcs.org/books/itlaw**

Business Analysis

Debra Paul and Donald Yeates (Editors)

A practical introductory guide for improving the effectiveness of IT and its alignment with an organization's business objectives. Workable business analysis skills and techniques, underpinned with academic theory. Covers strategy analysis, modelling business systems/processes, business case development, managing change, requirements engineering and information resource management.

1-902505-70-0 (ISBN 13: 978-1-902505-70-1).
Cover Price: £25.
Paperback: 256pp.
Published: April 2006. **www.bcs.org/books/
businessanalysis**

A Pragmatic Guide to Business Process Modelling

Jon Holt

Explores all aspects of process modelling from process analysis to process documentation by applying a standard modelling notation UML. Guidance for directors and managers on business process modelling to improve processes, productivity and profitability.

1-902505-66-2 (ISBN 13: 978-1-902505-66-4).
Cover price: £30.
Paperback: 184pp.
Published: September 2005. **www.bcs.org/books/
processmodelling**

Business Process Management – A Rigorous Approach

Martyn A. Ould

A rigorous way of understanding the mass of concurrent, collaborative activity that goes on within an organization, giving a solid basis for developing IT systems that actually support a business's processes.

1-902505-60-3 (ISBN 13: 978-1-902505-60-2).
Cover Price: £35.
Paperback: 364pp.
Published: January 2005. **www.bcs.org/books/bpm**

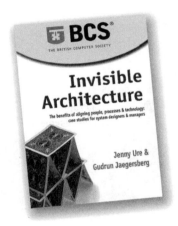

Invisible Architecture – The Benefits of Aligning People, Processes and Technology

Jenny Ure & Gudrun Jaegersberg

The biggest problems faced in implementing computer systems, especially across different countries, are often not technical – they are 'socio-technical'. Invisible Architecture uses real examples to highlight the potential for harnessing 'soft' factors to competitive advantage.

1-902505-59-X (ISBN 13: 978-1-902505-59-6).
Cover Price: £25.
Paperback: 104pp.
Published: March 2005. **www.bcs.org/books/ invisiblearchitecture**

Professional Issues in Information Technology

Frank Bott

This book explores the relationship between technological change, society and the law, and the powerful role that computers and computer professionals play in a technological society. Designed to accompany the BCS Professional Examination core Diploma module: 'Professional Issues in Information Systems Practice'.

1-902505-65-4 (ISBN 13: 978-1-902505-65-7).
Cover price: £20.
Paperback: 248pp.
Published: May 2005. **www.bcs.org/books/ professionalissues**

Project Management for IT-Related Projects – Textbook for the ISEB Foundation Certificate in IS Project Management

Bob Hughes (Editor), Roger Ireland, Brian West, Norman Smith and David I. Shepherd

The principles of IT-related project management, including project planning, monitoring and control, change management, risk management and communication between project stakeholders. Encompasses the entire syllabus of the 'ISEB Foundation Certificate in IS Project Management'.

1-902505-58-1 (ISBN 13: 978-1-902505-58-9).
Cover Price: £20.
Paperback 148pp.
Published: August 2004. **www.bcs.org/books/ projectmanagement**

A Guide to Global Sourcing – Offshore Outsourcing and Other Global Delivery Models

Elizabeth A. Sparrow

The opportunities and obstacles associated with offshore outsourcing and other global delivery models. Country-by-country analysis of offshore services available.

1-902505-61-1 (ISBN 13: 978-1-902505-61-9).
Cover Price: £25.
Paperback: 196pp.
Published: November 2004. **www.bcs.org/books/ globalsourcing**

More new books coming soon!
Visit: **www.bcs.org/books**

BCS products and services

Other products and services from the British Computer Society that might be of interest to you include:

Publishing

BCS publications, including books, magazine and peer-reviewed journals provide readers with informed content on business, management, legal and emerging technological issues, supporting the professional, academic and practical needs of the IT community. Subjects covered include business process management, IT law for managers and transition management. www.bcs.org/publications

BCS professional products and services

The BCS promotes the use of the SFIA*plus* IT skills framework, which forms the basis of a range of professional development products and services for both individual practitioners and employers. This includes BCS Skills*Manager* and BCS Career*Developer*. www.bcs.org/products

Qualifications

Information Systems Examination Board (ISEB) qualifications are the industry standard both in the UK and abroad. With over 100,000 practitioners now qualified, it is proof of the popularity of the qualifications. These qualifications ensure that IT professionals develop the skills, knowledge and confidence to perform to their full potential. There is a huge range on offer, covering all major areas of IT. In essence, ISEB qualifications are for forward-looking individuals and companies who want to stay ahead and who are serious about driving business forward. www.iseb.org.uk

BCS professional examinations are examined to the academic level of a UK honours degree and are the essential qualifications for a career in computing and IT. Whether you seek greater job recognition, promotion or a new career direction, you will find that BCS professional examinations are internationally recognized, flexible and suited to the needs of the IT industry. www.bcs.org/exams

The European Certification of IT Professionals (EUCIP) is aimed at IT professionals and practitioners wishing to gain professional certification and competency development. www.bcs.org/eucip

European Computer Driving Licence (ECDL) is the internationally recognized computer skills qualification that enables people to demonstrate their competence in computer skills. ECDL is managed in the UK by the BCS. ECDL Advanced has been introduced to take computer skills certification to the next level and teaches extensive knowledge of particular computing tools. www.ecdl.co.uk

Networking and events

BCS's specialist groups and branches provide excellent professional networking opportunities by keeping members abreast of latest developments, discussing topical issues and making useful contacts. www.bcs.org/bcs/groups

The society's programme of social events, lectures, awards schemes and competitions provides more opportunities to network. www.bcs.org/events

Further information

This information was correct at the time of publication but could change in the future. For the latest information, please contact:

The British Computer Society
First Floor, Block D
North Star House
North Star Avenue
Swindon SN2 1FA
UK

Telephone: 0845 300 4417 (UK only) or +44 1793 417424 (overseas)
Email: customerservice@hq.bcs.org.uk
Web: www.bcs.org